Life Skills for All Learners

Life Skills for All Learners

How to Teach, Assess, and Report Education's New Essentials

Antarina S. F. Amir and Thomas R. Guskey
with Henny Astuti, Ilsa Nurina,
Piesesha Hartiyana, and Ratih Larasati

Arlington, Virginia USA

2800 Shirlington Road, Suite 1001 • Arlington, VA 22206 USA
Phone: 800-933-2723 or 703-578-9600 • Fax: 703-575-5400
Website: www.ascd.org • Email: member@ascd.org
Author guidelines: www.ascd.org/write

Richard Culatta, *Chief Executive Officer;* Anthony Rebora, *Chief Content Officer;* Genny Ostertag, *Managing Director, Book Acquisitions & Editing;* Bill Varner, *Senior Acquisitions Editor;* Mary Beth Nielsen, *Director, Book Editing;* Katie Martin, *Senior Editor;* Thomas Lytle, *Creative Director;* Donald Ely, *Art Director;* Daniela Aguera/The Hatcher Group, *Graphic Designer;* Valerie Younkin, *Senior Production Designer;* Kelly Marshall, *Production Manager;* Shajuan Martin, *E-Publishing Specialist;* Christopher Logan, *Senior Production Specialist,* Kathryn Oliver, *Creative Project Manager*

Copyright © 2024 Thomas R. Guskey and Antarina S. F. Amir. All rights reserved. It is illegal to reproduce copies of this work in print or electronic format (including reproductions displayed on a secure intranet or stored in a retrieval system or other electronic storage device from which copies can be made or displayed) without the prior written permission of the publisher. By purchasing only authorized electronic or print editions and not participating in or encouraging piracy of copyrighted materials, you support the rights of authors and publishers. Readers who wish to reproduce or republish excerpts of this work in print or electronic format may do so for a small fee by contacting the Copyright Clearance Center (CCC), 222 Rosewood Dr., Danvers, MA 01923, USA (phone: 978-750-8400; fax: 978-646-8600; web: www.copyright.com). To inquire about site licensing options or any other reuse, contact ASCD Permissions at www.ascd.org/permissions or permissions@ascd.org. For a list of vendors authorized to license ASCD ebooks to institutions, see www.ascd.org/epubs. Send translation inquiries to translations@ascd.org.

ASCD® is a registered trademark of Association for Supervision and Curriculum Development. All other trademarks contained in this book are the property of, and reserved by, their respective owners, and are used for editorial and informational purposes only. No such use should be construed to imply sponsorship or endorsement of the book by the respective owners.

All web links in this book are correct as of the publication date below but may have become inactive or otherwise modified since that time. If you notice a deactivated or changed link, please email books@ascd.org with the words "Link Update" in the subject line. In your message, please specify the web link, the book title, and the page number on which the link appears.

PAPERBACK ISBN: 978-1-4166-3246-7   ASCD product #121026   n1/24

PDF EBOOK ISBN: 978-1-4166-3247-4; see Books in Print for other formats.

Quantity discounts are available: email programteam@ascd.org or call 800-933-2723, ext. 5773, or 703-575-5773. For desk copies, go to www.ascd.org/deskcopy.

Library of Congress Cataloging-in-Publication Data
Names: Amir, Antarina S. F., author. | Guskey, Thomas R., author.
Title: Life skills for all learners : how to teach, assess, and report education's new essentials / Antarina S.F. Amir and Thomas R. Guskey ; with Henny Astuti, Ilsa Nurina, Piesesha Hartiyana, and Ratih Larasati.
Description: Arlington, Virginia : ASCD, 2024. | Includes bibliographical references and index.
Identifiers: LCCN 2023032422 (print) | LCCN 2023032423 (ebook) | ISBN 9781416632467 (paperback) | ISBN 9781416632474 (pdf)
Subjects: LCSH: Education—Aims and objectives—United States. | Career education—United States. | Life skills—Study and teaching—United States.
Classification: LCC LA217.2 .A48 2024 (print) | LCC LA217.2 (ebook) | DDC 372.37/0440973—dc23/eng/20230809
LC record available at https://lccn.loc.gov/2023032422
LC ebook record available at https://lccn.loc.gov/2023032423

---

33 32 31 30 29 28 27 26 25 24   1 2 3 4 5 6 7 8 9 10 11 12

*To the students at HighScope Indonesia, past and present,
who helped us develop our ideas, create truly meaningful learning experiences,
and deepen our understanding of how learning can be demonstrated.
They inspire us to continue this important work.*

Life Skills for All Learners

How to Teach, Assess, and Report Education's New Essentials

Introduction 1

1. Meta-Level Reflection 7
2. Expert Thinking 29
3. Creativity and Innovation 53
4. Adaptability and Agility 73
5. Audience-Centered Communication 91
6. Synergistic Collaboration................................... 122
7. Empathetic Social Skills 149
8. Ethical Leadership 180
9. Grading and Reporting Systems 203
Conclusion... 231
Acknowledgments 234
References... 236
Index 239
About the Authors 248

Introduction

Are you confident your school is providing students with the knowledge and skills they most need for their futures? Are you sure your students will look back on the learning experiences you offer today and feel well-prepared for the challenges they will face as adults?

Societal change is accelerating at a mind-boggling pace, not only in the field of technology but also in terms of economic, social, and environmental shifts. Despite this reality, students throughout the world still learn in classroom environments that, in some ways, have remained unchanged for generations.

In the early 20th century, schools prepared students for an industrialized society that required workers to operate machines that made the products the world needed. But today, most of those products have changed beyond recognition or are no longer needed. Furthermore, the products that are most needed now are no longer put together by human hands but by automated, computer-controlled robots. Yesterday's industrialized societies have been transformed into today's information societies that require skills very different from those schools have long prioritized.

In 2004, Frank Levy and Richard Murnane published eye-opening research on how computers have changed the trajectory of employment and how the right education program can help people succeed in the new job market. With that in mind, in this book we highlight the importance of expert thinking and complex communication skills, two crucial capabilities that humans must master to do tasks that computers cannot do. Similarly, the Partnership for 21st Century Skills (P21) focuses on the 4 C's: critical thinking, communication, collaboration, and creativity.

This book highlights how educators should begin reframing the objectives of their classroom practice by aiming toward mastery of what are now known as 21st century skills. It differs from other books on the topic in that we discuss more skills in far more detail and include value-related components. Specifically, we refer to 21st century skills as the essential skills that students need to master to be visionary, self-regulated leaders and to succeed in life. Our framework proposes eight essential skills that need to be practiced and developed from early childhood through the high school years:

- **Meta-Level Reflection**—the conscious and deliberate process of thinking about one's own thinking.
- **Expert Thinking**—the ability to maximize the mental capacity of the brain by processing multiple aspects of perception, emotion, cognition, and action (knowledge) systematically, analytically, and critically, to make decisions and solve problems effectively.
- **Creativity and Innovation**—the ability to create novel and useful ideas/products/blueprints by generating possibilities and synthesizing them to solve problems and to improve situations.
- **Adaptability and Agility**—the ability to read and decode signals, quickly shift focus, and act on anticipated changes, as well as crises, by using learned skills and knowledge to maximize the result.
- **Audience-Centered Communication**—the ability to communicate ideas, information, values, and feelings clearly and persuasively by considering audiences' backgrounds and context as the key factors to determine the content, language usage, and expectations, both in language arts and across the curriculum.
- **Synergistic Collaboration**—the ability to work effectively on a team where each member commits to a personal role to accomplish a common goal through face-to-face or technology-mediated coordination or both.
- **Empathetic Social Skills**—the ability to function adaptively in the community by regulating one's own feelings and behavior to interact positively and develop a culture of respecting differences as a part of digital and global citizenship.
- **Ethical Leadership**—the ability to influence, motivate, and lead others based on responsibility, respect, excellence, and integrity.

As the names of the skills imply, we believe it is important to pair skills with values; hence, "ethical leadership" instead of just "leadership" and "empathetic social skills" instead of "social skills" alone.

Clearly, the skills students need to succeed in this rapidly changing and increasingly complex global society extend far beyond the traditional school curriculum. Students still need to understand who we are as a people, what we value as a society, and how we got to where we are. But more important, they must imagine how we can become better and how best to approach our future. They must be able not only to understand our current world but also to envision a world far better and to plan the necessary steps to get there. They must become responsible thinkers and creative problem solvers, ready to take on new challenges and social dilemmas—some of which we haven't yet imagined.

Developing such individuals requires a reimagined educational system based on an entirely new view of students. It requires educators to rethink and revise curricula to better develop and support this type of cognitive and noncognitive architecture.

Leading educational organizations throughout the world have taken up the task of defining the essential life skills they believe are most vital for students' success in school and beyond. Although this is valuable and important work, few of these organizations have taken on the greater challenge of describing how to help students develop these skills, how to assess these skills, or how to meaningfully report students' progress in developing these skills to the students themselves and to parents, families, and other stakeholders.

The faculty and school leaders of the HighScope Indonesia Institute in Jakarta, which comprises 14 networked schools through Indonesia, set out to do just that. Our goal was to change the education paradigm to help students at all grade levels develop these essential life skills by design. Our work involved constructing a continuum of stages of skill development, designing learning activities to help students acquire the skills, and planning a system of assessment and continuous progress monitoring appropriate from preschool through high school.

Our work was guided by the scholarship of renowned Indonesian educator Ki Hajar Dewantara, who developed the 3N concept of "Niteni, Nirokke, and Nambahi." This concept identifies three distinct stages of learning. The first stage involves observing the end result of what we aspire to learn and become; the next is replicating the best practices we can model in order to advance our learning; and the last is adding value to learning by incorporating our own unique expertise and character, considering our individual learning needs and goals.

Our Purpose

Our primary purpose in this book is to share this important work with educators throughout the world who are engaged in similar efforts to help students to develop these or comparable essential life skills. Although most modern educators are keenly aware of the need, many lack the time, resources, or expertise to embed this skill development in their curricula, instruction, assessments, and reporting procedures. Having addressed these challenges and gathered evidence on the effects of our work, we want to share our approaches, products, and experiences with others to facilitate their efforts in developing these or similar important life skills in their students. By sharing how we approached the task and the details of what we developed, we hope to streamline the process for others. Our goal is to extend this important work, broaden its application, and provide a framework on which others can build and improve still further.

How the Book Is Organized

The eight essential life skills are the focus of Chapters 1 through 8. These chapters describe each life skill in turn and address the following overarching questions:

- Why is this particular skill important?
- What are the key elements of this skill, and how can we encourage, teach, and develop the skill?
- How can we measure and assess this skill and report learning progress to students, parents, and other stakeholders?
- How can we integrate this skill into the curriculum and classroom practice?

Importance

In discussing the importance of a skill, we share our definition of the skill and offer examples of how students at different grade levels could demonstrate proficiency. We encourage readers to share our definition with students or create your own definitions. Describing the skill is an essential first step in understanding and implementing it in the classroom context. We also explain why we chose each particular skill area, why it is "essential" for students to develop, and the specific evidence (i.e., research studies, surveys, interviews) that identifies the skill area as important.

Key Elements

We describe the defining elements that contribute to the whole skill and deepen its meaning. For example, the skill Creativity and Innovation comprises three elements: novelty, risk taking, and beneficial contribution. We provide a detailed explanation of what we expect students to do in each element of the skill, how we guide them in developing the skill, the relationship among the elements that make up the skill as a whole, and how we expect students to respond to challenges they may face in learning them. We explain how these elements evolve developmentally as students mature, how teachers can encourage and facilitate skill development, and what constitutes evidence of students' performance. These key elements also form the basis of rubrics that provide students with feedback on their performance.

Each chapter contains illustrations and sample lessons to show how the skills can be taught, along with practical examples of how students' mastery is revealed through written materials, performances, and demonstrations in all subjects and across all grade levels. We include descriptions and illustrative examples of classroom activities, displays, graphic organizers, and student projects, as well as explanations of the rubrics and forms developed for the reporting process. Some of the assessment procedures involve exhibits, projects, videos, and demonstrations that can be filed in students' digital portfolio as well as physical portfolio.

Measurement and Assessment

Descriptions of essential skills provide a continuum of expected behaviors at each stage of students' development and show how such skills extend far beyond the learning goals set forth in typical school curricula. We clarify those descriptions by presenting rubrics for each skill from early childhood through high school, using the developmental levels of Early, Beginning, Transition, Developing, and Expert. These illustrate how students' understanding and performance of the skills evolve and deepen over time, making the development of the skills happen by design, as noted earlier, instead of by chance. We also explain the distinction among the three specific stages of skill development: (1) needs consistent guidance, (2) needs minimal guidance, and (3) performs independently. We provide examples to demonstrate how the elements of the skills are measured at each stage.

We outline the assessment procedures used to evaluate the evidence related to students' performance to provide students with formative feedback and to offer guidance in correcting learning errors and making revisions. In descriptions of how we assess and report on students' mastery of the skills to students, parents, families, and other stakeholders, we offer specific, concrete suggestions for gathering data on skill development and reporting students' progress. They provide educators with a framework to plan strategies for implementation in the unique context of their school.

Integration into Curriculum and Practice

In the final section of Chapters 1 through 8, we list specific suggestions to provide guidance for incorporating skill development into the school curriculum and students' day-to-day learning.

Following Chapters 1 through 8, Chapter 9 focuses on grading and reporting. We describe the system we designed to offer specific feedback to students, parents, and families on the development and mastery of the life skills. In addition, we include examples of progress reports adapted for different grade levels, report card recording techniques, and transcript information.

A Final Introductory Note

As previously stated, we developed this book primarily for prekindergarten through high school teachers and school leaders. We hope teachers at all levels find it useful in their efforts to integrate activities that help develop essential life skills in their regular classroom activities. We hope curriculum developers who struggle to incorporate these skills in regular school curricula might find it a practical guide that will help steer their efforts toward greater success. We especially hope instructional directors and school leaders use the book to create changes in their schools and to facilitate professional learning activities that guide teachers in their implementation efforts.

Our main goal, however, is to help educators understand that developing essential life skills requires aligning all learning processes to that purpose. It means taking time to reflect on all aspects of our practice, especially instructional content, classroom interactions, assessment procedures, and grading and reporting practices. It means finding ways to integrate both the academic and nonacademic skills that are so important to students' success in school and in their lives beyond.

We hope this book will equip teachers at all levels with practical and immediately applicable strategies to improve their practice. We also hope it helps school leaders support teachers in those efforts and provides them with the guidance and inspiration they need to improve existing educational systems in purposeful, effective, and comprehensive ways. If we can accomplish these goals, we will consider our work truly successful.

1
Meta-Level Reflection

When the mind is thinking, it is talking to itself.
—Plato—

Students today face increasingly complex problems. To successfully address those problems, they need to be able to think deeply about the issues involved, analyze what needs to be done and why, plan how to do it, reflect on how they feel about it, and anticipate what must be done to follow up. These skills represent metacognition, which involves the capacity to self-manage, be self-reflective, and be a self-learner (Kallick & Zmuda, 2017). In essence, *metacognition* means to think about one's own thinking for the purpose of deciding what action to take or what to learn and to improve.

We have adapted aspects of metacognition into what we label *Meta-Level Reflection* (MLR), which we define as the conscious and deliberate process of thinking about one's own thinking. We believe MLR is a mindset that increases one's ability to transfer learning in different contexts and leads to becoming a self-directed learner. It includes the ability to be aware of and use effective thinking strategies to solve complex problems and achieve objectives when working on a task.

Why Is Meta-Level Reflection Important?

We consider Meta-Level Reflection to be important for two reasons. First, it develops awareness of the thinking process used in problem solving and achieving objectives. Second, it helps individuals make a habit of planning, monitoring, and evaluating as a self-learner. Let's consider each of these.

Developing Awareness of the Thinking Process Used in Problem Solving and Achieving Objectives

Meta-Level Reflection occurs in every part of the learning process. It involves planning, executing the plan, and reflecting on the execution strategies. As students go through the process, they become more aware—more conscious—of *how* they think. Teachers help students develop this awareness by encouraging them to ask questions throughout their learning. For example, students ask questions about their interests, goals, problems they want to solve, information they need, and the kind of thinking skills they are engaged in. As students are planning, they need to think of various possibilities, from the expected learning goal to their own interest. As they are executing their plans and working on a project, they need to be aware of the kind of thinking they are using—for example, "Am I using analytical thinking or critical thinking now?" Also, when they encounter a problem during the learning process, they need to switch their thinking into a problem-solving mode and think of alternative solutions. And finally, as they are reflecting on their work, they need to be thinking to evaluate their productivity—how they have or have not achieved their goal.

Teachers can help students develop awareness of their thinking by prompting them, using questions or graphic organizers, to be mindful of their thoughts at each step of the learning process—planning, learning, and reflection. For example, a preschool teacher can use a simple visual map showing various classroom areas and give each student a token or game piece to move around the map as they state their plans, as in "I want to play in the Block Area and build a dinosaur zoo. Then I want to play games in the Computer Area." The idea is to teach children to think before they act. With practice beginning in early preschool, the aim is for the skill to become a mindset in older students.

In upper-elementary grades, graphic organizers can make thinking more concrete and help students learn to differentiate between copying and pasting information and being aware of the result of their own thinking process. For example, in a language arts class, teachers might ask students to fill out a graphic organizer (see Figure 1.1) to become aware of their thinking process. Students first write down the information as it is and then record their deeper understanding of the information.

FIGURE 1.1
Graphic Organizer for Developing "Thinking Process Awareness"

Directions: In the first column, record information you have read in the text. In the second column, use your own thinking process to analyze and evaluate the information.

Copied Information	After Applying Thinking Process

Making a Habit of Planning, Monitoring, and Evaluating as a Self-Learner

When teaching Meta-Level Reflection skills, we encourage students to practice and adjust their thinking depending on the situation. The High-Scope preschool program, for example, offers students many opportunities to engage in planning and reviewing, both of which require cognitive and metacognitive skills. Preschool children practice thinking before they act and recalling the actions in their daily routines. In the elementary grades through high school, developing students' habits of planning, monitoring, and evaluating is part of everyday instruction, and the habits are a critical aspect of project-based learning in a program we call "Making Good Choices." Giving students opportunities to practice conscious planning, to be aware of the kind of thinking they are engaged in, and to reflect on what they have done daily helps them develop the habit and mindset of Meta-Level Reflection.

To facilitate this process, teachers introduce activities at the beginning of the term to familiarize students with the life skills related to Meta-Level Reflection. They engage students in activities to experience Meta-Level Reflection, present vocabulary activities to explore words in the related rubrics, and create a word wall. Teachers then introduce individual and collaborative activities to practice the new skills. Figure 1.2 (see p. 10) is an example of a poster reminder for Meta-Level Reflection made by Grade 2–3 students.

FIGURE 1.2
A Working Agreement for Meta-Level Reflection Reminder Created by Grade 2–3 Students

Conscious Planning	Thoughtful Learning	Reflection for Future Improvement
1. Think about what I like and what I need to learn. 2. Make plans to achieve it.	1. Think about how I went about my learning. 2. What thinking steps did I follow? Were they effective? 3. Do I need to change the thinking steps to get a better solution? 4. Get feedback from others.	1. Did I achieve my goal? 2. Did I do my best? 3. Here is my plan to be better....

Key Elements of Meta-Level Reflection

Our approach to Meta-Level Reflection includes three elements: (1) *conscious planning,* (2) *thoughtful learning,* and (3) *reflection for future improvement* (see Figure 1.3).

Conscious Planning

Successful Meta-Level Reflection begins with a well-conceived plan, which requires serious effort. We refer to the process as *conscious planning,* which we define as the ability to think purposefully before taking actions based on identification of multiple aspects of the learning goals and using them to create detailed plans with adaptive strategies in real-life contexts. *Conscious planning* encompasses two important concepts: (1) considering multiple perspectives and (2) creating a detailed plan with good choices.

Students' skill in planning while considering multiple perspectives can be nurtured by deliberately designing opportunities for them to make a plan, elaborate on their plan, and explain the multiple perspectives they considered during the process.

> *Conscious planning* encompasses two important concepts: (1) considering multiple perspectives and (2) creating a detailed plan with good choices.

FIGURE 1.3
The Key Elements of Meta-Level Reflection

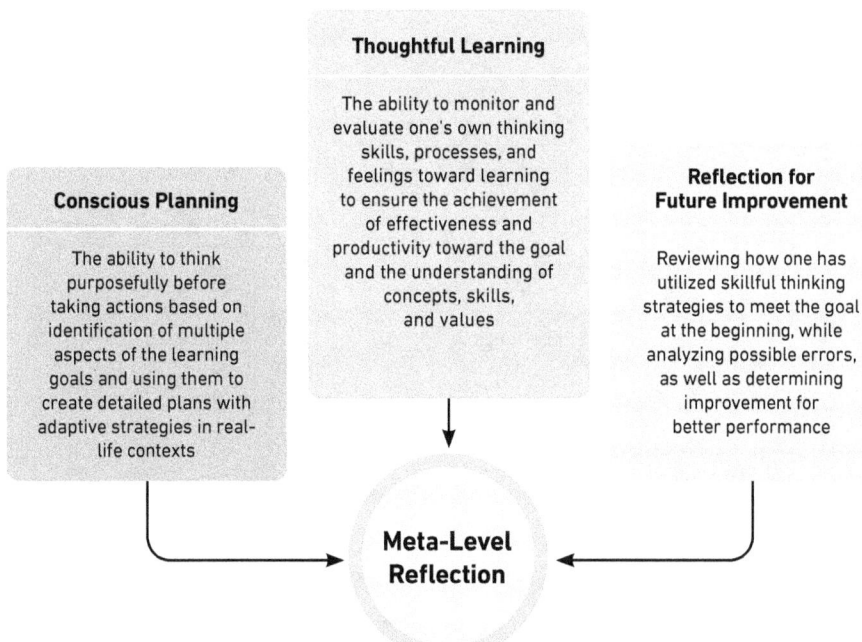

Students develop their habit of planning, monitoring, and evaluating by engaging in activities that have them doing exactly that—consciously planning at the beginning of a project, monitoring their execution of the plan, and engaging in daily and end-of-project reflection to evaluate their performance and create plans to improve in the future.

Teachers can create specific times to do each of these steps. "Planning time" is when students set direction and anticipate what they should be doing during "work/monitoring time," and "reflection/evaluation time" helps students make sense of the actions they took during "work/monitoring time."

Teaching the pattern of planning, monitoring, and evaluating can begin in early childhood. At HighScope, we do it by allowing the students to create a project, based on their own interest, using the steps of what we call "Plan-Do-Review" (PDR) for early preschool and preschool children. The counterpart for elementary, middle, and high school students is called "Conscious Planning–Thoughtful Learning–Reflecting for Future Improvement." Figure 1.4 (see p. 12) shows a graphic organizer for this process.

FIGURE 1.4
Graphic Organizer for Planning, Learning, and Reflecting

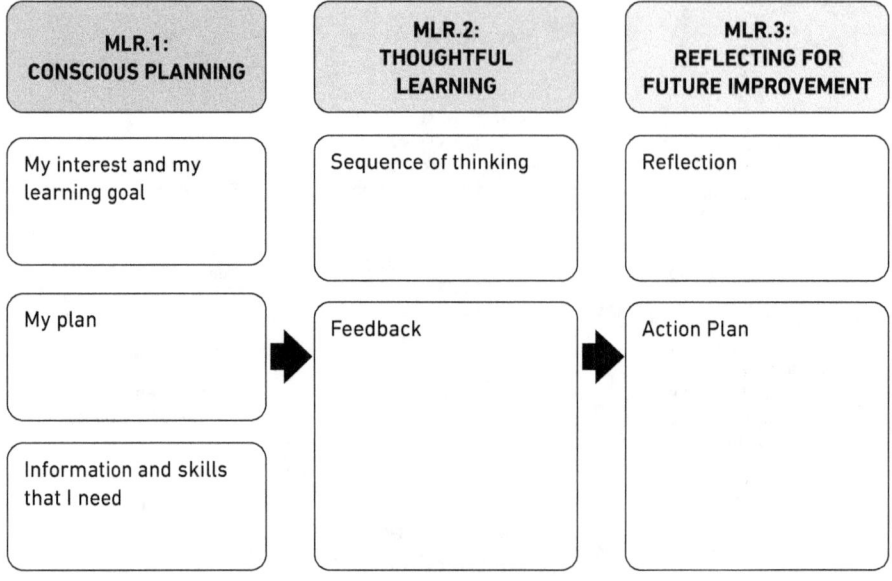

Nurturing the ability to plan based on multiple perspectives

To make a plan, one must make choices, and to make a choice, students need to consider various perspectives and opposing viewpoints that carry different consequences. For example, when proposing a solution to a waste management problem in the school cafeteria, a student might consider culture norms and logistics (e.g., how the school usually disposes of waste, other ways waste might be managed) as well as biases (e.g., personal preferences, attitudes about recycling). It's a process that promotes empathy and supports a more purposeful way to address problems that considers existing conditions.

Teachers should teach their students to make good choices, especially through passion-based projects, because these are a natural way to grow students' intrinsic motivation and ownership of learning. In our school, we have what we call the Making Good Choices project. In the planning stage, we want students to be conscious of what good project-related choices are. Their plans need to contain all the ingredients of such choices: clear project objectives, consideration of how the project is beneficial for themselves or the community, and use of previously learned knowledge and skills. Let's look at an example from a Grade 8–9 class.

In this case, the Making Good Choices project is related to sustainable development goals (SDG), which becomes the "big ideas" and the context for practicing the skills. For example, from a list of possibilities, a student chose goal number 15, "Life on Land." In his Making Good Choices log (see Figure 1.5), the student expressed the desire to "focus on deforestation because trees and plants are the things humans need the most to live. Without those things, humans won't be able to breathe, and there won't be any oxygen at all." He then described the plan, explained how his solution could make a difference and contribute to solving the problem, and identified the people who would benefit from his solution.

FIGURE 1.5
Conscious Planning in a Student's "Making Good Choices" Log

Goal: Life on Land (SDG Number 15)	**Problem:** Deforestation
Reason: I want to focus on deforestation because trees and plants are the things humans need most to live. Without those things, humans won't be able to breathe, and there won't be any oxygen at all.	
My plan to address this problem: I plan on making a supporter group where people who feel the same way can gather and do something to make a change. I will make a website to promote all that I have done and what the supporter group has done. It will serve as a promotion for both our activity and our supporters' group. It can also be used to write blogs or articles about what has happened on our planet and what we have done to reduce the effects of it. My first goal, as a person who opposes deforestation, is to make a hydroponic garden in my house to help my surroundings be greener.	
Here is how my solution will create a difference and address the problem: I have to create a hydroponic garden and a website. I can promote this method of planting through the website and can inspire others to do the same thing, thus making a difference because there'll be more people doing the things I do.	
Here are the people who will benefit the most from my solution and will serve as my sample for testing it: I will begin with my neighbors. I will inspire my neighbors to create their own hydroponic garden based on my campaign.	

Nurturing the ability to create a detailed plan

As noted, the student who was inspired by the problem of deforestation elaborated on the solution, how it is related to the SDG, how it creates a difference and addresses the problem, and what benefits it would bring. Later the student added details related to the information and skills needed to execute the project. In addition, as a component of his Making Good Choices log, the student answered questions about measuring the effectiveness of the proposed solution (see Figure 1.6). Finally, the student reviewed the plan and considered whether it would likely be effective. Figure 1.7 shows the graphic organizer that guided this process.

FIGURE 1.6
Sample Questions and Student Responses for Measuring Effectiveness of a Solution in a "Making Good Choices" Log

> **How will you measure the effectiveness/impact of your solution? Answer the following three questions.**
>
> **1. How will I determine if the sample's condition has improved?**
> I will create a comparison before and after my campaign to create a hydroponic garden in my neighborhood.
>
> **2. What will be my measuring tools to ensure I have objective data?**
> • I will use surveys distributed to my neighbors where they can upload pictures of their garden.
> • Comments and uploaded pictures from people who visit my website.
>
> **3. What are the criteria of success based on my sample and solution?**
> • Able to finish my hydroponic garden.
> • Able to attract my neighbors by educating them to make a hydroponic garden.
> • Able to inspire the larger community through my website to create their own hydroponic garden and make a change in the surrounding environment.

Thoughtful Learning

Thoughtful learning is the second element of the Meta-Level Reflection skill. We define *thoughtful learning* as the ability to monitor and evaluate one's own thinking skills, processes, and feelings toward learning to ensure the achievement of effectiveness and productivity toward reaching the goal and the understanding of concepts, skills, and values. This element emphasizes the importance of students being fully mindful of *what* and *how* they are thinking and feeling while executing their plans. It comprises two important concepts: (1) the ability to *monitor* one's own processes and feelings and (2) the ability to *evaluate* one's own processes and feelings.

> *Thoughtful learning* comprises two important concepts: (1) the ability to *monitor* one's own processes and feelings and (2) the ability to *evaluate* one's own processes and feelings.

FIGURE 1.7
Graphic Organizer for Reviewing a Plan and Considering Its Effectiveness

My solution to achieve the SDG that I have chosen is:	
How is my solution related to the SDG:	How can my solution create a difference and solve the problem:
Who are the people who will benefit the most from my solution? (This will be your sample for testing the solution.)	

The procedures to achieve my goal are:

1. _____
2. _____
3. _____
4. _____
5. _____
6. _____
7. _____
8. _____
9. _____
10. _____

Nurturing the ability to monitor one's own thinking processes and feelings

As students work on their project, they should be able to identify their thinking processes. They start by asking, "Is the way I think and feel effective and productive enough to help me reach my learning goal?" Next, they consider the thinking skills they will use. They should ask, "What thinking skills should I use? How can I use Expert Thinking [discussed in Chapter 2] in this project? What are the procedures for accomplishing the project? Which skills or concepts should I use? Which data should I use? Where can I find reliable data?"

Students also need to understand the role of feedback in improving their learning and to feel comfortable with it. Feedback may affect their feelings, but when they are able to manage those feelings, they will also be able to manage related distractions and control impulsivity. As a result, both individual and group productivity can increase.

Figure 1.8 shows a form that students can use to monitor their thinking throughout all stages of Meta-Level Reflection. The example is from a Grade 2–3 student who was working on a project on raising a healthy rabbit at home.

FIGURE 1.8

Example of a Student's Thinking Process Throughout Meta-Level Reflection

Project Phases	Questions to Guide My Thinking Process	Answers
Conscious planning	What is my interest?	My interest is rabbits.
	What is my plan?	I plan to raise a rabbit.
	What information should I find?	I need to know about rabbits' habitat and food.
	What information should I compare and contrast?	I need to compare/contrast different types of habitat and food and find which one is best to raise a rabbit at my home.
Thoughtful learning	How can I get the information?	• I can get information about rabbits from my uncle, who has lots of rabbits in his garden. • I can read books about rabbits. • I can search for and watch online videos about how to raise rabbits.
	How can I get feedback?	I can ask my uncle to give me feedback on my habitat and food ideas.
	How will I use the feedback?	I will use the feedback to improve my choice.
	What should I do if the feedback doesn't make me happy?	I will ask again until I understand.
Reflecting for future improvement	How did I perform?	I had a clear plan and the right resources to get information.
	What can I do to do better?	I will find more information about rabbits in different countries.

Meta-Level Reflection   17

Nurturing the ability to evaluate one's own thinking processes and feelings

When students monitor their own thinking, they also need to evaluate that thinking by asking themselves questions such as these: "Am I following the right procedure in using my thinking skills? Am I thinking skillfully? Have I used the right skills and concepts? Have I applied the right procedures or methods? Is my strategy effective?" If the answer is yes, then the students should go on. But if the answer is no, then they must pause and think of a more efficient way of thinking and feeling.

One way to facilitate students' thinking process is by providing a "Monitoring My Own Thinking Parking Lot" poster or whiteboard display where students can record the thoughts, questions, or ideas that occur to them as they work through the various stages of their project (see Figure 1.9). The parking lot provides a place for students to capture their thinking without disrupting the learning process of other students.

FIGURE 1.9
"Parking Lot" for Questions

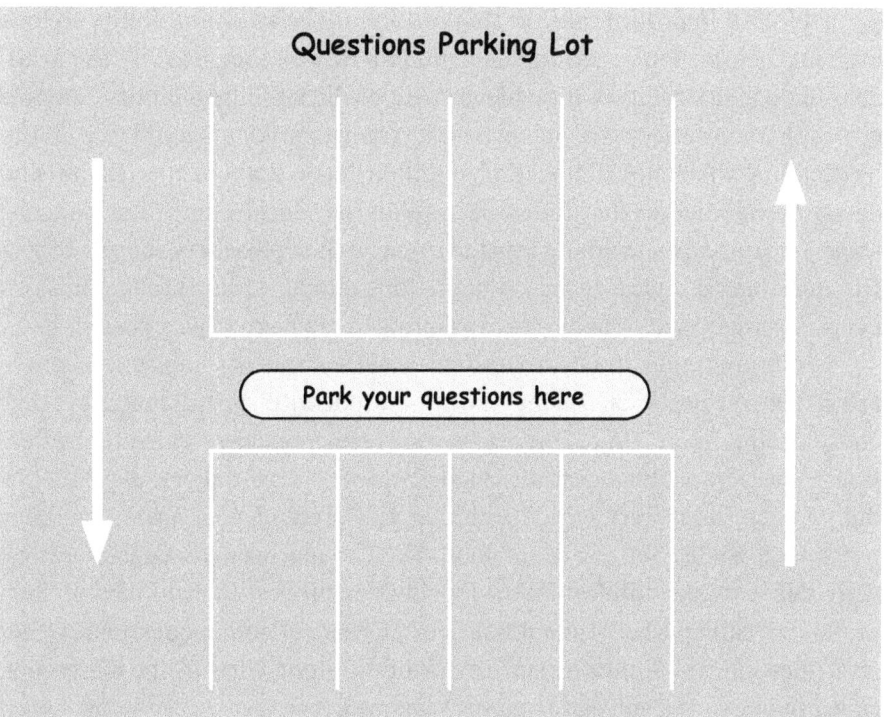

Reflection for Future Improvement

The third element of Meta-Level Reflection is *reflection for future improvement*. We define this as the ability to review how one has used goal-focused, skillful-thinking strategies from the beginning, analyzed possible errors, and determined ways to improve for better performance.

We believe that reflection goes beyond considering what has been done; it also must yield insight into what needs to be done differently *next time* in order to perform better.

> There are two important concepts in *reflection for future improvement*:
> (1) nurturing the ability to reflect and
> (2) developing a plan for improvement.

There are two important concepts in reflection for future improvement: (1) nurturing the ability to reflect and (2) developing a plan for improvement.

Nurturing the ability to reflect

Students need to self-evaluate their plans, reflect on the strategies they used, and consider alternative strategies that might improve their performance in the future. To help them do so, teachers must design reflective activities that are meaningful and aim to explore student's insight, learning, questions, and ideas. An important part of this process is the students' ability to look back on their performance and determine how well they used all the available tools and strategies to achieve their goals, and also identify possible errors that may affect goal achievement. Younger students build this ability by recalling what they did, identifying their feelings about the results, and determining whether they followed the plan they decided on at the planning stage. Depending on the daily routine in each school, teachers can ask reflective questions at any relevant moment—for example, after a student has finished an assignment or before transitioning to the next subject period.

In our preschool, the Plan-Do-Review (PDR) routine enables teachers to ask reflective questions. During "do" time, students play with materials they chose during "plan" time. During "review" time, teachers guide the reflection process by asking questions such as these: "What did you play?" "How did you use the materials?" "I saw that you pretended to have a birthday party with Shelly. Tell me more about it." The teachers can design various activities to engage children in the recollection process, such as having them pretend to call another student to ask or answer reflection questions. Other strategies may incorporate visual maps of different areas in the classroom, finger puppets, or a hot-potato game, to name a few.

Teachers in upper-elementary grades can use graphic organizers to help students practice reflecting on the thinking strategies they used during the thoughtful learning stage and also to identify possible errors (see Figure 1.10 for an example). High school teachers can develop their students' ability to evaluate their performance through reflection essays that include their thoughts on whether they have used tools and strategies skillfully. The prompting sentence stems in graphic organizers like the one in Figure 1.11 (see p. 20) can also be used as the basis for end-of-term reflection essays.

FIGURE 1.10
Graphic Organizer for Reflection for Future Improvement

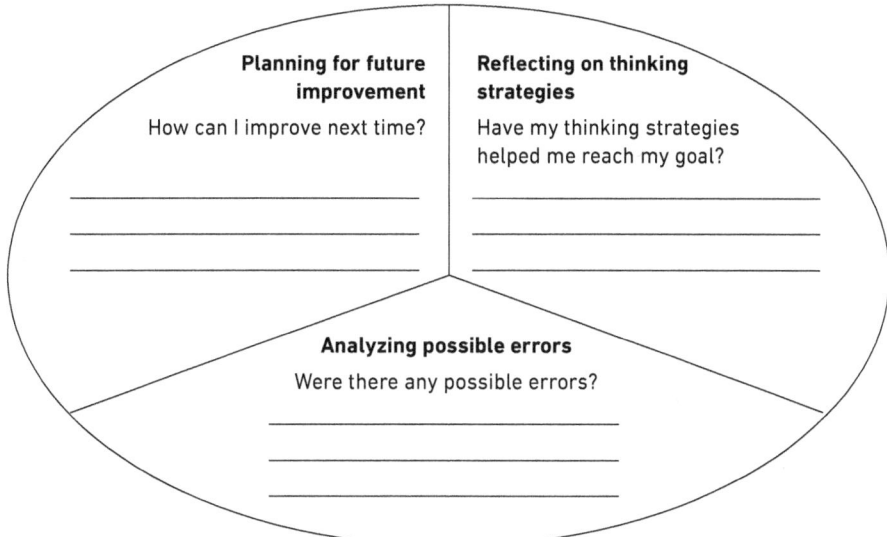

Nurturing the ability to develop a plan for improvement

Teachers need to help students develop the habit of wondering, "How can I do better in the next projects? What would I do differently in order to have a better result?" They can nurture students' ability to learn from errors. To make this process explicit, teachers can allocate a specific time at the end of the day or at the conclusion of the project during which students evaluate their performance and brainstorm ways to improve for the next one. Teachers can use prompting questions to initiate this process and graphic organizers to illustrate each step. They may also have students take turns sharing their reflection in front of their peers. That way, students can learn to give and receive feedback.

FIGURE 1.11
Prompts for High School Students' Reflection

When I think about ALL of my projects in this term,

1. I set **thoughtful plans** to _____, based on my purposeful interest in _____, my visions of sustainable future of _____, and my learning goals of _____.

2. The clear measurement criteria for my plans in this term were _____.

3. I supported my plans with reasoned arguments of _____ and used the adaptive strategies of _____, based on the following interdisciplinary knowledge and skills: _____.

4. When I look back on ALL my projects in this term, I think I (have/ have not) made a good choice because _____.

5. I regulate myself by _____ to manage my projects.

6. When working on my projects this term, I made decisions on the best solution of _____, based on _____.

7. I evaluated the solutions by _____.

8. The thinking skills I used in my projects were _____, and I used them skillfully by _____.

9. I independently processed diverse bits of information by _____, and I monitored and checked to make sure I attained productivity, effectiveness, and efficiency toward the goal by _____.

10. I have utilized **appropriate tools and strategies** skillfully by _____, and I have **transferred the learning** I gained from all my projects into _____.

11. I'm proud of the following ways in which I've applied my project management skills: _____.

12. My action plans to follow up the areas for improvement are as follows: _____
_____

It is best to start nurturing this ability in early childhood. Recall Time is a part of our routine in which teachers ask students to describe what they did during the work or play time ("Do") and how they did it. Students progress at their own pace with the teachers' encouragement, becoming more capable of answering questions such as these: "How did you solve that problem?" "What did you do when you didn't get the materials you needed?" and "How did you come up with your idea?"

In higher grades, teachers can increase the complexity by ensuring that students can explain how their work has clear objectives, is beneficial to themselves and others, uses their knowledge and skills, and upholds the values they believe in. And, as stated before, they also need to be able to reflect on the thinking processes they used, analyze possible errors, and plan for future improvement. Figure 1.12 illustrates how questions to guide students' reflections can increase in complexity.

FIGURE 1.12

Sample Questions to Prompt Students' Reflection for Future Improvement (Transition Level)

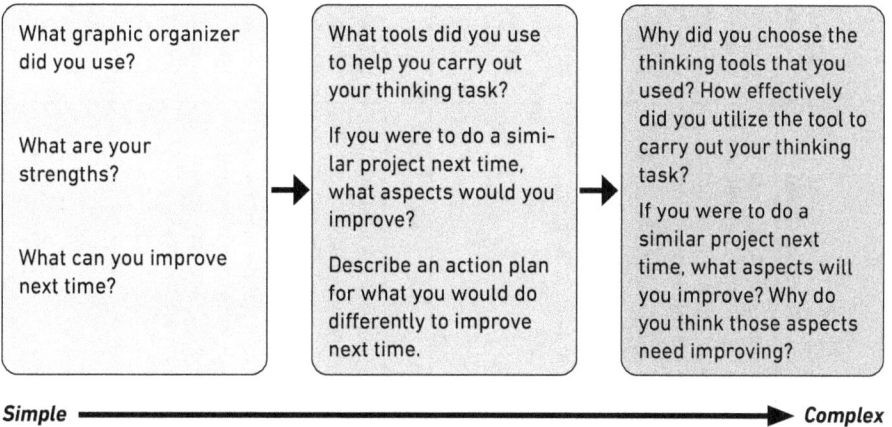

Simple ⟶ Complex

How Is Meta-Level Reflection Measured and Assessed?

To assess students' development in each element of Meta-Level Reflection, we designed a growth-related rubric to describe the behaviors that we expect to see at each continuum level, from Early (preschool–kindergarten) to Expert (high school). As shown in Figure 1.13 (see p. 22), the description for each developmental level becomes gradually more complex. (We describe the levels in detail later in this section.)

Recall that Meta-Level Reflection consists of three elements: *conscious planning, thoughtful learning,* and *reflection for future improvement,* which the rubric identifies as MLR.1, MLR.2, and MLR.3, respectively. Also in the rubric, Stages 1, 2, and 3 indicate the level of support a student needs to perform the behavior.

FIGURE 1.13
Meta-Level Reflection Rubric

	Early (Preschool–K)	Beginning (K–3)	Transition (3–6)	Developing (6–9)	Expert (9–12)
MLR.1 Conscious Planning	• Creates plans based on self-interest with detailed description (what, when, with whom) and sticks to the plan.	• Creates plans based on interest and learning goals. • Identifies information and skills needed and creates steps to achieve plans.	• Sets goals that are beneficial for self and others based on purposeful interest and learning goals. • Analyzes learned knowledge and skills needed and creates procedures to achieve the goals.	• Sets thoughtful and responsible plans based on purposeful interest and learning goals. • Supports the plans with arguments and procedures based on learned knowledge and skills to ensure adaptive approaches to achieve the goals.	• Sets thoughtful plans with clear measurement criteria, based on purposeful interest, vision of a sustainable future, and learning goals. • Supports the plans with reasoned arguments and adaptive strategies based on interdisciplinary knowledge and skills to surpass the goals.
	Stage 1 2 3	Stage 1 2 3	Stage 1 2 3	Stage 1 2 3	Stage 1 2 3
MLR.2 Thoughtful Learning	• Identifies activities that refer to the thinking process. • Understands input (feedback) from others and follows feedback to improve the learning process.	• Identifies the sequence of the thinking process s/he is engaged in. • Understands the important role of feedback to improve the learning process.	• Identifies the thinking skills s/he is engaged in. • Understands the important role of feedback and is able to digest the information to ensure the attainment of efficient approaches toward the goals.	• Explains the thinking skills s/he is engaged in and the thinking process involved. • Looks for feedback to be digested to ensure the attainment of an efficient and effective thinking and feelings management process to make decisions based on the goals and the concepts, skills, and values learned.	• Evaluates the thinking skills s/he is engaged in and why and how they were used skillfully. • Independently processes diverse bits of information (rational and emotional) by continuously (self-aware) monitoring and checking to make sure efficiency, effectiveness, and productivity toward the goal are attained.
	Stage 1 2 3	Stage 1 2 3	Stage 1 2 3	Stage 1 2 3	Stage 1 2 3

Meta-Level Reflection

	Early (Preschool–K)	Beginning (K–3)	Transition (3–6)	Developing (6–9)	Expert (9–12)
MLR.3 Reflecting for Future Improvement	• Reflects on own performance on a given task (e.g., what s/he did, how s/he felt about the result, whether s/he followed the plan).	• Explains whether s/he has met the objective set at the beginning and is able to explain the steps to achieve the plan. • Identifies action plans to improve for the future.	• Identifies whether s/he has used appropriate tools to carry out a thinking task toward the achievement of the goals (e.g., using a cause–effect graphic organizer to identify a causal-effect relationship). • Explains the areas for and identifies action plans for the future.	• Evaluates whether s/he has used appropriate tools and strategies to carry out a thinking task based on the goals (e.g., using a thinking map/asking the right questions for problem solving to find a solution to a problem). • Explains the areas for improvement, elaborates the reasons, and develops plans for areas for improvement.	• Evaluates how s/he has used appropriate tools and strategies skillfully and transfers the learning in the right contexts based on the goals. • Creates the action plans to follow up the areas for improvement. • Internalizes the whole process of reflection as a mindset in any activity.
	Stage 1 2 3	Stage 1 2 3	Stage 1 2 3	Stage 1 2 3	Stage 1 2 3

Stage 1: Student performs a task somewhat accurately with consistent guidance from others (teachers and peers).

Stage 2: Student performs a task accurately with little guidance and redirection from others (teachers and peers).

Stage 3: Student independently performs a task with ease, speed, and accuracy.

Here is how the levels of support break out:

- Stage 1: Student performs a task somewhat accurately with consistent guidance from others (teachers and peers).
- Stage 2: Student performs a task accurately with little guidance and redirection from others (teachers and peers).
- Stage 3: Student independently performs a task with ease, speed, and accuracy.

To assess Meta-Level Reflection skills and other essential life skills, we use four types of assessment: (1) assessment to determine a student's position before beginning new learning, (2) ongoing formative assessment to keep track of the student's progress in order to provide immediate feedback and support, (3) self-assessment as a way for students to reflect on their work and their performance using rubrics as the basis for judging where they are in relation to the expectations, and (4) summative assessment to determine the point of development at a certain time in the learning journey.

Teachers continuously conduct formal and informal formative assessment to check students' understanding of the rubric's expectations and to determine where each student is in relation to the expectations. Formative assessment methods include quizzes, questioning, and hand-signal assessments. For example, teachers can ask students to indicate their understanding of conscious planning using these sentence stems, with students responding with an appropriate hand signal:

- I understand that conscious planning should be based on my learning goals and involve strategies. (*thumbs up*)
- I don't understand yet how to create a thoughtful plan. (*thumbs down*)
- I am still confused about.... (*waving hand*)
- I am not sure about.... (*positioning thumbs horizontally*)

Students' progress on Meta-Level Reflection skills will be apparent in their work. Teachers can gain insight by considering students' goals as seen in their project logs, their thinking process as described in the graphic organizer they use, and the discussion they engage in with fellow classmates or teachers as well as the constructive feedback they get from peers.

A Closer Look at Continuum Levels

The continuum levels in the Meta-Level Reflection rubric obviously cover a broad expanse of understanding. Let's look at each level in greater detail, using the element of MLR.2, thoughtful learning.

Early (Preschool–K)

At the Early level, students begin to identify activities that are related to the thinking process. The word *think* is not easy for students at this level to understand. They may not be able to name the thinking process accurately, but they can simply use the word *think* or more specific action verbs. At this level, teachers help students to understand the key words and phrases, with the goal of full understanding.

Preschool teachers collect evidence of thoughtful learning during students' working process, when they execute their plans, and during the designated reflection time. Students' readiness levels determine how detailed a teacher's review is. An appropriate prompt can help teachers gather relevant information—even something as simple as "I noticed that you ran out of modeling clay while you were trying to make the birthday cake. What did you do to solve the problem?"

Beginning (Grades K–3)

At the Beginning level, students start to identify the sequence of the thinking process they engage in—that is, the elements of Expert Thinking (the topic of Chapter 2) that they currently employ (systems thinking, analytical thinking, and critical thinking).

Teachers can assess students' progress in thoughtful learning at this level by examining how they use sequence in explaining their thinking steps. For example, Darryl, a Grade 2–3 student, demonstrated thoughtful learning in describing his thinking process during a science experiment. Darryl said, "I want to see how fast solid matter changes to liquid" and explained each step of his learning process. "First, I was thinking about what objects I could melt using heat. To see which one melts faster, I picked butter and cheddar cheese." He continued, "Then, I compared and contrasted. Throughout the process, I do self-questioning by asking, *Have I selected the right materials and tools to support my experiment? Have I used the right steps in the experiment?* My teacher helped me melt butter in one pan and cheese in another pan. I observed that butter melts faster than cheddar cheese." He added, "My teacher reminded me to use a graphic organizer to compare and contrast, so I can note down the results of my experiment. I observed the speed and what they look like before and after." Darryl used the graphic organizer shown in Figure 1.14 (see p. 26) for comparing and contrasting. He then stated, "When I'm using this graphic organizer, I'm using analytical thinking."

FIGURE 1.14
Example of a Completed Graphic Organizer for Comparing and Contrasting

Categories	Object 1 Butter	Object 2 Cheese
Similarities		
Matter	Solid	
Basic Ingredients	Milk	
Differences		
Time to melt	2 minutes	5 minutes
Result	Watery	Gooey
Smell	Milky and salty	A bit smokey
Conclusion		
Butter melts faster than cheese.		

Given the expectations in the Meta-Level Reflection rubric, the anecdotal evidence gained from Darryl's conversation with his teacher and his use of the graphic organizer suggest that Darryl was in Stage 3 of the rubric. He was able to articulate the expectations in the rubric and recalled the thinking skills he engaged in during the experiment. Additionally, he was able to use his teacher's feedback to guide his next steps without additional guidance. In comparison, students in Stage 1 would need the teacher to explicitly prompt them to identify the thinking skills through questioning and giving examples.

Transition (Grades 3–6)

As students reach the Transition level, teachers assess their ability to identify the thinking skills they engaged in when solving a problem or doing their research. Another skill that teachers assess is how the students monitor and use feedback from others to ensure that they take approaches that can help them to be more productive in reaching the goal. Students modify their approach based on critical and constructive feedback and conduct self-monitoring to ensure that their actions are effective and productive to achieve the goal.

Developing (Grades 6–9)

Students at the Developing level are capable of not just identifying but also elaborating on the elements of Expert Thinking they are using. They are clear about their learning goals and proactively look for feedback.

As an example, a Grade 8–9 student named Reuben explained the thinking skills and thinking process he engaged in while designing a plan to solve a waste management problem at his school related to littering and trash disposal in the cafeteria. He explained how he would use data analysis, scientific thinking, and analytical thinking skills to solve the problem. He also looked for feedback from an expert in this area, his teachers, and his peers to gain more understanding and brainstorm possible solutions.

During a conversation, his teacher asked Reuben how he used self-questioning to monitor his own thinking. The teacher also assessed whether Reuben was able to monitor his progress toward achieving the learning objectives.

In addition, Reuben documented which thinking skills he engaged when he did a gap analysis comparing current and ideal conditions regarding littering and trash disposal. During a class meeting where he presented his ideas for a prototype product, he also reached conclusions about what to improve and maintain in order to achieve effectiveness and efficiency in his project.

Based on his project log and anecdotal notes from the conversation with the teacher, we can infer that Reuben is at Stage 2 on the rubric. Determining factors include the need to be prompted by the teacher to explain the thinking skills he engaged in and how he looked for feedback.

On the other hand, students who are at Stage 3 on the rubric do not need a teacher's prompt or support to reflect on their thinking skills and look for feedback. For example, a student named Cameron independently explained the thinking skills she engaged without the teacher's guidance. She also described how the feedback she received helped her identify her product's strengths and weaknesses. From this evidence, we can infer that Cameron is at Stage 3.

Expert (Grades 9–12)

At the peak of development, the Expert level, students are not only able to explain their thinking skills but also to evaluate why and how they used them. They monitor and check the use of thinking skills to maximize the attainment of concepts, skills, and values and to ensure progress toward the goal. They modify and make changes along the way, ensuring the most effective method to achieve their goals. Students at this level monitor their thinking automatically.

To assess students' skills in thoughtful learning, teachers can prompt students through questioning or observe students during their learning activities when they are finding solutions to problems, conducting an experiment, or doing some research. As part of the learning process, teachers can provide immediate feedback for each student and examine how those students follow up the feedback. Then, teachers can interview students to explain their thinking process—which thinking skills they engaged in during the learning activity.

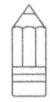

Suggestions for Integrating Meta-Level Reflection into Curriculum and Classroom Practice

- Infuse a Meta-Level Reflection rubric into curriculum standards and project-based learning by expecting students to consciously plan their projects, learn thoughtfully, and continuously reflect.
- Integrate the Meta-Level Reflection process into all aspects of learning to provide multiple opportunities for student practice.
- Allow students to discover their purposeful learning goals, guide them to create a detailed plan based on good-choices criteria, and ensure that they can measure the success of their plan.
- Continuously ask students to revisit their goals and monitor their progress.
- Allocate time for students to reflect on how they feel about and do their learning. Encourage them to find their areas for improvement and create their own action plan to increase their ownership of learning.
- Encourage students to actively ask questions to monitor their thinking processes.
- Provide graphic organizers for students to map their thinking process.
- Develop students' habit to ask for and receive feedback.

2
Expert Thinking

No problem can withstand the assault of sustained thinking.
—Voltaire—

Self-regulated leaders consciously think about and monitor their own thinking. When challenges arise, they set goals, devise plans, and select effective strategies to tackle those challenges after having considered multiple perspectives. This series of processes confirms that Meta-Level Reflection and Expert Thinking skills are inseparable.

We use the term *Expert Thinking* to refer to a set of thinking skills that are essential for self-regulated leaders. We define *Expert Thinking* as the ability to maximize the mental capacity of the brain by processing multiple aspects of perception, emotion, cognition, and action (knowledge) systematically, analytically, and critically, to make decisions and solve problems effectively.

We purposefully use the term *expert* to differentiate these skills from those of novice thinkers. Whereas expert thinkers possess a mental framework for organizing their knowledge, novice thinkers lack such structures (Adams et al., 2008). Novice thinkers tend to remember pieces of information, jump to conclusions, and memorize new ideas rather than integrating them with any related information. Expert thinkers are able to perceive structure, notice relevant structure that cues them to the next steps, recognize patterns, find structures, and identify discrepancies based on empirical data to revise ideas. They can effortlessly retrieve information, effectively perform reasoning through a chain of possibilities, recognize information that contradicts existing knowledge, and integrate newly acquired information with related schemas.

Why Is Expert Thinking Important?

We consider Expert Thinking central and important for three reasons: it (1) helps us see patterns and connections, (2) critically filters information we receive, and (3) allows us to make better decisions. Let's explore each of these in turn.

Seeing Patterns and Connections

Expert Thinking helps us see patterns and connections in information. Some children go through school simply memorizing facts. Because of the rapid pace of change in today's world, those facts may soon become obsolete. True learning occurs when children make connections between the facts they learn, see relationships, and are able to transfer what they have learned to new and different contexts. For this reason, schools must specifically teach students the kind of thinking that allows them to make these connections.

Teachers can intentionally develop this skill by helping students to observe, compare, contrast, and categorize objects or information based on certain attributes, thereby identifying and interpreting patterns, and reaching conclusions or generalizations based on pattern. Intentional development of Expert Thinking skills helps students develop the process of patterning in the brain so they can make sense of information and efficiently produce higher-order thinking.

Filtering Information

Expert Thinking helps us critically filter the information we receive rather than simply rushing to accept it. This ability is especially important in today's world, where children learn through social media and information they download on multiple devices. Expert Thinking is the brake that allows them to pause and ask important questions such as these:

- How can I tell if this is true?
- Is it logical?
- Who said this? Is that person a credible source?
- On what data is this based?
- Has anybody else said the same thing?

Expert thinkers use systems thinking, analytical thinking, and critical thinking skills when processing new information. With new information bombarding us daily, attention spans shortening, and problems becoming more complex, these skills must be developed from early childhood through high school with increasing sophistication and complexity.

Making Better Decisions

Expert Thinking facilitates better decision making. When students see patterns and connections in information, they gain a deeper understanding of a topic or problem, which leads to better ideas and solutions. When they question the reliability and reasonableness of information, they make smarter choices. According to Jensen (1994), it takes a vast number of neural circuits and connections for the brain to make the most effective decisions possible. These connections do not happen automatically—at least not optimally. They can, however, be stimulated through intentional efforts.

Teachers can purposefully create opportunities for students to hone this skill by actively having them assess their own decision-making process through questions such as these:

- Which perspective should I consider?
- How do I support my arguments?
- Have I supported my arguments with valid information?
- How does my decision-making process affect myself and others?

We believe students need to be taught to develop "the ability to bring together many diverse bits of information to create new understanding, maximize potential, and provoke solutions" (Jensen, 1994, p. 145).

Key Elements of Expert Thinking

Expert Thinking comprises three elements: (1) *systems thinking*, (2) *analytical thinking*, and (3) *critical thinking* (see Figure 2.1, p. 32). It is worth noting that we do not consider these three elements as having a hierarchy or order of precedence. Indeed, they not only are interconnected but also can occur at the same time.

Systems Thinking

We define *systems thinking* as the ability to examine the interconnectedness of elements that make up a system (big picture) through a horizontal perspective with the intent to understand how its structure influences the behavior of elements and how the cause-and-effect relationship is represented.

FIGURE 2.1
The Key Elements of Expert Thinking

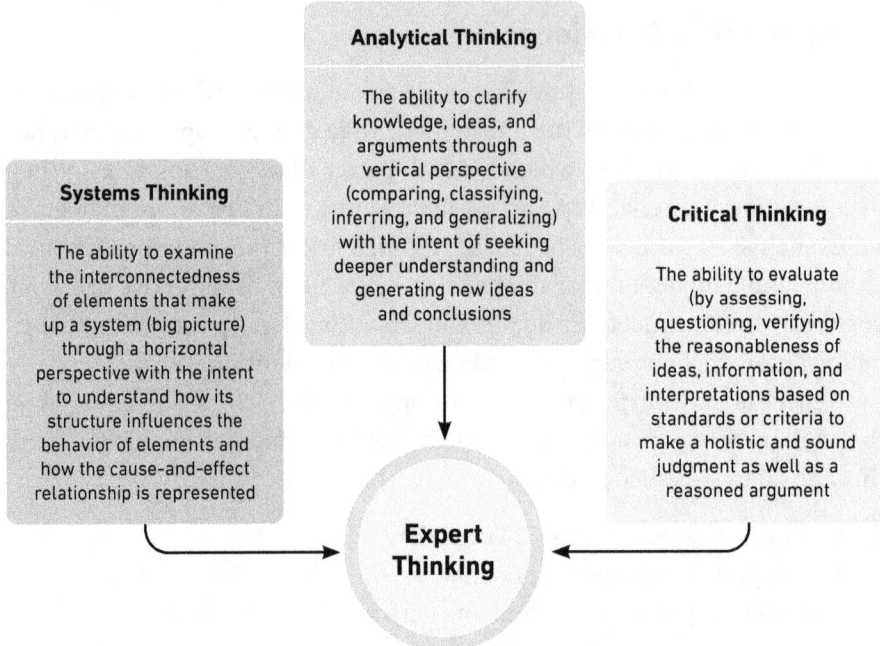

Systems thinking encompasses six important concepts: (1) big-picture thinking, (2) elements, (3) interconnectedness, (4) structure, (5) patterns of behavior, and (6) cause and effect. Big-picture thinking emphasizes understanding the part-whole relationship and how the elements in it are structured and interconnected. The cause-and-effect relationship focuses on how sub-elements are interconnected and show patterns of behavior. For that reason, the explanation that follows is organized into two main parts: (1) nurturing big-picture thinking, including elements, interconnectedness, and structure, and (2) nurturing the ability to identify patterns of behavior and cause and effect. (See Figure 2.2 for a graphic organizer and prompting questions that can help students understand systems thinking.)

> *Systems thinking* encompasses six important concepts: (1) big-picture thinking, (2) elements, (3) interconnectedness, (4) structure, (5) patterns of behavior, and (6) cause and effect.

FIGURE 2.2
Graphic Organizer for Conceptualizing Systems Thinking

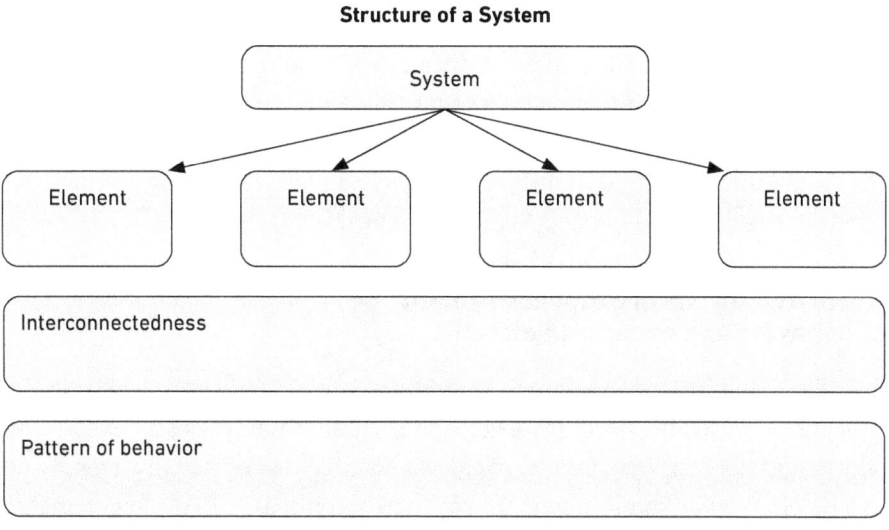

Prompting questions:
1. What is the system?
2. What is the system's objective?
3. What are the system's elements?
4. How are the elements and sub-elements connected to one another?
5. How does the structure of the system support its objective?
6. What is the elements' pattern of behavior?
7. What are the system's boundaries?
8. What insights can we gather?

Nurturing big-picture thinking

The basic concept of big-picture thinking is the part-whole relationship, and the key to understanding the part-whole relationship is to identify the various elements and their functions.

Preschool and early-elementary students can start their study of this concept using concrete objects: each part, what it does, and how it connects with the other pieces to form a whole. Teachers can introduce the relevant vocabulary through discussion and ask students to choose from among objects around them and to describe the objects' structure and how that structure operates within the whole. In Grades 4–5, students should be introduced to the words *element, interconnectedness, boundaries,* and *big picture.*

In our school, we create a different "big question" for each term. It's an idea or concept explored across all subjects, framed into a question that our students need to answer based on their analysis of cross-multidisciplinary learning. Students learn about the concept from a horizontal perspective across all subjects. At the end of the term, they need to be able to answer the big question using the perspectives that they have learned in the different subjects. This approach helps students develop a mindset that recognizes that small topics learned in different subjects all lead to one big picture that needs to be addressed—hence, big-picture thinking.

Nurturing the ability to identify patterns of behavior and cause and effect

Preschool and lower-elementary students at our school begin learning the concept of cause and effect by observing their surroundings and explaining why things happen. Discussions of cause and effect occur in daily events and can be planned or spontaneous. In planned activities, STEAM experiments provide concrete opportunities to experience cause and effect—for example, an oil-water-soap experiment to explore cause and effect in chemistry. An example of a more spontaneous event comes from our preschool class, when the teacher noticed a student spilling some of the water that he was trying to pour into a friend's cup during snack time. She turned the situation into a teachable moment: "Oops! When Jay was pouring the water, his aim was off, causing the water go on the table, not in Ali's cup. What was the effect on the table? That's right—the table got wet."

At the higher grade levels, discussions of cause and effect usually get more complex as abstract concepts are incorporated. Social and natural phenomena in the environment provide great context. Students can observe their surroundings, find a problem to solve, and propose and try out solutions. In Grades 10–12 at our school, students are introduced to the dynamic pattern of behavior among the elements using the "dynamic-thinking" method, which allows them to study an issue or a phenomenon from a wide horizontal perspective. This perspective asks students to distance themselves from the detailed behavior of each element in a system. Instead, they identify the elements, the connection among the elements, and the pattern of the elements' behavior over time, as well as the boundaries of the system. This thinking process enables students to see a dynamic pattern, rather than a static one, due to a cause-and-effect relationship among elements. An example would be when students identify the criteria, interactions, or interconnectedness of the elements of good government.

Analytical Thinking

After students are able to see a particular problem from a horizontal perspective—the "big picture" in systems thinking—they need to look into details of elements or issues within the system to better understand the case being examined and to come up with a conclusion or generalization—the vertical perspective. This process calls for a skill called *analytical thinking*. We define *analytical thinking* as the ability to clarify knowledge, ideas, and arguments through a vertical perspective (comparing, classifying, inferring, and generalizing) with the intent of seeking deeper understanding and generating new ideas and conclusions.

This element consists of three sub-elements: (1) comparing and contrasting, (2) sorting and classifying, and (3) generalizations and conclusions. Comparing and contrasting primarily emphasizes students' ability to find similarities and differences between two or more objects or ideas in order to gain insights from multiple perspectives. Sorting and classifying refers to the ability to group certain objects or ideas based on multiple perspectives and patterns found as a result of comparing and sorting. Generalizations and conclusions are about making a general statement based on multiple perspectives from a number of ideas, bits of information, or concepts.

> *Analytical thinking* consists of three sub-elements: (1) comparing and contrasting, (2) sorting and classifying, and (3) generalizations and conclusions.

Nurturing the ability to compare and contrast and to sort and classify

Robert Swartz and Sandra Parks (1994) define *analytical thinking* as the thinking process that provides us with insight and understanding by clarifying the information we have. Clarifying involves basic analytical skills such as determining key elements of a system, comparing them to other things, and classifying. Comparing and contrasting helps us detect patterns by finding similarities and differences, with the goal of gaining insight and understanding.

There are two forms of expert classification: classifying from the top down and from the bottom up. Classifying from the top down facilitates our understanding of new objects by identifying them as belonging to certain categories in an existing classification system and providing guidance on how to use these objects effectively to achieve a certain purpose. Our brain typically processes new information in this way. Classifying from the bottom up is a more complex process that involves exploring a variety of ways that objects can be grouped to reveal different patterns and relationships, then choosing a classification system that best serves a specific purpose. By Grades 6–9, students should be able to expertly organize and classify. Although comparing and contrasting naturally involves sorting, learning to expertly categorize or classify typically requires explicit teaching.

Young children can develop analytical thinking through practice comparing, sorting, and classifying concrete objects and direct experiences. It is important that younger students become familiar with the concept of "same" and "different." At the beginning of the academic year, teachers at our school give students concrete experiences to help familiarize them with vocabulary words related to analytical thinking, such as *compare*, *sort*, *characteristics*, *conclude*, and so on.

Exposure to these concepts can came from labeling things that are the same or different—for example, describing how one's hair is the same or different from someone else's (same color, different style), describing what students see during a neighborhood walk (kinds of plants, types of businesses), or sorting the books in the classroom library by author, size, type, topic, and so on. Students in kindergarten can be introduced to a simple Venn diagram to visualize their thinking. As an example, during a collaborative math workshop in one of our K–1 classes, the teacher used masking tape to create a large Venn diagram on the floor. A student picked two different shapes of wooden blocks—a prism and a cube. Other students could jump into the two circles and describe the attributes of each shape, or they could jump into the intersection of the diagram and describe the similarities or shared attributes.

At the beginning level of analytical thinking, children are able to describe the characteristics of the objects and sort them into categories based on things such as size, color, and shape. Plenty of activities can be designed for the purpose of comparing and contrasting real objects. For example, a preschool or kindergarten teacher reading a story aloud might distribute hands-on props connected to the story, such as sets of colorful plastic animals and colorful wooden blocks, and give students prompts to practice classification by color ("The family of red bears are heading out to the picnic in a red car. The yellow bears are going in a yellow car. Find a car that matches the color of your bears") and by size ("The smallest bear lives in the smallest house; the biggest bear lives in the biggest house").

To help students structure their thinking, we use graphic organizers, posters, and questions. Graphic organizers are a great way to encourage the development of desirable patterns of thinking and reasoning. Their complexity increases as students progress through the developmental stages.

As students mature and are able to think more abstractly, we have them advance to comparing and sorting ideas and perspectives based on categories and patterns, which may result in establishing new criteria and then justifying their classification decisions. A more complex graphic organizer (see Figure 2.3 as an example) is needed to help students organize their thinking as they learn to compare and contrast. (We describe a higher-level example of a learning activity later in this chapter.)

FIGURE 2.3
Graphic Organizer for Comparing and Contrasting

Categories	Object 1 _____	Object 2 _____
Similarities		
Differences		
Insights Gained		

Prompting questions:
1. What categories do you use?
2. What are the similarities?
3. What are the differences?
4. What categories or patterns do you see in the similarities and differences?
5. What insights do you get from this process (compare, contrast, sort)?

Nurturing the ability to draw conclusions and make generalizations

After using the skills of comparing and contrasting, sorting, classifying, and categorizing, students can eventually learn to draw conclusions and make generalizations based on the pattern they find in their earlier analysis. For example, after comparing and sorting daily objects into various types of simple machines, students find it easy to identify a new object that makes daily work easier as a simple machine. Throughout the learning process, teachers intentionally develop this ability in their students.

Younger students in preschool and lower-elementary grades begin making simple conclusions by comparing and contrasting concrete objects and experiences around them. For example, children in our preschool compared and contrasted the taste of different types of fruit. One of the students said, "I thought only yellow fruit like lemon tastes sour, but then I tasted the green kiwi. It's also sour." The teacher said, "Right. Even the small red strawberry is sour sometimes." Another student said, "So we cannot say that a fruit is sour or not based only on its color."

To further facilitate the development of the ability to generalize, each class has a "question of the day" corner where students can write questions, before and during learning, related to a targeted concept in multiple subjects. They can discuss the questions during morning meeting or subject-area time. The concept changes every day to spark students' curiosity and build their ability to ask the right questions. For example, students in Grade 2–3 who were exploring the concept of "pattern" wrote the following questions before the class began:

- What is pattern?
- Where can I find pattern?
- Is there a pattern in our class?
- How can I identify pattern?
- What makes a pattern?
- What can I do with pattern?

Teachers could initiate a discussion by selecting some questions and allowing students to share their answers and ideas. The question of the day and related discussion provide an opportunity for students to become self-learners, to own their learning and develop their own knowledge, as opposed to teachers providing questions for students to consider. Furthermore, the questions in the example were also discussed in different subjects, so students could see the transferability of the concepts. For example, during morning meeting, students and teachers discussed "Where can I find a pattern?" Students came up with various answers, noting the day-and-night pattern in daily life and the pattern of their school schedule and school hours.

Beginning in Grade 4–5, students can learn to identify complex relationships among elements and make generalizations. We teach more mature students to question the rationale behind their own ideas in order to define the limits of their own generalizations. For example, students in a social studies class were exploring human actions that affect the environment. The teacher used the thinking map for skillful generalization as modeled by Swartz and Parks (1994):

- What generalization can we suggest from the case?
- Which sample can we select to support the generalization based on our previous compare, contrast, and sort?
- How many samples do we need to collect?
- How can we justify that the selected sample is representative?

In another example of building Expert Thinking skills, a Grade 8–9 teacher designed an experiment at the beginning of the academic year in which students compared and sorted three substances—salt, sugar, and pepper—that might make ice melt. Before doing the experiment, the students were asked to make a hypothesis based on the question "Which one of the ingredients will melt the ice faster?" After the experiment, the students compared and sorted their observations using a table, as shown in Figure 2.4.

FIGURE 2.4
Example of a Table Comparing Results of an Observation

Compare the results of your observation of ice melting.

Criteria	Ice + Sugar	Ice + Salt	Ice + Pepper	Ice Only
Amount of time needed to start melting	50 seconds	40 seconds	60 seconds	60 seconds
Temperature of the overall mixture (C°)	9°C	10°C	7°C	7°C
Amount of water melted (mL)	1 mL	2 mL	0.8 mL	1 mL
Similarities	They all melt in 60 or less seconds.			

From your observation, which ingredient can melt the ice the fastest?
From my observation, I believe that salt melts the ice the fastest.

During the discussion, the teacher introduced the phrase *classification scheme* and engaged the students in a vocabulary activity referring to the table they had made to compare and sort their observation data. When one student shared her conclusion with the class, noting that different materials would have different effects on the melting rate of an ice cube, the teacher identified the type of conclusion the student had just made as a *generalization*. Once again, the teacher was using a vocabulary activity to introduce the key words related to Expert Thinking.

The next day, the students studied the key elements of Expert Thinking. They were asked to recall how their experience from the previous day related to this essential life skill. They brainstormed their ideas on a virtual whiteboard and summarized their understanding for each key element of Expert Thinking in a poster (see Figure 2.5).

FIGURE 2.5
Example of a Poster Reminder for Expert Thinking, Grade 8–9

Systems Thinking	Analytical Thinking	Critical Thinking
Find the big picture. Explain the elements and structure. Explain how elements impact the system and how this can create problems in the system.	Make compare-contrast and categories to see patterns in data. Analyze data to find relationships and connections to create generalization.	Evaluate information to ensure reliability and validity. Use criteria when analyzing data.

The students were now ready to personalize their new knowledge. To guide their personalization, the teacher asked them to write about how they applied Expert Thinking in the experiment. Students used sticky notes in the virtual whiteboard to write their personalization. (Teachers can provide different tools such as sticky notes or a one-minute writing exercise in which students write what they understand and "still wonder.") This personalization served as a formative assessment for the teacher to give appropriate feedback and corrective activities before the students practiced the skill collaboratively.

Based on the formative assessment, the teacher identified students who needed corrective activities to enhance their understanding of analytical thinking and show the expected behavior based on the rubric for Expert

Thinking. The teacher helped them to understand the expectation by understanding the vocabulary related to analytical thinking. The teacher selected key words such as *category, classification,* and *implication,* and used certain strategies, such as a "vocabulary detective" graphic organizer (see Figure 2.6), to build students' understanding.

FIGURE 2.6
Vocabulary Detective Graphic Organizer for Grade 8–9

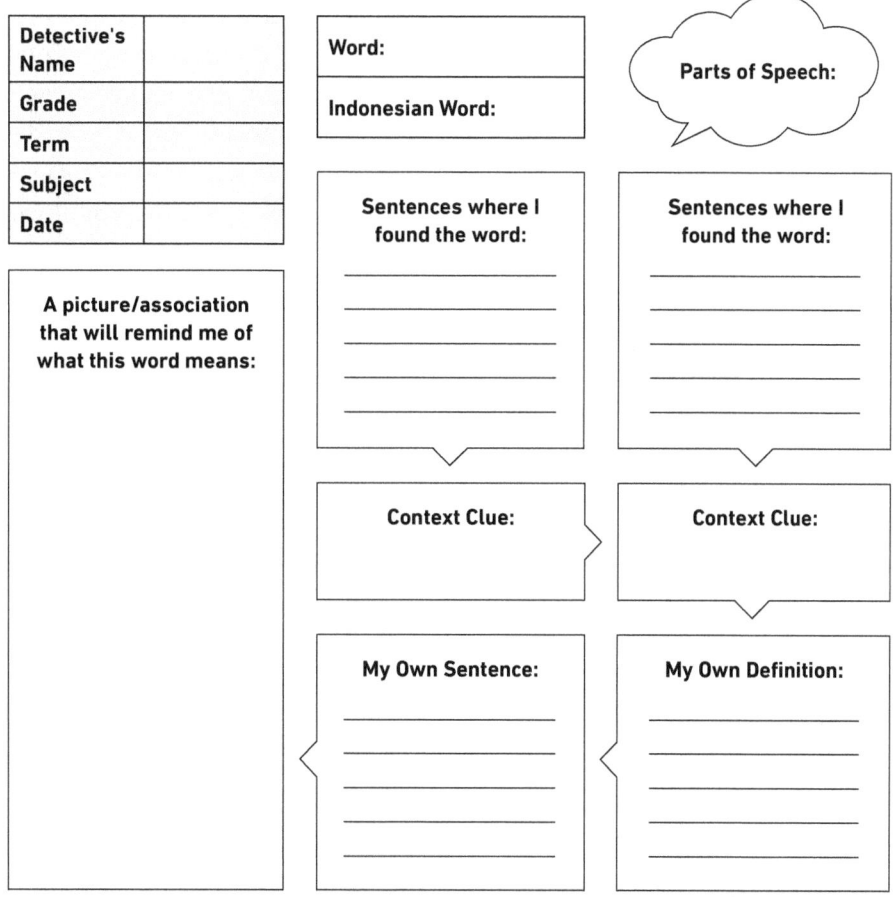

At the Expert level on the rubric for Expert Thinking, we expect students to be able to evaluate the credibility of the information they use to form their generalizations and to determine the limits of the generalization. When students develop generalizations, teachers ask them to consider a few questions, such as the following:

- Are the data big enough to support my generalization?
- What patterns support my generalization?
- Is this generalization applicable/transferable to all contexts?
- What is the limit of my generalization?

Critical Thinking

Evaluating new knowledge and ideas cannot be accomplished effectively without critical thinking. Individuals must think critically to ensure their judgments are valid, accurate, and align with the existing evidence. We define *critical thinking* as the ability to evaluate (by assessing, questioning, verifying) the reasonableness of ideas, information, and interpretations based on standards or criteria to make a holistic and sound judgment as well as a reasoned argument. Teachers use a deliberate process to nurture students' ability to ask questions about the reliability and accuracy of information and to use appropriate graphic organizers as a tool to map their thinking process.

Critical thinking consists of three sub-elements: (1) reliability of resources, (2) reasonableness of ideas, and (3) evaluation of errors. Finding reliable resources, both primary and secondary, involves assessing bias. Determining the reasonableness of an idea requires making claims or arguments based on evidence, as well as considering counterclaims and qualifiers. Evaluation of errors involves reflection, comparing and contrasting, questioning, and identifying criteria.

> *Critical thinking* consists of three sub-elements: (1) reliability of resources, (2) reasonableness of ideas, and (3) evaluation of errors.

Nurturing the ability to determine reliability of resources and reasonableness of ideas

Students learn how to determine the reliability of resources and the reasonableness of ideas by developing the habit of asking questions when receiving information rather than just accepting it. Teachers can model how to consider the concept of reliability by suggesting questions such as these:

- Where can I find reliable information online or offline?
- What are the important keywords to find information online?
- Who are the authors?

- Which authors are more credible than others when they have different opinions or perspectives?
- How can I justify its reliability?

As students move up in grade level, they can discuss more detailed factors for judging reliability of information. Our upper-elementary students are even expected to make their own criteria. For example, a teacher guided her Grade 6–7 students in making the following thinking map, based on the model by Swartz and Parks (1994), to establish criteria for reliability:

- What source is being evaluated?
- How does the source fit or support the argument?
- What are the factors to consider? For example,
  - Publishing (date, reputation of the publisher)
  - Author (expertise, possible bias, special interest, primary or secondary, corroboration/confirmation)
- Weigh all the factors and judge the reliability.

After discussing the thinking map, the students answered the questions in a graphic organizer (see Figure 2.7, p. 44) to determine reliability of sources and reasonableness of ideas.

Nurturing the Ability to Evaluate Errors

To ensure their thinking leads to an accurate result, students need to learn to recognize and analyze errors that may occur in the validity and accuracy of information they gather, their thinking process, their reasoning, or their execution of a procedure.

Younger students can practice finding errors in processes that are concrete and visible, such as completing a puzzle by finding, through trial and error, the pieces that go together. Another example involves teachers explicitly asking their students to recheck their own work after finishing a task.

Students in upper grades are expected to analyze errors in more abstract concepts, such as their thinking process or reasoning when they execute plans or procedures. High school students should be able to develop their own criteria to identify errors in a system based on their understanding of its structure. For example, a high school student was writing his senior thesis on how to solve traffic congestion in Jakarta, Indonesia. Using his big-picture thinking, he wrote the following thesis statement:

The core of the problem is the lack of coordination between departments that handle mass transportation and the department that takes care of city planning.

FIGURE 2.7
Graphic Organizer for Evaluating Reliability and Reasonableness of Information

Insights gained from the primary and secondary sources:	Secondary Sources		Reliability and Reasonableness
	Source 1:	Who:	
		What:	
	Source 2:	Who:	
		What:	
	Source 3:	Who:	
		What:	
	Conclusions, generalization, and my judgment on this issue:		

Prompting questions:
1. Who is the author/publisher (secondary source)?
2. What is the background and credibility of the source?
3. Why do you include this source?
4. What does the source say about…?
5. What is the general conclusion of the source?
6. What is the author's purpose for writing the text? Is there any bias?
7. How do you evaluate the reasonableness, relevance, and representativeness of the source?

After carefully analyzing the problem, he found that coordination was not the main cause of traffic congestion. Other factors played bigger roles, such as affordable gasoline and the decreasing cost of vehicles (which led to more drivers on the roads) and Jakarta's limited transportation infrastructure, with road construction not keeping pace with the increase in the number of private vehicles.

In the student's second draft, he revised his thesis statement to say this:

The gap between road construction and the number of private vehicles is the fundamental problem that contributes to traffic congestion in Jakarta.

When his teacher asked him why he had revised his statement, the student replied,

> I wrote the first draft mostly based on a single aspect only, which is internal coordination among departments. However, on second thought, I thought I needed stronger arguments by analyzing other aspects such as government policy on gasoline, vehicle ownership, and infrastructure in Jakarta. I support my thesis with more reliable data from existing research that explains the causes.

How Is Expert Thinking Measured and Assessed?

To ensure that Expert Thinking skills are consistently measured and assessed within our school program, we created a rubric to describe the behaviors we expect to see at each developmental level (see Figure 2.8, p. 46). We wrote descriptions and specified indicators for each of the three elements of Expert Thinking: *systems thinking, analytical thinking*, and *critical thinking*. The rubric represents *systems thinking* as ET1.a and ET1.b; *analytical thinking* is ET2.a and ET2.b; and *critical thinking* is ET3. Also in the rubric, Stages 1, 2, and 3 indicate the amount of support a student needs to perform the behavior:

- Stage 1: Student performs a task somewhat accurately with consistent guidance from others (teachers and peers).
- Stage 2: Student performs a task accurately with little guidance and redirection from others (teachers and peers).
- Stage 3: Student independently performs a task with ease, speed, and accuracy.

The following discussion examines the second element, *analytical thinking*. The rubric for this element focuses on students' skills in comparing, sorting, and generalizing knowledge with the intent of seeking deeper understanding of ideas and generating new and relevant conclusions. Whereas in systems thinking students view the situation or problem from a horizontal perspective, analytical thinking requires them to view it from a vertical perspective as they go deeper into a specific element or aspect of the system.

This element consists of two sub-elements: (1) comparing, contrasting, and sorting and (2) developing generalizations. Comparing, contrasting, and sorting primarily emphasize students' ability to find similarities and differences between two or more objects or ideas in order to gain insights from multiple perspectives. Generalizing involves not only these skills but also

FIGURE 2.8
Rubric for Expert Thinking

		Early (Preschool–K)	Beginning (K–3)	Transition (3–6)	Developing (6–9)	Expert (9–12)
ET1.a	Systems Thinking	• Identifies what something is and what it is not. • Identifies parts and whole of a concrete object and how they make up a whole.	• Identifies how parts are arranged together to make up a whole and achieve a purpose.	• Identifies the big picture of a system that includes relevant subsystems with its elements and how they are structured to achieve a specific purpose.	• When trying to solve a problem, explains and justifies the big picture, the elements and structure of the system from multiple perspectives.	• When trying to solve a complex problem with different perspectives, develops and justifies a mental model to represent the big picture of a complex system.
		Stage 1 2 3	Stage 1 2 3	Stage 1 2 3	Stage 1 2 3	Stage 1 2 3
ET1.b	Systems Thinking	• Identify the relationship among parts of an object.	• Explains how parts work together in "part-whole relationship" that make up a whole of an object or an experience.	• Explains the cause-and-effect relationship among elements within a system in achieving its purposes.	• Explains how the interconnectedness in a structure of a system works and how it influences the larger system.	• Uses the model to simulate the "dynamic cause-effect relationship" and explains the interconnectedness in a system to achieve its objective within the boundaries of the system.
		Stage 1 2 3	Stage 1 2 3	Stage 1 2 3	Stage 1 2 3	Stage 1 2 3
ET2.a	Analytical Thinking	• Compare-contrasts two or more concrete objects or experiences. • Identifies and creates repeating patterns using concrete objects to categorize.	• Compare-contrasts two or more concrete objects or experiences. • Explains the patterns found (repetition or sequence) in the comparison. • Sort them into categories based on the patterns.	• Compare-contrasts and sorts three or more objects or ideas. • Explains the patterns, trends, and relationships found in the analysis. • Sorts them into categories and subcategories based on the patterns.	• Compare-contrasts and sorts ideas/elements/information/data into multiple categories. • Explains the patterns, trends, relationships, and interconnectedness found in the analysis. • Identifies subordinate and superordinate categories and explains the implications.	• Compare-contrasts and sorts ideas/elements/information/data into a variety of classification systems, with considerations of multiple perspectives. • Explains the patterns, trends, interconnectedness, and dynamic nature of cause-effect relationships found in the analysis.
		Stage 1 2 3	Stage 1 2 3	Stage 1 2 3	Stage 1 2 3	Stage 1 2 3

Expert Thinking   47

		Early (Preschool–K)				Beginning (K–3)				Transition (3–6)				Developing (6–9)				Expert (9–12)			
ET2.b	Analytical Thinking	• Explains reasons behind her/his own choices or actions in deciding the category.				• Makes conclusions/simple arguments and explains the reason based on experiment/concrete experience.				• Develops generalizations/ideas/conclusions with reason and evidence, including from own experiment.				• Develops arguments/hypotheses/conclusions/generalizations/solutions with reasons and evidence and addresses the counterclaims.				• Develops and defends valid arguments/hypotheses, conclusions/generalizations/solutions/insights with well supported reasoning and evidence, and addresses the counterclaim and the limits of the generalizations.			
		Stage	1	2	3	Stage	1	2	3	Stage	1	2	3	Stage	1	2	3	Stage	1	2	3
ET.3	Critical Thinking	• Asks clarifying questions about another person's idea.				• Selects information for a specific purpose and identifies the reason and the source. • Asks relevant and critical questions to identify possible errors.				• Compares, questions, and selects information from a range of (primary and secondary) sources of information and explains the reasons for choosing. • Identifies errors in information, procedures, and systems.				• Questions and evaluates a range of information sources to recognize their values and limitations, and to make conclusions about their reliability. • Uses and justifies explicit criteria to question and to evaluate reasonableness in information/ideas, and identify errors in procedures and systems.				• Develops, justifies, and applies well-supported criteria to question and evaluate the reasonableness of information/ideas. • Identify errors in a system, based on an understanding of its structure.			
		Stage	1	2	3	Stage	1	2	3	Stage	1	2	3	Stage	1	2	3	Stage	1	2	3

Stage 1: Student performs a task somewhat accurately with consistent guidance from others (teachers and peers).

Stage 2: Student performs a task accurately with little guidance and redirection from others (teachers and peers).

Stage 3: Student independently performs a task with ease, speed, and accuracy.

the ability to identify patterns. In other words, comparing, contrasting, and sorting are prerequisites for making a generalization.

The continuum levels in the Expert Thinking rubric obviously cover a broad expanse of understanding. Let's look at each level in greater detail.

Early (Preschool–K)

At the earliest level, students are expected to be able to find answers related to their own curiosity through the process of comparing, contrasting, and sorting objects and experiences. Being able to define an object's characteristics is helpful for answering their own questions and building intrinsic motivation. Our research has shown that even children in preschool and kindergarten can do simple analyses using comparing, contrasting, and sorting for concrete objects.

To collect evidence of analytical thinking, preschool teachers record anecdotal notes during small-group time or students' work on the Plan-Do-Review process. Teachers can determine students' stage of progress based on their ability to identify and create patterns using concrete objects. They can prompt students with questions such as these: "What is the pattern?" "Why do you think this is a pattern?" "What is the rule of the pattern?"

Beginning (Grades K–3)

Students at the Beginning continuum level are expected to be able to build upon their skill of comparing, contrasting, and sorting concrete objects and experiences learned in the Early level and elevate it by adding subcategories within each category. They are then expected to be able to provide reasons and justification for the categorization and make conclusions.

Throughout the year, students practice the skill of comparing, contrasting, and sorting through various learning activities. Project-based learning provides the context needed for students to practice the skills. As an example, Adam, a Grade 2–3 student, undertook a project to create a simple machine to help him work efficiently in daily life. At the beginning of the learning, he observed his daily habits and found out that he had a problem with cleaning up his LEGO bricks. He tried out three simple lever-based machines—a broom, a shovel, and tongs—to determine which one would help him complete the chore the fastest. He concluded that a small shovel was the best choice. However, he found that the metal shovel he used left scratch marks on the Legos, so he decided to make his own. He compared three materials—cardboard, acrylic, and wood (in the form of Popsicle sticks)—and assembled the shovels using hot glue. Using a graphic organizer (see Figure 2.9), Adam described the strengths and weaknesses of each material; he also reached a conclusion as to which one was best for his project: wood.

FIGURE 2.9
Example of a Completed Compare-Contrast Graphic Organizer

Categories	Subcategories	Materials		
		Cardboard	Popsicle sticks	Acrylics
Strengths	Capacity		Strong enough to hold up to 15 LEGO bricks	Hold a pile of LEGO bricks, up to 30
	Level of difficulty to make	Easy. It was quick to make. I could choose to use hot glue or tape.	Medium. It took longer to make since I needed to glue each stick one by one.	
	Endurance		Medium. As long as the glue hardens well.	Long
Weaknesses	Capacity	Hold only 10 LEGO bricks		
	Level of difficulty to make			Hard. I needed to buy the exact size for the pre-cut. I could not cut the acrylic based on my needs.
	Endurance	Short. Cannot get wet.		
Conclusion	Popsicle sticks are the most suitable material to make a shovel for my LEGO. Although it took longer to make, the materials are easier to get than acrylic and endure longer than cardboard.			

Throughout the learning, Adam did all the steps independently. Based on his graphic organizer, his product, and anecdotal notes from a conversation with him, his teacher concluded that Adam was already at Stage 3 of the rubric for the Beginning level.

Transition (Grades 3–6)

As children move to the Transition level, they begin thinking in more abstract ways. At this stage, they are able to move beyond comparing concrete objects to comparing ideas and sorting them into multiple categories and subcategories. They also begin to go from reaching conclusions to making generalizations.

At this level, we introduce students to more sophisticated methods, which are open and focused compare and contrast (Swartz & Parks, 1994). *Open compare and contrast* asks students to identify as many differences and similarities as possible, while *focused compare and contrast* asks students to compare items based on identified or selected elements. Both the open and focused forms of comparing and contrasting go beyond listing similarities and differences. Both involve more organization and deeper analytical thinking, and both generate a conclusion or interpretation (Swartz & Parks, 1994). Teachers ask students how they came up with certain categories to sort, how they identified patterns and trends, and how they interpreted them to form generalizations. Teachers gather multiple pieces of evidence from conversations with students, the students' graphic organizers, and their products.

Developing (Grades 6–9)

Students at the Developing level must be able to move beyond simple categorization to classification systems. They must be able to identify changes, patterns, and trends based on data from multiple resources and then use these insights to develop generalizations. Students at this level also continue to advance in their use of sophisticated methods of comparing ideas.

To assess students' progress at this level, teachers can ask them to demonstrate their ability to classify from the top down and from the bottom up. Teachers assemble evidence based on how students use graphic organizers to classify information into multiple categories, how they develop conclusions/generalizations/arguments based on patterns, and how they back up their arguments with evidence during their presentations.

Expert (Grades 9–12)

By the time they graduate from high school, we expect students to be able to demonstrate greater cognitive flexibility by comparing and sorting ideas into multiple classification schemes, considering multiple perspectives when doing so, and explaining the insight they gain from the analysis. The product of analysis should be a new conclusion or insight, a decision made, or a problem solved. We consider anything less to be no more than comprehension.

As students draw conclusions and make generalizations based on their analysis, they must keep in mind the limits of making generalizations—including the context in which they can be applied. For example, a Grade 12 student wrote a report for Sociology on "Teenager Stereotypes," basing it on multiple resources that identified *rebelliousness* and *adventurousness* as characteristics of teenagers. In her report, she surveyed teens in her class on their hobbies/areas of interest (dance, gymnastics, cheer, visual arts) and asked questions design to gauge whether they possess the two "teen traits." Although she found high rates of rebelliousness and adventurousness in teens who were interested in visual arts, the rates were low in those who were interested in dance, gymnastics, and cheer. In her report, she concluded that the statement "teens are rebellious and adventurous" is a generalization limited by teens' areas of interest. But she noted the generalization might be expanded if her research had included factors beyond interest, such as socioeconomic status or family parenting style. She further explained that her research was limited to the group of teenagers she surveyed in her specific area of South Jakarta, Indonesia. Based on this report and a teacher interview, this student had reached the Expert level in analytical thinking at Stage 3. She had independently developed a valid, well-supported generalization, along with the limit, based on her analysis of credible data gathered from her research.

Suggestions for Integrating Expert Thinking into Curriculum and Classroom Practice

- Infuse Expert Thinking rubrics into the standards and subject rubrics.
- Help students become familiar with and understand the expectations in the Expert Thinking rubrics.
- Allow students to demonstrate their understanding of Expert Thinking expectations by making visual reminders they can reference throughout the academic year.
- Provide graphic organizers with different purposes for students to choose from, based on their goals.
- Help students see the big picture by understanding part of the whole relationship.
- Provide ample opportunities for students to observe, ask questions, and identify patterns.

- Allow students to assess their arguments by evaluating reliability, accuracy, reasonableness, and logic of information.
- Provide graphic organizers for students to use when practicing the Expert Thinking skills.
- Provide continuous, immediate, descriptive, and actionable feedback based on Expert Thinking rubrics.

3

Creativity and Innovation

*We must not let our expectations be dictated
by what we think is possible.*
—Benjamin Bloom—

Creative and innovative individuals come up with novel ideas, are not afraid to make mistakes while calculating the associated risks, and, most important, transform the ideas into a concrete product or blueprint that offers value to the society. We define *Creativity and Innovation* as the ability to create novel and useful ideas, products, or blueprints by generating possibilities and synthesizing them to solve problems and to improve situations.

Why Is Creativity and Innovation Important?

All children are born with curiosity. They are open to accepting various ideas, use imagination in what they do, and come up with unpredictable ideas. The skill of Creativity and Innovation enables students to see a problem from a fresh perspective and devise workable solutions—an ability that is important in our increasingly challenging world, where sustainable solutions to large-scale problems are needed.

What kind of environment nurtures Creativity and Innovation? We point to two main factors. The first is intrinsic motivation. Kids who are intrinsically motivated are enthusiastic about learning and persevere when they encounter challenges. The second is a supportive, secure atmosphere that allows students to stay curious, make choices, voice their opinions, and take risks.

Intrinsic Motivation

We believe children learn best and think most creatively when they are intrinsically motivated. One way that teachers can build students' interest is by allowing them to observe and explore different areas of expertise. It's inspiring to have opportunities to explore and to develop the skills associated with different kinds of expertise.

Consider the example of Keisha, a Grade 2–3 student. In presenting her project, titled "Knives and Scissors Super," she stated that she had observed how cooks in her father's restaurant needed a long time to chop vegetables. Her fluent explanation of her product and how she came up with the idea reflected her genuine interest in her dad's profession. That interest drove her to learn the information and skills needed to come up with an innovative solution to the chopping-time problem. Her desire to do the necessary work without being pressured by others is what we mean by the phrase *intrinsic motivation*.

In contrast, *extrinsic motivation* is based on an expectation of rewards coming from an external source, such as a teacher. Although many educators believe in extrinsic motivation, in our school we don't use rewards, praise, and punishment as motivators. Instead of praising students when they perform well, teachers give students opportunities to talk about what they have done. Carol Dweck (2006) has stated that giving praise does not support the development of a growth mindset.

Consider the example of Amare, a preschool student. During Plan-Do-Review time, as he was spinning a hula hoop around his arms, he called out to his teacher, "Miss Julie, look!" The teacher approached Amare and said, "I see that you're spinning the hula hoop in circles around your arm." She described Amare's exact action instead of praising him with vague terms such as "Good job!" or "Awesome." In our school, instead of offering praise, we describe the positive things we see: "I see you've used a lot of purple in your drawing!" or "You landed very gently from that jump." Such acknowledgment is more meaningful because it not only shows students that we're really paying attention to what they do, but also enriches their vocabulary and can encourage more discussion that develops their thinking.

It's also worth noting that punishment does not exist in our classrooms. We believe it is more important to apply a related and respectful consequence and to discuss with the students how to fix a problematic situation while examining the root of the problem. Teachers strive to instill the mindset that mistakes are opportunities to learn. They also encourage students to actively seek feedback as a tool for growth, not as punishment or criticism. That way, making mistakes, learning from them, and seeking feedback are parts of the process of being creative and innovative.

Supportive, Secure Atmosphere

In the book *Educating Young Children* (Hohmann et al., 2008), David Weikart, the founder of the HighScope Educational Research Foundation, envisions democratic classrooms in which teachers and students share control in a mutual give and take. Teachers and students take turns as leaders and followers, speakers and listeners. This kind of democratic atmosphere, in which students are given opportunities to choose their focus and share their ideas and teachers act as facilitators, is a great catalyst for developing students' creativity and innovation skills.

Teachers may apply shared control in various contexts, from choosing activities in a certain routine (e.g., which books to read or what problem-solving strategies to use) to deciding what projects to do. For example, during morning meeting time, the teacher may ask the students, "What kind of greeting would you like to do this morning?" Choosing from a chart posted on the classroom wall, the students can vote for a high-five, a handshake, or another kind of greeting.

For shared control to be effective, students need to understand the expectations—that is, the rubrics. A combination of clear expectations and opportunities for students to direct their own learning (as in choosing a focus for a project) provides a sense of safety and confidence for students. They know what to expect, hence safety. They also get to work on a topic of interest, hence confidence. All this, when combined with support from teachers as facilitators, will result in an ideal learning atmosphere.

In facilitating creativity, teachers need to empower students to "create, invent, discover, imagine if, ... suppose that, and predict" (Sternberg & Grigorenko, 2003, p. 216). This is why many schools adopt project based learning (PBL), inquiry learning, experiential learning, and similar approaches that give students opportunities to explore, experiment, and apply thinking patterns using logic and scientific procedures.

A consistent approach in all aspects of a learning experience contributes to a supportive, secure environment. Teachers should focus not only on learning strategies but also on other components, such as classroom atmosphere and the assessment system. Schools that use PBL, which gives students more control over the learning experience than more traditional approaches, still need to ensure that teachers interact with students in ways that grow students' sense of responsibility and ownership toward the learning. Teachers should also make sure that students' projects show a deep understanding of the topic, measured by authentic assessment.

Key Elements of Creativity and Innovation

The skill of Creativity and Innovation has three key elements: (1) *novelty*, (2) *risk taking*, and (3) *beneficial contribution* (see Figure 3.1). Let's look at each of these in greater detail.

FIGURE 3.1
The Key Elements of Creativity and Innovation

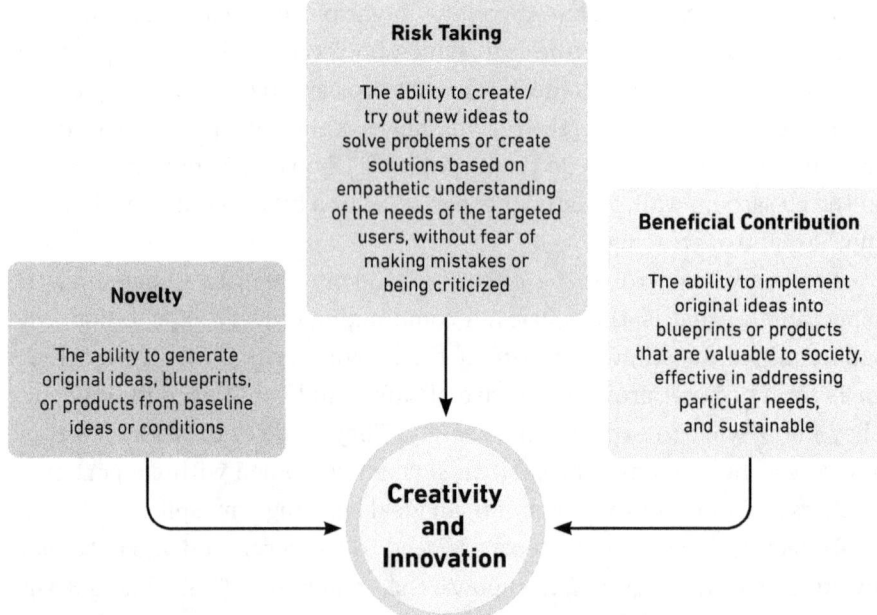

Novelty

To be deemed creative and innovative, an idea or a product must display novelty, the first and foremost element in our definition of Creativity and Innovation. We define *novelty* as originality in ideas, blueprints, or products generated by the ability to synthesize baseline ideas or conditions.

Novelty comprises two important concepts: (1) original ideas and (2) synthesis of baseline ideas or conditions. To successfully come up with novel ideas, students need to understand the concept of "original ideas," because originality is essentially judged on how far removed the idea is from the already existing or baseline ideas or conditions. For that reason, students also need to learn how to synthesize baseline ideas or conditions so they can come up with an idea that is as novel as possible. Teachers can help students learn these skills by exposing them to multiple baseline ideas that they can then use as a foundation for creating novel ideas. Because the concepts of "original ideas" and "synthesis of baseline ideas or conditions" are so interdependent, we discuss them together in the following section.

Novelty comprises two important concepts: (1) original ideas and (2) synthesis of baseline ideas or conditions.

Nurturing "original ideas" and "synthesis of baseline ideas or conditions"

Determining whether something is novel or not requires a starting point or a baseline. The question is whether you're looking at a brand-new product or idea resulting from a creative undertaking, or whether the outcome reflects existing elements combined into a greater or more complex system (Sawyer et al., 2003). Consider Apple's iPhone as an example of the latter. We already had mobile phones with keypads and tablets with touch-sensitive screens, but it wasn't until Apple synthesized those two products that the iPhone was born.

Novelty emerges from a combination of imagination, complex knowledge and thinking processes, and empathy with users and their needs. Students in preschool and lower-elementary grades are limited in their understanding of novelty because their experience derives primarily from familiar concrete objects. The level of novelty they display is limited to imitation, as they produce objects that are simply variations in content or form of an existing object. Students can use unstructured play time to make their own creation using materials available in their classroom or elsewhere in their surroundings. For example, a student who loved aircraft and had read a number of books about planes and airports built a hangar using wooden blocks from the play area.

During the first weeks of school in elementary grades, teachers can introduce students to the concept of "ideas" and related terms, such as *create* and *imagination*. Activities that can turn abstract concepts into concrete experiences include storytelling, "pretend" playtime, and "what-if" questions.

For example, after the morning meeting, a teacher announced to his students, "We are going to learn about something super-exciting!" Holding two dolls, he said:

Meet my friends Jennie and Jake. They have a collection of used boxes, bottles, and straws, but they do not know what to do with the materials. Can you help give them ideas on what to create? I will give you some used boxes, bottles, and straws as well. I wonder what you are going to build from them! You can create something from your imagination.

As the students worked, the teacher interacted with them and took notes on the skills they showed or statements they made related to the targeted life skill, Creativity and Innovation. He also asked students a few questions about what they were making and used key vocabulary words—for example, "How did you come up with the *idea*?" "What *idea* did you have?" "When you were making something with the materials, what did you *imagine* them to be?" The teacher wrote down words such as *idea*, *create*, and *imagination* on flip-chart paper. He then asked students to guess what the life skill might be, and some of his students replied, "Creativity and Innovation."

Even transition times can be opportunities to use relevant vocabulary. For example, teachers and students can play "Imagine if...," as in "Imagine if you could move very fast. What would you do?" Students' appropriate responses to such prompts can be evidence that they understand the word *imagination*. For those who do not yet understand, books are among the tools teachers can use to inspire students' creativity. For example, in the earlier scenario about creating something new with recycled materials, the teacher read aloud a book entitled *Not a Box*, by Antoinette Portis. The story is about a rabbit who is asked about what he can do with a large box. He creates many things, including a spaceship, a race car, and a mountain.

To make sure that his students understood the concept behind Creativity and Innovation, the teacher did a personalization activity. He asked his students to draw or write about their favorite activity from the series of Creativity and Innovation activities they had done. The students also had to write one vocabulary word that they learned that day.

In the end, the whole class, guided by the teacher, created a digital poster titled "Our Agreement" as a visual reminder of what to do to demonstrate Creativity and Innovation. The teacher reminded the students that they already had some words on the flip chart that they could include in the poster, as well as more words they had learned during vocabulary activities. Now, the class could refer to the poster whenever they were doing activities that required Creativity and Innovation.

Gradually, as students' knowledge and thinking become more developed, their process of coming up with ideas becomes more complex. The concepts, too, are more abstract. Vocabulary development continues to be essential in aiding students' understanding. Figure 3.2 is an example of a completed version of the "vocabulary detective" graphic organizer we mentioned in Chapter 2. The example in the figure shows a student's understanding of the English word *transformation*, which is *transformasi* in Indonesian. The dual-language approach helps to develop students' literacy in both English and Indonesian.

FIGURE 3.2
Example of a Completed "Vocabulary Detective" Graphic Organizer

Detective's Name	Reuben
Grade	9
Term	1
Subject	Social Studies
Date	19 July 2021

A picture/association that will remind me of what this word means:

English Word:
Transformation

Indonesian Word:
Transformasi

Parts of Speech: Noun

Sentences where I found the word:
Innovation and transformation are often used synonymously, but they are different in the digital world. In some instances, transformation can lead to innovation; it's a mutually causal relationship that is often overlooked because the two terms are mistakenly thought to mean the same thing.

Sentences where I found the word:
Transformation takes time—moving from one state to another is a process. Innovation, on the other hand, usually refers to a sudden spark for creativity, and the incipient actions that lead to implementing that spark into a company's strategy.

Context clues:
Difference and similarities with innovation

Context clues:
Additional information

My Own Sentence:
Transformation triggers innovation.

My Own Sentence:
Transformation takes place in a long time.

In addition to vocabulary activities, teachers should design activities to help students develop the specific skills related to finding original ideas and synthesizing baseline ideas. One of the common techniques in our is SCAMPER (**S**ubstitute, **C**ombine, **A**dapt/adjust, **M**odify/minimize/maximize, **P**ut to other uses, **E**liminate, **R**everse or revise). A similar technique is called FEOF (**F**luency, **E**laboration, **O**riginality, and **F**lexibility) (Cash, 2016).

An example of the use of FEOF comes from a Grade 2–3 class in which the teacher asked her students to list ideas for new uses of various objects in the classroom. Later she upgraded the originality challenge by asking students to "Come up with a new ending, beginning, or characters for a popular story." Based on their performance on these activities, she decided which students needed more practice or minilessons on generating original ideas.

Grade 8–9 students are required to demonstrate their ability to transform a baseline idea, and high school students are expected to be able to synthesize the baseline ideas to create original ideas. As an example, for the latter, a teacher used the SCAMPER strategy. He purposefully focused on the "MPER" elements because these four actions require the students to break down the content (e.g., functions) or form (e.g., shape, visuals) of the baseline ideas or conditions. He asked his students to sketch a new object out of an existing object in their surroundings, such as a smartphone, a laptop, or a chair. They were expected to modify/minimize/maximize or even eliminate a function or a feature of the object. At the end of the activity, students shared their experience with their peers, which led to working together to create a visual reminder, shown in Figure 3.3, about the elements of Creativity and Innovation.

FIGURE 3.3
Example of a Poster Reminder

Novelty	Risk Taking	Beneficial Contribution
Appreciate other people's ideas in order to see their potential and always try to find another way to develop it. Modify and improve what we have (work and skill).	Critics are inspiration! Take risks to try new things to keep improving our creativity and innovation.	Use our learning skills to benefit others and ourselves. Make a product that is useful for us and others.

Risk Taking

Creative and innovative individuals understand the risk taking these skills require. They acknowledge that without risks, we can never really creatively generate anything new and meaningful to solve problems. We define *risk taking* as the ability to create/try out new ideas to solve problems or create solutions based on empathic understanding of the needs of the targeted users, without fear of making mistakes or being criticized.

Developing the skill of risk taking involves two important concepts: empathy and persistence. Empathy is about understanding the needs of the people affected so that only necessary actions and risks are taken. Students must also show persistence to learn from mistakes and distinguish judgmental criticism from productive feedback. Teachers can nurture risk takers by creating a safe environment where students can try out different ideas and evaluate the related risks.

> *Risk taking* involves two important concepts: empathy and persistence.

Nurturing empathy

Being a creative individual involves more than just creating innovative products. The innovation must be relevant and bring added value for the users, solving a problem they face. Based on the "design thinking" problem-solving process (see Hasso Plattner Institute of Design at Stanford University, n.d.) we begin teaching elementary students to build empathy with the potential users of their targeted innovations. We want them to understand what these users feel and need so that a solid connection develops between the student designers and the targeted users. Figure 3.4 (see p. 62) shows part of a graphic organizer we use for this purpose; it guides students through the process of interviewing potential users to understand their problems, perspectives, and needs. (In this case, the students were working on innovations related to light and sound.) Even as early as Grade 1, we encourage students to observe their surroundings and interview the users before they design a solution.

For example, Casey, a Grade 2–3 student, was learning about the properties of materials (e.g., physical appearance, state of materials, brittleness). Casey observed her mom, an avid gardener who also cared about the environment, engaged in her hobby. Casey noted that her mom used plastic containers to grow plants, but because the containers held water instead of allowing it to drain, the plants' roots decayed, and their leaves withered. Casey interviewed her mom, asking the following questions:

- "What are the problems, Mom?"
- "How do you feel about this?"
- "Can you tell me what causes the problems?"
- "Do you consider using different types of containers?"
- "What are your preferences?"

FIGURE 3.4
Graphic Organizer for Interviewing Potential Users of Innovations

---

INTERVIEW

✓ Ask about their **EXPERIENCE:**
"Tell me about your experience with light and sound."

✓ Ask about **WHAT & WHY:**
"What was your problem with light?"
"Why did it happen?"

✓ Ask about their **FEELING:**
"How did you feel when that happened?"

✓ **LISTEN TIME > TALK TIME**
Your job is to get the other person talking.

Notes from your interview (You may write your notes here if you need more space.)
_____
_____
_____
_____
_____

The interview revealed a lot to Casey about her mother's concerns and priorities. Casey documented and reflected on her findings and identified the problem, as shown in Figure 3.5.

Nurturing persistence

Building students' persistence requires developing a classroom culture that reflects several important attributes. Such a culture encourages students to do their best, with a clear understanding that if they do not reach a particular goal by a certain time, they should keep trying and not give up. An important part of the "not give up" aspect requires ensuring that students realize that it's OK to make mistakes, that mistakes are not cause for punishment, and that we can all learn from our mistakes. Fostering this kind of culture is crucial if we want students to become responsible risk takers as they develop the skill of Creativity and Innovation.

FIGURE 3.5
Example of a Grade 2–3 Project Log on Building Empathy by Identifying the Problem

What is the need?	Who has the problem?	Why is it important to solve?
A new container that won't hold the water.	My mom	Gardening helps mom stay happy.
It should allow water to flow and maintain the medium dry.		It helps our environment stay green.
The reusable container.		

Follow the rule to make the problem statement: **Who** *needs* **what** *because* **why**

My Problem Statement: Mom needs a reusable container that allows the water to flow and keep the medium dry because it will keep the plants healthy.

Beneficial Contribution

The central concept related to *beneficial contribution* is value added. Novelty and risk taking are not enough when it comes to Creativity and Innovation, because novel ideas, in extreme forms that may result from excessive risk taking, can be outright absurd or senseless. Creative ideas are only useful when they are relevant to a problem and actually provide real value in resolving the issues at hand. To us, producing *beneficial contributions* is "the ability to transform original ideas into blueprints or products that are valuable to society and effective in addressing particular needs."

> The central concept related to *beneficial contribution* is value added.

Nurturing the concept of "value added"

Preschoolers and lower-elementary students usually create products based on their personal interests. That said, starting in the elementary grades, students can learn the concept of improving the function of an existing, or baseline, product. Starting at the beginning of the school term, teachers can conduct a vocabulary activity to ensure that students understand the meaning of the word *function*. The activity can start with simple discussions about the function of ordinary classroom objects such as a whiteboard, a computer, or a file folder. Questions that prompt students to explore and gain a deeper understanding about an object's function—*What is this for? What is it made of? What is the shape? What if we change the shape or materials? What would happen?*—can lead students to wonder how they might add to or improve the function of these things. At the start of a project-based learning cycle, students can formulate a project focus question and brainstorm possible solutions that stem from their effort to improve the function of an existing object or idea. Figure 3.6 is a graphic organizer to use for this activity.

FIGURE 3.6
Graphic Organizer for Brainstorming a Project Focus Question

1. Framing the Project Focus Question
Working in groups, create a project focus question that you will answer in your project.

2. Brainstorming the Possible Hypothesis
Think of at least three (3) different solutions.

Draw a sketch to illustrate your ideas
(You may attach your ideas here if the space in the boxes is not enough.)

Idea 1	Idea 2	Idea 3

Pros and cons of Solutions 1, 2, and 3.

	Pros	Cons
Solution 1		
Solution 2		
Solution 3		

My Hypothesis
Based on my considerations of cost and benefit, the most fitting hypothesis to answer my project focus question is:

In upper-elementary classes, students develop their empathy (as discussed earlier) for users when they observe existing ideas and products with a laser-like focus on users' needs. They determine whether the existing ideas or products are still relevant, or if there's a disconnect between the ideas or products and the problems they are intended to solve. Students research the current condition and compare it with the ideal conditions to "find the gap." For example, in a Grade 4–5 social studies class, Anthony, who knew that many of his friends liked to use organic products, researched the prospect of making and selling organic soap. While drafting a comparison of three different organic soaps, he asked the following questions:

- What are the current products?
- What aspects should I consider when comparing the products?
- Which information/standard of organic soap can I use as reference for ideal conditions?
- What are the problems with the current product?
- How much does it cost? What is the price range?
- When was the current idea/product invented?
- Which information/standard can I use as reference for ideal conditions?
- What is the most liked organic soap?
- What are the added values of the most expensive soap?

Anthony compared the soaps in terms of three aspects—health-related factors, environment, and price—and recorded his findings in the table shown in Figure 3.7.

FIGURE 3.7
Example of a Table Comparing Three Aspects of Different Products

	ASPECTS		
Soap	Health	Environment	Price
Soap A	• No fragrance • No bleach	• Animal testing free • Nonsustainable packaging	$5
Soap B	• Essential oils added • No bleach • It moisturizes the skin	• Animal testing free • Sustainable packaging • Unique and sustainable packaging	$12
Soap C	• No fragrance • No bleach • It moisturizes the skin	• Animal testing free • Nonsustainable packaging	$7

After doing the comparison, Anthony surveyed his friends to ask what they preferred. In a subsequent gap analysis, he found that although the majority preferred to use eco-friendly organic bar soaps, the existing options were too deemed too pricey, not aesthetically packaged, or unappealingly scented. Based on what he had learned, Anthony brainstormed potential ideas, including the pros and cons related to existing products. After experimenting with various possibilities, he finally decided to produce and market an affordable organic bar soap with a unique look and a pleasant fragrance derived from flowers and herbs. An essential oil from a local producer and honey used as a moisturizing element provided added value. He named the soap Le Quartz.

How Is Creativity and Innovation Measured and Assessed?

We use a rubric that we developed to measure and assess students' progress and achievement in attaining the Creativity and Innovation skill (see Figure 3.8). It describes the behaviors we expect to see at each developmental level. As previously stated, this essential skill has three elements: *novelty, risk taking*, and *beneficial contribution*. The rubric represents these as CI.1, CI.2, and CI.3, respectively. The rubric also describes three stages of development:

- Stage 1: Student performs a task somewhat accurately with consistent guidance from others (teachers and peers).
- Stage 2: Student performs a task accurately with little guidance and redirection from others (teachers and peers).
- Stage 3: Student independently performs a task with ease, speed, and accuracy.

As with the other essential life skills, vocabulary and concepts related to Creativity and Innovation need to be introduced at the beginning of the school year across all continuum levels. The practice and assessment of the skills goes on throughout the year, with grading conducted toward the end of the year.

Teachers design various learning experiences for students to practice and showcase their abilities in Creativity and Innovation. The most common experiences involve project-based learning (PBL). This approach provides a certain context or phenomenon as a starting point for students to be creative and innovative in solving problems. Another option is the passion project, or what we refer to as the "Making Good Choices" project. Compared to PBL,

FIGURE 3.8
Rubric for Creativity and Innovation

	Early (Preschool–K)	Beginning (K–3)	Transition (3–6)	Developing (6–9)	Expert (9–12)
CI.1 Novelty	Reproduces an object with details based on imagination and imitation. Stage 1 2 3	Produces an object with variations in content and/or form to improve functions based on imagination. Stage 1 2 3	Creates an innovation based on a combination of original ideas (content and/or form) and investigation of the surroundings. Stage 1 2 3	Creates an innovation based on the transformation of content and/or form in a variety of ways after investigating the surroundings. Stage 1 2 3	Creates an innovation based on the synthesis of multiple ideas (content and/or form), using cross-disciplinary knowledge and insights gathered from investigation. Stage 1 2 3
CI.2 Risk Taking	• Explores new ideas without fear of making mistakes. • Is persistent in his/her own ideas. Stage 1 2 3	• Comes up with new ideas and attempts to build empathy based on the needs of users. • Is persistent without fear of making mistakes. Stage 1 2 3	• Tries out new ideas to make an effort to empathize with the needs of the users, although not completely (e.g., does not accept criticism). • Is persistent without fear of making mistakes. Stage 1 2 3	• Develops an innovator mindset with the ability to – Empathize with the needs of the users, including considering criticism as input. – Be persistent in defending own ideas with arguments without fear of making mistakes. Stage 1 2 3	• Has an innovator mindset with the ability to – Be persistent against conventional ways, with arguments. – Empathize with the needs of the users, including considering criticism as input. – Assess risk for minimizing negative impacts. Stage 1 2 3

(continued)

FIGURE 3.8
Rubric for Creativity and Innovation—*(continued)*

	Early (Preschool–K)				Beginning (K–3)				Transition (3–6)				Developing (6–9)				Expert (9–12)			
CI.3 Beneficial Contribution	• Creates useful ideas or products for him/herself.				• Begins to create products to solve problems related to sustainability by considering the needs of the surroundings, using relevant technology and materials.				• Creates products that attempt to efficiently solve problems related to sustainability that are accepted by the surroundings, using relevant technology and materials.				• Creates solutions or products that contribute to a sustainable future, using relevant technology and materials.				• Creates a systematic solution that contributes to a sustainable future with measurable outcomes, using relevant technology and materials.			
	Stage	1	2	3	Stage	1	2	3	Stage	1	2	3	Stage	1	2	3	Stage	1	2	3

Stage 1: Student performs a task somewhat accurately with consistent guidance from others (teachers and peers).

Stage 2: Student performs a task accurately with little guidance and redirection from others (teachers and peers).

Stage 3: Student independently performs a task with ease, speed, and accuracy.

which is undertaken within a specific, curriculum-guided topic, passion projects allow students to explore various topics based on their individual interests.

As we continue our discussion of measurement and assessment, we focus on the first key element of Creativity and Innovation: *novelty*. The rubric section for *novelty* focuses on students' skills in generating original ideas, blueprints, or products through synthesis of baseline ideas or conditions. The emphasis is essentially on how fresh the students' ideas are. There is always a baseline, in the form of either existing ideas or conditions or objects that students want to depart from. As the continuum level gets higher, the modification becomes more varied and less similar to the baseline—hence, it shows a higher level of novelty. Let's take a closer look at the indicators of the various developmental levels for novelty.

Early (Preschool–K)

Students at the Early level are able to *reproduce* an object with details based on imagination and imitation. They add details as they wish.

Teachers can assess students' novelty while interacting with them during student-initiated play time. For example, during the Plan-Do-Review time, when a student was creating a construction out of building sticks, the teacher joined in and used targeted vocabulary as she asked a few questions. "Your building has so many details," she said. "What did you imagine this to be?" Then, "Let's imagine what would happen if we added more sticks on the right or left side of your building." "What would happen if we took some sticks out of the building?" In situations like this, teachers record students' responses as anecdotal notes that can be used as evidence for assessment.

Beginning (Grades K–3)

At the Beginning level, students are able to *produce* an object with variations in content or form, or both, to *improve functions* based on imagination.

PBL provides contexts in which the students are empowered to choose to focus on certain aspects of the project and teachers can find evidence of Creativity and Innovation. For example, in a project related to the topic of the five senses, the students are free to choose which sense to focus on, based on their observations or experiences. One student focused on the sense of touch—specifically, the need to protect her hand when helping her mom cook. Based on a problem she experienced (her hand often felt the heat from the stove), she created a mitten that was thick enough to provide heat protection. By adding layers of fabric to make her mom's existing mitten thicker, she created a new product with improved functionality. A product like this can be one piece of evidence for the novelty element of Creativity and Innovation at the Beginning level. If needed, teachers can prompt students to assess whether their products vary enough from the original product to improve the functions.

Transition (Grades 3–6)

As students progress to the Transition level, they are able to create an innovation based on a *combination* of existing ideas related to content or form, or both, and investigation of the surroundings. At this level, we expect students to take two or more existing ideas and combine them to create an innovation based on their observation of the surroundings. Teachers can assess the skills when students are working on their projects. Students' investigations of the surroundings consist of observations, interviews, and engaging with users—the people who will benefit the most from their solution—as well as consulting with experts. Teachers can assess students' process in coming up with their ideas by looking at their research journal or log (refer back to Figure 3.6 on p. 64 for a graphic organizer that can be part of this record) and interviewing the students to elicit more details.

Developing (Grades 6–9)

Students at the Developing level are able to create an innovation based on the *transformation* of content or form (or both) in a variety of ways after investigating the surroundings. The following example describes the development of Reuben, a Grade 8–9 student.

For his digital literacy project, Reuben created an innovation using skills and knowledge related to STEAM (science, technology, engineering, the arts, and mathematics). He noticed that his friends were not scrupulous when it came to throwing away trash after eating in the cafeteria. He came up with an idea to create a "smart trash bin." As he explained, "I designed a trash bin that motivates people to put trash in it. This trash bin has a sensor inside, [so] when people put trash in, the screen will show a check mark, the word thank-you, and give you a quote to inspire and motivate you."

This example illustrates how Reuben investigated his surroundings and noticed that his friends were not properly using the cafeteria trash bins. Based on the rubric's expectations, when it comes to the Creativity and Innovation element of Novelty, Reuben is a Stage 3 student. He transformed a regular trash bin into a smart trash bin with a sensor and a screen to motivate people to dispose of their trash properly.

His classmate, Lara, was also bothered by the mess surrounding the cafeteria trash bin. Lara expressed interest in creating a better bin but wasn't sure where to begin. Her teacher suggested she observe the trash bin's current shape; was there something about it that was contributing to the current problem? After studying the bin, Lara determined that there was. "This trash bin's opening is too small for cafeteria trash," she explained. "We need something with a bigger opening, so that you can put more of the tray inside before tipping out the trash." The teacher recorded anecdotal notes on her conversation with Lara, which served as formative assessment. The teacher also observed the process Lara used to make the improved trash bin. Using her anecdotal notes and observations, as well as the design plans Lara drew up as her final product, the teacher concluded that Lara is a Stage 2 student; sometimes she was able to transform ideas or objects independently, but at other times she needed the teacher's help.

Expert (Grades 9–12)

Students at the Expert level are able to create an innovation based on the *synthesis* of multiple ideas related to content or form (or both), using cross-disciplinary knowledge and insights gathered from investigation. Students are expected to look at the problem from multiple perspectives and therefore be able to create an innovative product based on thorough investigation of the surroundings.

At this level, we expect students to conduct research and gain knowledge from multiple fields, integrating their knowledge from different disciplines to create an innovative solution. Teachers can assess the skills through projects that ask students to generate solutions to real problems.

For example, in the Global Citizenship course, students are asked to identify and analyze current global issues from multiple perspectives (e.g., economic, political, social, cultural, and health-related). Then they are asked to develop and propose innovative and effective solutions to solve the issue based on the framework of "global citizen."

One student decided to address the issue of gender equality in the Indonesian workplace. Her thorough research identified not only the problems but also other relevant and useful information, such as where victims could reach out for help. As she came to realize the importance of raising awareness about the issue, she noticed that most of the available information appeared on websites. She decided to use her computer-coding skill to create a user-friendly, attractive, and informative app. Users could download the app and use it to find out about current issues, related efforts, and solutions as opposed to reading websites that reported nothing but news.

Suggestions for Integrating Creativity and Innovation into Curriculum and Classroom Practice

- Infuse into the curriculum standards a Creativity and Innovation rubric for the purpose of measuring skills related to students' ability to propose solutions or create innovative products.
- Allow students to identify their passion by observing and exploring different occupations.
- Have students explore new ideas by observing and comparing existing ideas.
- Provide plenty of opportunities for students to take ownership of their learning by making their own choices based on their interests and passion.
- Have students give feedback on their own work and that of others.
- Create a safe learning environment that encourages students to try, to make mistakes, and to learn from those mistakes.
- Structure the creative thinking process by using graphic organizers.
- Use brainstorming strategies for generating creative and innovative ideas, such as SCAMPER and FEOF during project-based learning.

4

Adaptability and Agility

Intelligence is the ability to adapt to change.
—Stephen Hawking—

In Chapter 3, we talked about how our students need Creativity and Innovation to deal with the speed of change and the more complex challenges the world presents. Equally essential is Adaptability and Agility. To *adapt* is to adjust to a certain condition or challenge, and to be *agile* is to be swift enough to act in response to or in anticipation of more possible changes.

We define *Adaptability and Agility* as the ability to read and decode signals, quickly shift focus, and act on anticipated changes, as well as crises, by using learned skills and knowledge to maximize the result. We have designed and implemented a learning model that promotes the mastery of Adaptability and Agility as part of our efforts to achieve the goal of our education system—for our students to have the abilities of a self-regulated leader. Therefore, we need to see "change" as more than a buzzword and, as educators, establish a serious plan to develop this life skill.

Why Is Adaptability and Agility Important?

As we have noted, Adaptability and Agility is the skill we need to respond to changes or crises; and in today's world, as we face challenges on a colossal scale, this skill is more important than ever. With Adaptability and Agility, students learn to develop cognitive and mental flexibility, which enables them to anticipate and face changes and crises with a positive state of mind. As students come to understand that changes are natural parts of life and as they practice dealing with change strategically, they will be able to turn challenging situations into opportunities. They will display the key qualities of optimism and grit.

Optimism and Grit

Adaptive and agile individuals treat mistakes as learning experiences. Thomas (Guskey, 2015) posits that people who attribute mistakes to their personal growth factors believe they are capable of improving themselves and therefore have the motivation to continue working toward their goals. They move forward with grit and a sense of optimism that things will get better.

The mindset of being agile can be developed from early childhood through an inclusive, multiage, and multicultural environment. Being immersed in an environment where school members respect differences will instill open-mindedness that becomes the starting point of an agile mindset.

Every year, our school alternates between celebrating a national multicultural week and an international multicultural week. Each class chooses the culture of a certain region that they agree to explore for an entire term. Starting in elementary grades, each student can pick an aspect of the chosen culture to research deeper—for example, the cuisine, the music, or the language. To attain deeper learning, students engage in a project mission to solve a sociocultural problem and provide a solution using the cultural understanding they develop. This opportunity lets students become more open to various perspectives. For example, people in certain cultures, such as the Korean culture, do not feel comfortable addressing somebody older by name. Korean women and girls address an older female friend as "Eonnie" and an older male friend as "Oppa," and Korean men and boys use the parallel terms "Noona" and "Hyung." Similarly, in a region of Indonesia, younger folks usually call an older female friend "Mbak" and an older male friend "Mas." It would be understandable that a Korean or an Indonesian would feel awkward addressing anyone older by name alone, especially if they have never interacted with people from cultures in which this is the norm.

A grading system can also contribute to the growth of an agile mindset that leads to optimism and grit. In our school, we use the grade *NY*, or "Not Yet," to replace the aggravating *F*. The grade signifies that all students have a second and even third chance to improve. If they are not on target yet, teachers can provide scaffolding to assist them. Moreover, "Not Yet" means students should never stop learning, and they will eventually be able to reach the expected stage of their learning journey. In contrast, an *F* grade labels students as failures for the rest of their life.

To nurture the development of Adaptability and Agility, as with the other essential life skills, teachers can use activities to introduce students to its important concepts and vocabulary, taken directly from the rubric. To ensure that students understand the vocabulary and the rubric expectations, teachers need to conduct formative assessment, paying attention to students' interactions, particularly during project work, when the need for Adaptability and Agility is high.

It is also important to design a daily routine in which students can make choices and decide what to do if they face a challenge. An example of such a routine in our preschool program is Plan-Do-Review. The comparable routine for elementary, middle, and high school students is called Making Good Choices, as we've mentioned in earlier chapters. As an example, a Grade 6–7 teacher always asks students to make a Plan A and a Plan B. He describes Plan B as "an extra plan in case Plan A does not work." He also encourages his students to write down in their Making Good Choices log what changes happened and how they dealt with the changes. As these students get used to changes and challenges, they learn to view them as learning opportunities. This realization is the beginning of the development of optimism and grit.

Key Elements of Adaptability and Agility

Highly adaptive and agile students have the capacity to perform the two elements that shape our model of Adaptability and Agility: (1) *agile mindset* and (2) *versatility*. (See Figure 4.1.)

FIGURE 4.1
The Key Elements of Adaptability and Agility

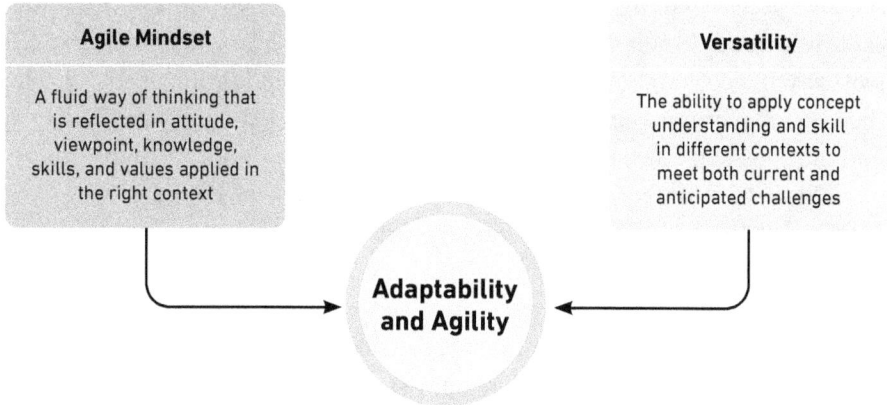

Agile Mindset

Students with an agile mindset are aware of changes in the world, accept them as natural parts of life, and understand that nothing remains the same. Accordingly, they will try to use the knowledge, skills, and values that they have learned and transfer them to the context or change that they are facing to match the needs of the situation. We define *agile mindset* as a fluid way of thinking reflected in attitude, viewpoint, knowledge, skills, and values used in the right context. In internalizing this mindset, students need to understand two important concepts: (1) viewing changes or challenges as natural parts of life and (2) transferring learned knowledge, skills, and values in different contexts.

> In internalizing an *agile mindset*, students need to understand two important concepts: (1) viewing changes or challenges as natural parts of life and (2) transferring learned knowledge, skills, and values in different contexts.

Nurturing the concept of "viewing changes or challenges as natural parts of life"

Changes or new challenges are not always easy to accept or deal with. Those who handle them well typically feel themselves capable of rising to challenges. Fortunately, this positive mindset can be built through deliberate effort.

In the preschool years, teachers need to lead young children in the visualization and discussion of changes so that they feel prepared. In our preschool, teachers use a countdown chart to help students anticipate upcoming school events or changes in the daily schedule. As an example, a preschool class was about to take a field trip to a farm. The teacher drew three small pictures of a cow and one picture of a bigger cow and laminated them. The three small pictures represented the number of days left before the field trip, and the biggest picture represented the "D-day"—the day of the trip.

Older students are expected to be more prepared for possible unannounced changes. For that to happen, teachers need to create opportunities to discuss with students how to deal with changes or crises. For example, during our "Conscious Business Day," each class, as a group, turns into a "company," with students deciding what to sell to families and students from other classes when they come to shop. Usually, plenty of unexpected situations occur on the D-day, such as running out of cash for change, spilled food or drink, or running out of items to sell. These are occurrences that students need to respond to promptly. For that to happen, teachers and students gather during the planning phase to brainstorm possible changes and challenges that might occur and ideas for how to deal with them. The graphic organizer in Figure 4.2 can provide a structure for the brainstorming process.

FIGURE 4.2

Graphic Organizer for Brainstorming Responses to Changes and Challenges

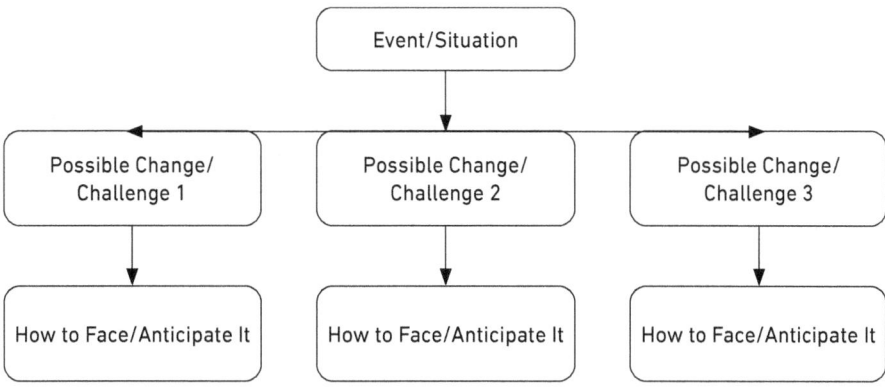

In lower-elementary grades, where the concept of "change" is still abstract, teachers can design concrete activities that show changes in the surrounding environment and have the students examine and discuss the cause and effect. These kinds of activities should help create a mindset that changes are natural parts of life.

A K–1 teacher, for example, froze a couple of solid objects (e.g., coins, beads) in ice cube trays filled with water. The next day, the students gathered in small groups to observe what happened to the solid objects in the ice cubes and the ice cubes themselves when left at room temperature. The teacher used this opportunity to introduce the concept of "change." The teacher asked if the students saw anything different from before. Some students noticed that only the ice melted, whereas the solid objects kept their form. The teacher then wrote the word *change* on a paper strip and stuck it on the classroom's vocabulary wall. The students wrote their own examples of the word *change*, based on their observation of the ice cube experiment, on their own paper strip and added it to the classroom's vocabulary wall. Afterward, the students did a "turn and talk" to share their experiences with other changes in their lives. From the discussion, the class concluded that changes are natural parts of life. As for the vocabulary wall, the teacher continuously referred to this display every time the class had a discussion about change.

Nurturing the concept of "transferring learned knowledge, skills, and values in different contexts"

Being agile means being able to transfer knowledge, skills, and values learned in one context to different contexts. Identifying learned knowledge, skills, and values can help students to be more aware of how they can transfer them to their current situation. This process may not come naturally to young learners, and teacher prompts can help them recall what they have learned and guide them into making connections with their current work.

As discussed in previous chapters, learning activities that provide contexts based on real-life phenomena are perfect catalysts for students to practice essential skills. Project-based learning and passion projects are two activities that we ensure are part of our learning design.

As an example, during the planning phase of our school's passion project, or Making Good Choices (MGC) project, students need to list what knowledge, skills, and values they have learned that can be used in a new context for their project. For example, a Grade 6–7 student who was swimming in Physical Education (PE) class and loving it wanted to explore his interest more deeply for his MGC project. After identifying three possible project topics, he chose to explore how swimming can help reduce stress. He identified skills he had learned in other subjects that could be transferred and used in the context of his interest in swimming, including creating a graph to represent swimming performance and stress-level data (a skill learned in math class), persuasive writing about the benefits of swimming (a skill learned in language arts), and digital literacy skills to research workouts that hone particular swimming skills and learn more about the history of swimming for exercise. These and other aspects of the student's planning process are shown in the project log in Figure 4.3.

After the student had gathered the data on his stress level following swimming practice, he created line graphs to illustrate his findings on stress levels in relation to swimming. He then used his persuasive-writing ability to create a campaign and a short video clip promoting swimming as a way to manage stress. This example shows that the student was, indeed, able to transfer multiple skills to a different context.

FIGURE 4.3
Example of a Project Planning Log

MAKING GOOD CHOICES PROJECT PLANNING

1. **My learning goals:**
   a. **Essential life skills:** Expert Thinking, Creativity and Innovation, Adaptability and Agility
   b. **Interest-based content:** Swimming
2. **My plan to achieve my goal based on my interest and essential life skills:**

Options of project	Benefit if I turn the idea into a workable project	
	For myself	For others
How to swim properly	I can improve my swimming skill.	They can learn how to swim.
The history of swimming	I will appreciate the sport better from learning the history.	They can have deeper information about swimming
How swimming can help reduce stress	I can learn to manage my stress through swimming.	They can be more interested in doing exercise, especially swimming.

From the options above, I choose:

My Project: How swimming can help reduce stress	My arguments (Why my choice of project matters): Students tend to have numerous assignments. If we cannot manage our stress, the work will take a toll on our physical and mental health. Swimming is usually associated with recreational activity, especially when it is done with our family as we go on a vacation on the beach. With this mindset, I believe it is a good start to offer the idea of swimming as a sport that is fun and beneficial to reduce our stress level.

3. **The knowledge, values, and skills I need to achieve my goals**

Knowledge	Values	Subject-Specific Skills
• The definition of stress • The cause of stress • The effect of stress • The solution for stress • Swimming traits that are beneficial to reduce stress • How to measure stress level	• Responsibility • Respect • Integrity • Excellence	• Observation skills • Research skills • Analysis skills • Digital literacy skills • Creating graphs to represent data • Persuasive writing skills

I will use the knowledge, skills, and values to ensure adaptive approaches to achieve my goals by:

• Upholding values that will help guide me throughout the project. For example, I will be responsible and follow my set timeline.
• Applying skills to help me find and process the information. For example, I will use my analysis skills to compare and contrast various valid and reliable resources about stress and swimming techniques. I will use my math skills to create a graph to represent data on stress levels. I will also apply my digital literacy skills (developed during the digital literacy subject) as well as my persuasive writing skills to create a short video clip that presents the result of my research.

Versatility

In managing unexpected changes, versatile individuals are able to apply one of their qualities or a combination of their virtues according to the demands of the circumstances. When it is required, people with versatility can easily change their approach in an unbiased, appropriate, proportionate, and effective manner. These capabilities are influenced by their "range of motion," which enables them to know what moves to take and when to take them (Jordan, 2020).

We define *versatility* as the ability to have deep understanding of interdisciplinary concepts and mastery of skills to be applied in different contexts to match the needs of the current and anticipated challenges in life. To understand the concept of *versatility*, students need to understand and practice two important concepts: (1) viewing from multiple/ interdisciplinary perspectives and (2) adaptive expertise.

> To understand the concept of *versatility*, students need to understand and practice two important concepts: (1) viewing from multiple/interdisciplinary perspectives and (2) adaptive expertise.

Nurturing the ability to view from multiple/interdisciplinary perspectives

Students in preschool and K–1 are characterized by egocentrism. Given this trait, we may not expect them to be able to see things from multiple perspectives yet, but we can have them practice being aware of others' perspectives through certain approaches. One way to do this is by building the habit of having a problem-solving discussion when conflicts between students occur, with the teacher as the facilitator. In our preschool, we adopted HighScope's conflict resolution approach, which the teachers use to mediate such situations. One of the steps requires the teacher to ask the students in conflict to describe what happened. Afterward, the students are asked to come up with solutions. Teachers can contribute ideas or solutions after the students listen to each other and try to come up with their own ideas. Through this approach, students begin to learn to listen to others' perspectives.

At the elementary level, starting with Grade 2–3, learning expectations outlined in the rubric require students to make an effort to see multiple perspectives as they apply the knowledge they are acquiring and work on a task.

For example, students may be asked to write about one topic using information from two different books.

In a Grade 6–7 science class, the teacher organized a debate activity on organic versus synthetic food coloring, addressing the claim "Synthetic food coloring brings more harm than good." Students were divided into affirmative and negative groups. Before the debate, almost everyone agreed that organic food coloring was the best option from the health perspective. But after the debate, they began to see the case from various perspectives, including economics. One student concluded, "Some brands of synthetic food coloring are FDA-approved. Because of that, and the lower price this type of coloring offers, it makes more sense to use synthetic food coloring for the food industry."

Nurturing adaptive expertise

Students with versatility have adaptive expertise. They have a flexible and creative approach in applying their knowledge, skills, and values in different contexts innovatively, effectively, and efficiently. Equipped with adaptive expertise, versatile individuals have the fluidity that allows them to efficiently use knowledge to handle new problems and are not limited to performing predefined practical routines (Timperley, 2010).

To nurture this mindset, teachers need to provide plenty of opportunities for students to practice their ability to solve unexpected problems. Teachers can create scenarios where unexpected problems occur or observe the students' problem-solving process during their project. To achieve this, teachers need to ensure that the design of the project is complex and unstructured enough for an unexpected problem to occur. A project that is too structured, with a predictable outcome, will not yield the challenges and problems we are looking for as part of the learning experience.

Recall that for the element of agile mindset, students need to be familiar with the idea of transferring their learned knowledge, skills, and values to a new situation. For this element of versatility, they need to learn how to find the most appropriate way to face the new situation using the learned knowledge, skills, and values so that the solution or strategy will be innovative and effective, as well as executed efficiently.

Adaptive expertise can be practiced through "metacognitive awareness, goal-setting behaviors, the ability to self-assess against goals, to ask questions and have the tools to go about answering those questions" (Grotzer et al., 2021). For older students, teachers can use a Meta-Level Reflection journal to help students be more aware of their goal, to brainstorm innovative ideas to reach the goal, to plan accordingly, to monitor how effective and efficient the work is compared to the goal, and to reflect on the whole process. Figure 4.4 is a graphic organizer that can help students with the initial steps in the process.

For younger students, teachers can expose them to new materials and new situations. One way to do this is through a message board. To introduce new materials, teachers can draw an announcement picture on the message board, accompanied with a word or a simple phrase to explain the drawing. The actual materials can be taped to the board or simply put nearby. The students and the teacher can then discuss what the new material is and how to use or play with it.

FIGURE 4.4
Graphic Organizer for Project Planning

My Goal for This Project (Problem Statement)
I aim to solve a problem of…
Research Question
Hypothesis
Use the space below to brainstorm possible solutions to answer the research question and come up with a hypothesis.
Possible solutions: **From the options above, what is the most fitting hypothesis for my research question?** **Why do I think the hypothesis fits the research question best? Support with argument and data.**

How Is Adaptability and Agility Measured and Assessed?

We have created and use a developmental rubric to measure and assess students' progress and achievement in the essential skill of Adaptability and Agility (see Figure 4.5, p. 84). It describes the behaviors we expect to see at each developmental level. As previously explained, Adaptability and Agility has two elements: *agile mindset* and *versatility*. In the rubric, *agile mindset* is represented as AA.1, and *versatility* as AA.2. The rubric also describes three stages of performance:

- Stage 1: Student performs a task somewhat accurately with consistent guidance from others (teachers and peers).
- Stage 2: Student performs a task accurately with little guidance and redirection from others (teachers and peers).
- Stage 3: Student independently performs a task with ease, speed, and accuracy.

In the following sections, we describe the expectations at each continuum level for the second element, *versatility*, along with examples of students' behavior for each level.

Early (Preschool–K)

Students at the Early level are expected to be able to perform and try out ideas using new materials and help others solve simple problems in a new situation. To assess a student's ability in handling new materials and new situations, teachers need to observe the student's reactions and responses in such conditions, as in the following example.

Playing with a big cardboard box, Queenisha pretended it was a house. She put layers of colorful scarves on top of the box for its "roof" and then put two boxes together to make a "bigger house." Another child joined in and wanted to add more scarves to wrap around the box as the "wall paint," but the scarves kept falling. Queenisha used duct tape to secure the scarves to every side of the box.

This anecdote indicates that Queenisha has reached Stage 3 for the *versatility* element for Adaptability and Agility. She tried out different ideas for the new materials, including using scarves as the roof and putting the boxes together to make a bigger house. She also helped her friend solve a problem by using duct tape to secure the scarves. She did all this independently—hence, she is at Stage 3.

84   Life Skills for All Learners

FIGURE 4.5
Rubric for Adaptability and Agility

	Early (Preschool–K)	Beginning (K–3)	Transition (3–6)	Developing (6–9)	Expert (9–12)
AA.1 Agile Mindset	• Shows readiness to face a change or new situation when informed of it. Stage 1 2 3	• Shows readiness to face and anticipate a change or new situation when informed of it. Stage 1 2 3	• Shows readiness when facing and anticipating a change or new situation by understanding the general nature of change. Stage 1 2 3	• Reflects positive attitude and open-minded viewpoints when facing and anticipating a change or new situation by understanding the specific background of the change and being able to explain the detailed causes of the change. Stage 1 2 3	• Reflects a fluid way of thinking (agile mindset) when facing and anticipating a change or new situation by understanding why it's necessary to change and convincing others to accept the change. Stage 1 2 3
AA.2 Versatility	• Performs and tries out ideas using new materials and helps others solve simple problems in a new situation. Stage 1 2 3	• Transfers and applies some knowledge, skills, and values from different subjects to meet a challenge presented by a change or new situation. • Explains how applying the chosen knowledge, skills, or values would effectively address the situation. Stage 1 2 3	• Transfers and applies essential knowledge, skills, and values from multiple subjects to meet a challenge presented by a change or new situation. • Explains how applying the chosen knowledge, skills, or values would effectively address the situation. Stage 1 2 3	• Transfers and integrates multiple and varied knowledge, skills, and values, including opposing approaches to come up with innovative and efficient solutions to meet a challenge presented by a change or new situation. Stage 1 2 3	• Transfers and synthesizes a contextually relevant approach based on multidisciplinary skills, values, and knowledge to come up with innovative and efficient solutions to meet a challenge presented by a change, a new situation, or an anticipated one without any bias. Stage 1 2 3

Stage 1: Student performs a task somewhat accurately with consistent guidance from others (teachers and peers).

Stage 2: Student performs a task accurately with little guidance and redirection from others (teachers and peers).

Stage 3: Student independently performs a task with ease, speed, and accuracy.

Beginning (Grades K–3)

Students at the Beginning level are able to transfer and apply some knowledge, skills, and values from different subjects to match the needs related to a change or a new situation and to explain how they match the needs. To assess this skill, teachers can prompt the students with questions such as "Where did you learn this?" or "How can you use the knowledge, skills, and values learned in other subjects to address this problem?" Consider the following example.

During the COVID-19 pandemic, school events were modified for virtual participation. One of the events affected by the change was our "Conscious Business Day," which we described earlier in this chapter as a day when students promote and sell products they have created. Under the COVID restrictions, students had to promote and sell through social media, as opposed to opening booths in their classrooms. Students in kindergarten through Grade 3 asked for their parents' help to promote and sell their products using their parents' social media accounts.

In preparation for the event, students had to present their promotion strategies. Bailey explained that he made sure that his display's background color was soft enough so that the picture of the product in the foreground could be the focus. When asked where he had learned about such factors, he said he learned about elements such as color and space in visual arts class. The teacher then asked how his skills in considering color and space were helpful in his new situation—promoting the online event through social media. Bailey paused and seemed to be unsure of how to answer the question, continuing only after the teacher prompted him with some ideas. Bailey's performance indicated he was on the targeted continuum level of "Beginning" because he was able to apply the visual arts skills to the context of a business-related activity in a new situation—the virtual Conscious Business Day. He was at Stage 2 in demonstrating the *versatility* element of Adaptability and Agility because he needed a bit of help from the teacher to explain how his skills were helpful in the new situation.

Transition (Grades 3–6)

Students at this Transition level need to be able to transfer and apply essential knowledge, skills, and values from multiple subjects to match the needs of a change or a new situation. The students must also be able to explain how these would match the needs of the situation.

For example, a Grade 4–5 student observed that online shopping increased during the COVID-19 pandemic because more people had to stay at home while still needing to shop for essential items. This situation led to an environmental problem: more plastic waste from the packaging, in the form of bubble wrap and single-use plastic. She explained that although the increase in online shopping helped the economic well-being of certain entrepreneurs, the plastic waste that ended up in the ocean was dangerous for marine animals and polluted the water. When asked to explain where she got the information, the student replied that she had learned it during social studies and science classes. As a solution, she presented ideas for using more sustainable packaging options, such as shredded, used paper, and avoiding plastic for items that did not need waterproof protection. She got the idea of using shredded paper from her visual arts class, where she was using it for a mixed-media art project and discovered that a pile of shredded paper is cushiony and thus can protect packages from breaking during shipping. The student was at Stage 3 for the *versatility* element of Adaptability and Agility because she independently used knowledge from multiple subjects and explained how it could be helpful in the new situation.

Developing (Grades 6–9)

Students at the Developing level need to be able to transfer and integrate multiple and varied knowledge, skills, and values, including opposing approaches, to come up with innovative and efficient solutions that match the needs of a change or a new situation. To assess this skill at the Developing level, teachers can gather evidence as students are working to find the solution for their projects. They can observe and interview the students during their brainstorming phase to gather insights about their thinking process.

Let's look at the following example of Reuben, the Grade 8–9 student we first mentioned in Chapter 1. In addressing the issue of trash in the school cafeteria, Reuben applied the compare-and-contrast skills he previously had learned in his social studies class. In that class, he also had learned about structured versus unstructured problems. He knew that structured problems are issues that are routine in nature and therefore need a system as the solution. Based on this knowledge, he analyzed the waste management problem in the cafeteria as something routine, and he aimed to create a waste-management system to solve it. To create the system, he worked collaboratively with some of his classmates. Each member had to research different details related to what might be the best features for waste management tools. Reuben's task was to research, compare and contrast, and sort trash bins in two categories—manual and automated—and find the type of bin that would best fit the needs of the people who used the school cafeteria. He demonstrated versatility when he analyzed the problem in his science class using knowledge, skills, and values he had learned from his social studies class. He also used his compare-and-contrast skills to analyze multiple options to create the system to solve his problem. He was at Stage 3 for the *versatility* element of Adaptability and Agility because he completed his part of the whole process independently.

Expert (Grades 9–12)

Students at the Expert level are able to transfer and synthesize a contextually relevant approach based on multidisciplinary skills, values, and knowledge to come up with innovative and efficient solutions that match the needs of both current and anticipated change or a new situation without any bias.

To help students comprehend key phrases and vocabulary words, such as *contextual* and *bias*, teachers use a vocabulary activity called "Pictionary Game," in which students have to find visual representations of the word or phrase, write a definition (using a dictionary, if necessary), and use it in a sentence (see the example in Figure 4.6). Cecil, an 11th grade student, found two images that represented the word *contextual* and one image for *bias*.

FIGURE 4.6
Example of a Student's Response to a Pictionary Game

	Contextual	Bias
Picture of representation	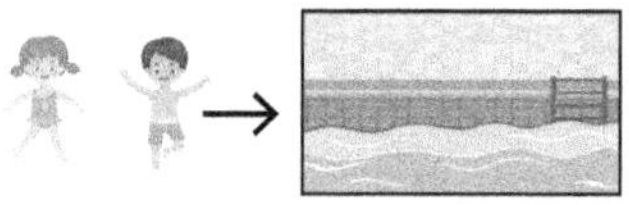  [two images: children → beach scene; child → forest scene]	 [image: balance scale and person]
Definition	depending on or relating to the circumstances	one-sidedness or unfairness
Sentence	Contextually relevant solutions should also be free from bias.	

To check students' understanding of the rubric's expectations related to versatility, the teacher asked them to write a one-minute reflection essay using the following prompt: "How does being versatile help you to overcome the situation? Write an example of a situation." Cecil wrote the essay shown in Figure 4.7, which led the teacher to conclude that she understood the expectation in the rubric.

FIGURE 4.7
Sample Reflection Essay

> Versatility helps me come up with efficient solutions that are beneficial for my decision making, as I exclude bias and consider opposing viewpoints.
>
> **Example:**
>
> My passion is creating 3D art. I'd like to exhibit my artwork to purposefully send a message about social problems happening around the world. This project will involve local artists in my area. My ideal concept for exhibition is to display the arts product at site-specific exhibitions as it will attract more audiences. This concept will likely enable me to spread the messages for wider ranges of audience. However, creating a site-specific art exhibition will be uneasy as there are many regulations that I need to comply with during the pandemic as the safety measures are strictly tightened. Therefore, I came up with another choice which is to hold the exhibition in a museum, which is safer although it is pricier and will only attract limited audiences. In this case, my opposing viewpoints are about the options of venues which ideally should be held in site-specific exhibitions. However, I need to exclude bias and consider every aspect to make this art exhibition happen. So, I'm being versatile in shifting my ideal exhibition concept from a site-specific art exhibition to a museum. The anticipation that I must work on, I will be promoting beforehand and creating effective strategies to reach out to more audiences through online platforms.
>
> _____
> *Note:* This essay has not been edited for grammar, punctuation, or spelling.

Cecil displayed *versatility* in her English language arts class, as she and two other students, Tony and Rendy, prepared to perform the scene from Shakespeare's play *The Tempest* in which a storm at sea is threatening a ship. On rehearsal day (a week before the performance), the audio setup wasn't working properly. The teacher observed the following discussion among the three students:

Cecil: This problem surely can be fixed today, but there's no guarantee that [it] would not happen again on D-day [performance day]. I'd say we have to come up with Plan A and B. Better yet, if we can come up with a plan that would work in both situations.

Tony: We can prepare our own speaker to be attached to the laptop for Plan A.

Rendy: I guess we should prepare for the worst—that the audio from the laptop might not work either. Let's go with manual background sound production for Plan B. Some of us can play percussion to make it sound like there's a storm.

Cecil: I think it's a good idea to prepare an extra speaker. However, regular PC speakers might not work so well in an auditorium this big. We might have to borrow or rent a huge speaker. But let's keep the idea since it might be possible to be done. We can definitely keep this as Plan B.... I guess the safer choice is the second idea: to use drums or objects to mimic the sound of the storm, because we won't have to rely so much on the technology. We still need the microphones to work, but I think the mic worked just fine. And in that case, I think we should just go all out. I think the problem of audio, when it happens, could occur in any part of the play. For that, some of us can play the piano, right? How about we play the background sound live instead of using a recording? Given the limited practice time, I think we can nitpick which major scene really needs background music.

Cecil's handling of the situation demonstrates Stage 3 of the *versatility* element for Adaptability and Agility. She was able to make a decision when her group members came up with two opposing ideas. She independently shared her consideration of cost and benefit for the two options and decided to go for the second idea. That said, she also acknowledged the first idea by saying that they should keep it as Plan B, demonstrating a lack of bias. She also added an innovative idea when she suggested upgrading the whole production with live background music.

Suggestions for Integrating Adaptability and Agility into Curriculum and Classroom Practice

- Infuse expectations for Adaptability and Agility into curriculum standards and subject area rubrics.
- Expose students to examples of changes around the world and global issues.
- Create a democratic learning environment for students to share, try out, and exchange ideas.
- Encourage students to come up with back-up plans.

- Avoid teaching using a one-way expression of knowledge, such as using close-ended worksheets or drilling to the tests. Instead, provide open-ended recording sheets or graphic organizers that students can use to organize their thinking for projects that involve or mimic the unpredictability of the real world. Graphic organizers that help students lay out alternative plans can help them anticipate possible changes.
- Allow students to brainstorm multiple ideas and consider pros and cons for each one.
- Give descriptive and actionable feedback.
- Provide multiple opportunities for students to transfer skills in different contexts.
- Continuously encourage students to reflect on their performance and create action plans for improvement.

5

Audience-Centered Communication

To effectively communicate, we must realize that we are all different in the way we perceive the world and use this understanding as a guide to our communication with others.
—Tony Robbins—

Today, people communicate through visual, auditory, and written means—everything from direct conversations and Zoom calls to text messages and email. However, any method of communication can be used well or used poorly, and even deeply knowledgeable individuals need to be able to effectively communicate their ideas to particular audiences in order to achieve their goals. And as social creatures, human beings communicate to connect, share our knowledge and experience, and organize action. We define *Audience-Centered Communication* as the ability to communicate ideas, information, values, and feelings clearly and persuasively by considering the audience's backgrounds and context as the key factors to determine the content, language usage, and expectations—in language arts as well as across the curriculum.

Why Is Audience-Centered Communication Important?

In line with our school's goal to develop self-regulated leaders, we view communication as one of the most important skills a leader must possess. Great leaders need to inspire and motivate to sell ideas and achieve their goals. More important, the content and the delivery of the message need to reflect an understanding of the audience.

Learning and practicing the skills of Audience-Centered Communication helps students develop two important abilities: (1) the ability to understand and relate better to their audience and (2) the ability to express themselves, their needs, what they know, and what they can do in a way that is effective, clear, and persuasive.

> Learning and practicing *Audience-Centered Communication* helps students develop two important abilities: (1) the ability to understand and relate to their audience and (2) the ability to express themselves, their needs, what they know, and what they can do in a way that is effective, clear, and persuasive.

Understanding the Audience

Even young students can begin to learn the skill of understanding an audience. In preschool, some students may initially prefer *solitary* play before gradually joining in *parallel* play (sitting near another student but not interacting), until they feel comfortable interacting with others during *associative* play, and finally *cooperative* play. Teachers should view parallel play as an opportunity to refer one student to another, building on the basics to gradually help them become more aware of what others are doing and to realize that others have their own stories.

Starting at the elementary level, teachers need to help students understand that what they share should have value in the eyes of their audience. The sharing section of morning meeting is a good forum for this work, as teachers can encourage students to ask themselves, "Why is this story important to share with my friends? What value will it have for them? Will it tell them something useful they can use to understand me better? Understand the world better? Understand themselves better?"

Middle school students can learn more detailed concepts related to ensuring that communication fits audience needs in terms of both content and delivery. In a Grade 6–7 English language arts class, a teacher designed stations for students to explore a number of important concepts. Station 1 was "Knowing Your Purpose and Key Messages," Station 2 was "Knowing Your Audience," and Stations 3 and 4 focused on the three key components of rhetoric: *ethos* (how to build credibility), *logos* (how to appeal to reason), and *pathos* (how to appeal to emotions).

- At Station 1, students read articles or watched videos about different purposes of communication—informing, persuading, collaborating, and motivating. As they did so, they also tried to find the key message of the texts or videos, which required them to put on their Expert Thinking hat to see the big picture. They used graphic organizers to distinguish between essential and nonessential information.
- At Station 2, students were asked to determine their own communication purpose and key message for an upcoming exhibition. Once they were sure about their purpose and key message, they had to find information about the audience, such as their age, what they wanted to know, or their interests. The students filled out a graphic organizer to jot down the purpose, the key message, the target audience, and the most fitting delivery method for their project exhibition.
- At Stations 3 and 4, students either watched a resource video or read articles about how to build credibility, appeal to the audience's reason, and appeal to the audience's emotions (ethos, logos, and pathos, respectively) by delivering comprehensible and reasoned ideas with appropriate and factually sound examples or statistics.

Producing Effective, Clear, and Persuasive Communication

To produce effective, clear, and persuasive communication, students need to combine the essential skills of Meta-Level Reflection, Expert Thinking, Creativity and Innovation, and Empathetic Social Skills to process the input they acquire from listening to or reading various resources. Meta-Level Reflection helps in consciously planning the content for communication, monitoring quality during the communication process, and reflecting for future improvement. As students plan, they need Expert Thinking to determine a big-picture sense of the audience's needs and the communication content being planned, to analyze the elements, to critically evaluate the information sources, and to generate accurate conclusions and generalizations to be communicated using their Empathetic Social Skills. At the same time, the essential skill of Creativity and Innovation is needed to make sure the content and delivery are novel enough to grab the audience's attention and match their needs. The combination of these skills results in communication that is effective, clear, and persuasive.

Key Elements of Audience-Centered Communication

People with well-developed reading and listening comprehension skills tend to be effective writers and speakers, as they are able to obtain information and look at it critically to determine its accuracy, to corroborate information from different resources, and even to challenge information before creating their own writing. These processes are directly related to Expert Thinking, as students evaluate the information through careful steps of systems thinking, analytical thinking, and critical thinking.

In our assessment system, these dynamics are captured and further explored in the form of four key elements of Audience-Centered Communication: (1) *active listening*, (2) *strategic reading*, (3) *effective speaking*, and (4) *impactful writing*. (See Figure 5.1.)

FIGURE 5.1
The Key Elements of Audience-Centered Communication

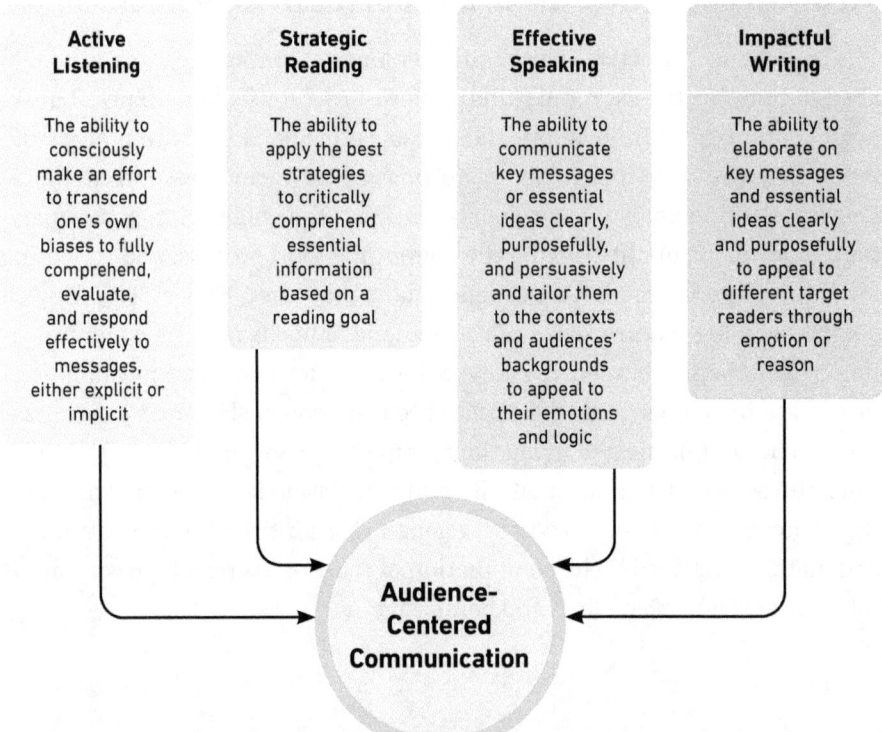

Active Listening

Active listeners are able to acquire, process, and retain information in a multitude of interpersonal contexts (Hargie, 2006). At the right moments, they ask good questions to clarify critical points and demonstrate attentive and positive body language. We define *active listening* as the ability to consciously make an effort to avoid one's own biases to fully comprehend, evaluate, and respond effectively to messages, either explicitly or implicitly. Explicit responses involve asking questions that help clarify the message, whereas implicit responses can be written responses, as in note taking. Implicit effort requires making connections through patterns and activating prior knowledge. For these purposes, it is important for students to understand the concept of "responding to verbal and nonverbal cues."

> In learning about *active listening*, it is important for students to understand the concept of "responding to verbal and nonverbal cues."

Nurturing the ability to respond to verbal and nonverbal cues

Teachers need to design a learning atmosphere that ensures a supportive condition—one in which students feel secure enough to share their thoughts and listen to each other in a respectful manner by paying attention to the other person's verbal and nonverbal cues. Verbal cues relate to what the other person says; nonverbal cues are about intonation, voice volume, facial expression, enthusiasm, tone, gesture, distance, and posture.

A supportive condition can be designed for various routines, such as reading-aloud time, shared reading, sharing time in morning meeting, or project presentation, to name a few. Teachers can also provide sentence stems to prompt the use of proper statements to express agreement with an opinion, to express disagreement, or to ask questions. Specifically for nonverbal cues, teachers can use opportunities such as morning meeting, advisory periods, and language arts or other subject times to discuss what nonverbal cues are through games or other activities. That way, students will learn to empathize with the speakers and understand their perspectives.

One of the routines to build a habit of responding to verbal and nonverbal cues is shared reading. Shared reading offers a great opportunity for teachers to model how to listen attentively as a book is read aloud (verbal cues) and how to respond to it properly—for example, by raising a hand before commenting or asking questions. For certain books, teachers can also point out characters' different facial expressions or gestures and mimic them to get students exposed to nonverbal cues. For example, using an echo-reading strategy, an elementary teacher read one sentence or phrase at a time from the book *Grumpy Monkey*, by Suzanne Lang, and invited students to repeat the sentence or phrase, trying to match her intonation. (Before she began, the teacher had reminded the students that to show that they were listening and responsive to the activity, they needed to follow along and participate.) Echo-reading the sentences "Grumpy! Me? I'm not grumpy!" the students furrowed their brows and scrunched up their noses. The teacher then discussed how it's possible to tell how others are feeling through facial expressions or gestures.

Another way to make students more aware of nonverbal cues, especially at the preschool and lower-elementary levels, is to make a class album of students' various facial expressions. Teachers can create photo albums of students showing different facial expressions—angry ones, sad ones, happy ones, and so on. These albums have proven very helpful in addressing classroom conflicts in a constructive way. For example, when two preschool students started squabbling over a toy, the teacher simply drew two "upset" faces on the board and invited the class to talk about the feeling those faces showed. This new activity got the squabbling students back on task without "calling them out," reviewed students' awareness that facial expressions are nonverbal cues that let us know what people are feeling even when they are expressing their feelings with words, and led to a useful discussion of ways to solve disputes when the people arguing are getting angry.

In elementary through high school, one of many opportunities our students have to listen to each other occurs during the project-based cycle segment called the "Constructive Friends Protocol," during which students present their project draft and get feedback from classmates. Teachers engage the students in listening to the content of the materials presented and sharing their opinion. As an example, a student in a high school's Bioliteracy class was describing her project on how to maintain good hygiene during the COVID pandemic. She planned to deliver her presentation later to a local community of vendors in a second-hand market near her house. As she was presenting, the teacher asked the other students to take notes on the speaker's key message while assessing the reasonableness of the arguments, the logic behind the reasoning, whether the evidence supported the arguments, and whether the word choice or presentation style fit the targeted audience. After the presentation, one student commented, "The word choices are very academic, which is good for a class presentation. However, your audience would be people in a traditional market whose education may not be as advanced. I suggest that you get to know your audience better and what they really need."

These students, ranging from upper-elementary to high school age, should be able to recognize more subtle cues like tone of voice and gestures. Teachers can first introduce students to the concept of nonverbal cues (e.g., tone and gestures) through the group activity segment in morning meeting or advisory, and practice more during project presentation or Constructive Friends' Protocol. In addition to teaching students how to interpret verbal and nonverbal cues from a speaker, it is important for them to learn to recognize an *audience's* nonverbal cues and know how to respond to speakers. Teachers can use cards that show gestures such as head scratching or yawning, and expressions such as a wrinkled forehead, and ask students to describe what they might imply and how a speaker might respond. For example, head scratching may indicate confusion, in which case the speaker should either speak more slowly or provide a clearer example of the material being presented.

Strategic Reading

Readers who are good at comprehending written information can look for and use relevant information and understand which parts are essential and which are not. To develop that ability, readers need to infer information and synthesize it using knowledge gained from personal experience, prior knowledge, and other texts (Fountas & Pinnell, 2011). We define *strategic reading* as the ability to apply the best strategies to critically comprehend essential information based on a reading goal. Successful *strategic reading* involves two important concepts that students need to understand and practice: reading goals and comprehension strategies.

> Successful *strategic reading* involves two important concepts that students need to understand and practice: reading goals and comprehension strategies.

Nurturing the understanding and practicing of reading goals

Strategic readers know what they are trying to find as they read a text. In reading informative texts, for example, they know what information they need to find. Students can learn about reading goals beginning in elementary school. Teachers can model reading based on a goal as they read aloud or during shared reading. Examples of goals include finding information, reading for pleasure, enriching existing knowledge and skills, or comparing and contrasting information from different resources.

Students should be made aware of learning objectives and how their reading relates to those objectives so they can be more strategic in finding information. For example, in a Grade 4–5 class, the teacher observed that a number of students seemed to be struggling to find information they needed for their project. The teacher grouped these students for a minilesson and modeled how to ask questions to help find specific information, using a think-aloud with the following structure:

1. Ask myself about the learning objectives.
   - What information do I need to find?
   - What keywords should I look for?
   - Where can I find the keywords—title, table of content, index page?
2. I want to find information about..., so the keywords I need to find are.... Let me first check the title.
   - What does the title tell me? Based on the title, what will the text be about?
   - Do I find the keywords I need? If not, are there similar keywords here? *[Highlights the keywords.]*
   - Where else can I find the keywords?
3. Let me check the table of contents.
   - Do I find the keywords I need? If not, are there similar keywords here?
   - Here I find the keywords. *[Highlights the keywords].* Which page is it?
4. Let me open the page and look for the keywords.
   - Where can I find the keyword on this page other than on the section title?
   - Now that I have found the keyword in some paragraphs *[highlights the keywords]*, let me look at other paragraphs and find similar keywords so I can see the pattern. That way, I can get the essential information.
   - What does the paragraph tell me about?
   - Does the paragraph contain important/essential information related to the reading goal?
   - How does the paragraph relate to the information that I need?
   - Do I need more information?

After modeling with the think-aloud, the teacher followed the same steps to find specific information together with the students, using the same text but searching for different keywords. The students then did the steps independently, using texts of their own choice.

Nurturing the ability to apply comprehension strategies

Because it involves analyzing, inferring, and synthesizing a text, reading itself is a strategic action (Fountas & Pinnell, 2017). Readers need to be able to choose one or more reading strategies that fit their reading goal. Students should be exposed to various strategies from an early age, so they have a repertoire to choose from and use to aid their comprehension as they progress through the grade levels.

In preschool, teachers begin modeling the strategies during read-aloud time. For example, as a teacher showed students the cover of a storybook, she asked, "When you see the picture, what do you think the story is about?" Her question was the beginning of exposure to *prediction* strategies. When she asked, "What happens in your life that is similar to the story?" she was introducing the students to the *making connections* strategy.

From elementary to high school, modeling and practicing strategies can occur during guided reading. Teachers need to introduce several reading strategies, such as *questioning, visualizing, making connections, summarizing,* and *synthesizing,* to name a few. They can also prepare cards like those shown in Figure 5.2, which students can choose from once they have learned the strategies. The goal is to be able to choose strategies that best fit their needs.

FIGURE 5.2
Reading Strategies Cards

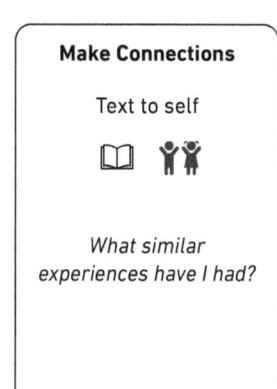
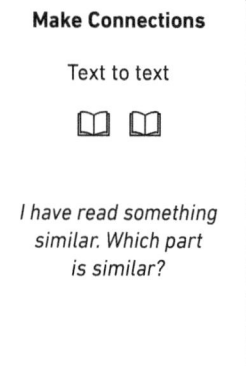

A strategy that is useful in tracking students' thinking as they read is *annotating texts* (Daniels & Zemelman, 2014). The basic concept is to stop, think, and react when encountering information that readers see as important because it is (1) related to the information being looked for, (2) connected to another text that has been read previously, or (3) an idea that contradicts a preexisting idea that the reader has in mind. After spotting particular phrases or sentences, the reader can jot down a thought or reaction. A high school history teacher modeled this strategy by annotating a text and then had her students practice it using the same text before choosing their own to read. For the practice, the teacher identified three concepts related to the topic at hand—how humans lived in the prehistoric era—that students were to focus on as they read the text: migration and settlement, tools advancement, and art making.

Effective Speaking

In essence, speaking is the distinctive process of distributing and reciprocating thoughts, ideas, and emotions through verbal means. As communicators, students are expected to be able to develop and arrange consistent key messages and present them with great clarity while adapting their delivery to suit the audience. We define *effective speaking* as the ability to communicate key messages or essential ideas clearly, purposefully, and persuasively, and tailor them to the contexts and audiences' backgrounds to appeal to their emotions and logic. Effective speaking includes two concepts that students need to understand and apply: content and effective delivery method. Both must fit the context and audiences' needs.

> *Effective speaking* includes two concepts that students need to understand and apply: content and effective delivery method.

Nurturing the ability to craft content

Crafting content is one of the two processes in speaking, the other being "performing the speech" (Palmer, 2014). For preschoolers, the first focus is building their vocabulary. The key to this development is the interaction between students and teachers. In classrooms with a supportive climate, teachers join students in their play and converse throughout, without dominating the conversation. Conversation works as a way to develop children's vocabulary alongside their thinking processes. Teachers can use this opportunity to introduce new words. For example, during planning time in a preschool class, a student pointed to the spatulas and pans in the House Area and said, "I want to play that and that." "Oh, you want to use a spatula and a pan?" the teacher replied, inserting the names of the objects. "What are you going to do with them?"

Beginning in upper-elementary grades, students should practice crafting formal presentations. After students acquire the information they need, teachers can facilitate the crafting skill by conducting workshops that center around students drafting and organizing their speech content within an outline, much like crafting content in writing. Here, students also need to use their Expert Thinking to make sure the message is credible and reliable—that is, to support it with a sound argument and with evidence from valid and reliable resources. The students must then organize the information they have gathered in a way that builds the key messages they want the audience to understand.

To foster students' independence, it is important that teachers facilitate the learning of various strategies for productive skills in language, such as brainstorming, analyzing, referencing, outlining, or using a checklist for self-editing. For example, a "Point-Reasoning-Example-Point" (or PREP) graphic organizer, like the one in Figure 5.3, can help students outline their presentations or generate effective presentations from papers they have written.

FIGURE 5.3
PREP Graphic Organizer

Item	Content
Point	
Reasoning	
Example	
Point	

Nurturing an effective delivery method

For effective delivery, teachers need to guide students in practicing the competencies a speaker needs in order to gain rapport with an audience, including how to establish a presence and how to create visuals that heighten the audience's message retention. Palmer (2014) identifies six essential competencies for speakers to elevate their presence: (1) poise that exudes confidence, (2) voice volume to make everything heard, (3) passion that brings life into the voice, (4) eye contact to engage the audience, (5) gestures that fit the message, and (6) speed pacing for a dynamic performance.

In addition to offering plenty of opportunities for students to present their ideas, teachers should use multiple strategies to have students reflect on their presentation skills. A reflection log can help students evaluate their presentation based on the six essential competencies for speakers.

Even students at the K–1 grade level have learned how to use formal manners when presenting their ideas in front of others. One opportunity to do so is during our end-of-term exhibition of learning, where students showcase their projects. Each classroom hosts an exhibition for around 45 minutes, during which all students are ready to explain their project to anyone who comes in and expresses an interest. For example, before presenting his project about the concept of "rights and responsibilities at home," a student asked, "Do you want me to present in English or Indonesian?" He presented his work and pointed, at appropriate times, to relevant parts of a poster he had created. As he wrapped up the presentation, the student asked, "Do you have any questions?"

In a Grade 6–7 class, a language arts teacher had the students watch short clips of some exemplary public speakers, from university debaters to presidents. The students had to write down and discuss the qualities that characterized these speakers. They used an observation form made by their teachers based on Palmer's (2014) six essential competencies (see Figure 5.4).

The teacher used the discussion as an opportunity to give immediate feedback before the students did their actual presentation. In addition, after noticing that some of her students tended to make wordy presentation slides, she did a minilesson to discuss the importance of visuals when speaking or presenting information, to hook the audience's attention and aid understanding. She modeled how to make a visual that shows just enough information that is easy to process and delivers the details verbally (see Figure 5.5).

FIGURE 5.4

Observation Form: Speakers' Six Essential Competencies

Criteria	Notes
Poise	
Voice	
Passion	
Eye contact	
Gesture	
Speed	

FIGURE 5.5

Examining Ineffective and Effective Use of Images

Let's explore how the information at left is presented in the image.

The Water Cycle	The Water Cycle
<ul><li>The water cycle is the continuous process by which water evaporates from Earth's surface, forms clouds in the atmosphere, and returns to Earth's surface as precipitation.</li><li>The water cycle is driven by the energy from the sun, which causes water to evaporate from bodies of water and the ground.</li><li>The water vapor rises into the atmosphere and cools, forming clouds. This process is called condensation.</li><li>When the clouds become heavy with water, the water falls back to Earth's surface as precipitation, which can take the form of rain, snow, sleet, or hail.</li><li>Precipitation can soak into the ground, run off into bodies of water, or be absorbed by plants.</li></ul>	 Image credit: Dennis Cain/NWS

Impactful Writing

It is important that students write skillfully and have an impact on others through what they write. We define *impactful writing* as the ability to elabo-

> To produce a piece of *impactful writing*, students need to understand the writing process and strategies.

rate key messages and essential ideas clearly and to appeal to different target readers emotionally or rationally. To produce a piece of *impactful writing*, students need to understand the writing process and strategies.

Nurturing an understanding of the writing process and strategies

Preschool and K–1 students can learn the basic skill of writing, progressing at their own pace and with different types of support, based on their needs. Teachers can provide various unconventional materials for students to practice writing, such as a tray filled with sand or a sealed plastic bag filled with flour. Both give students an easy way to practice making letter shapes with their finger. (If you try the flour method, make sure the plastic bag remains sealed—and that students create their letter shapes by pressing on the outside of the bag!)

Students who can more easily draw their ideas rather than capture them in writing should be allowed to do so, and teachers can always capture these students' ideas by writing them down while the students dictate. For students who write in invented spelling, teachers can first ask them to read what they have written and then record it. Figure 5.6 shows examples of these kinds of support.

Students who show more readiness in writing can benefit from various graphic organizers. One common example is the accordion graphic organizer, which looks like a folded brochure; each page is devoted to a different stage of the writing process, from prewriting to revising and editing (see Figure 5.7, on p. 106, for a "flattened" version, showing four stages and four organizers). Students begin with the prewriting organizer, working independently during writing workshops, and go to their teachers to ask for feedback. Then, when their ideas are taking a clearer shape, students can move to the drafting organizer to begin organizing their ideas. The center is for the thesis statement, the bubbles around it are for the main idea and supporting details for each paragraph. Then, for all drafts—from first to final—students use the Revising and Editing stage checklists to review their work and self-assess their process, including paying attention to the "6 + 1 traits": ideas, organization, voice, word choice, sentence fluency, conventions, and presentation.

FIGURE 5.6
Examples of Preschool and K–1 Students' Writing Stages

Writing from a student at the drawing stage:

Writing from a student at the invented spelling stage:

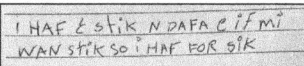

"I have 3 sticks and Dafa give me 1 stick, so I have 4 sticks."

Students should compare the qualities of their writing with the expectations described in the rubric. Once the students have fulfilled the expectation of their continuum level, teachers should encourage them to see the difference between that expectation and the expectation at the next level. Ask them, "What should you do to elevate the quality of your writing?" Phrasing like this can increase students' awareness of the rubric expectations and improve their writing quality accordingly.

FIGURE 5.7
Graphic Organizer for Different Stages in the Writing Process

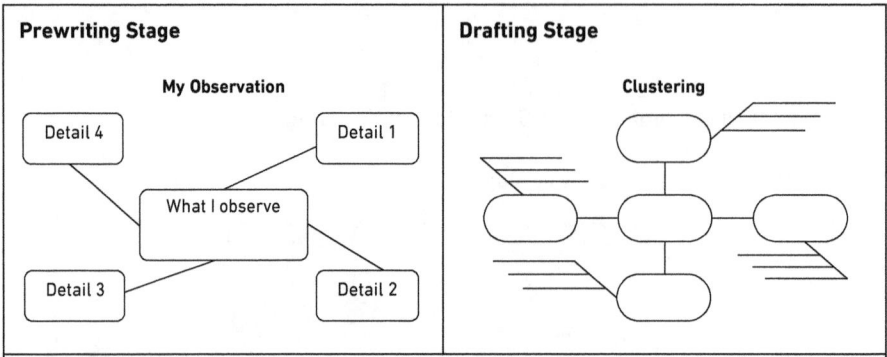

Revising Stage

CONVENTIONS	Checking Points	Note
Punctuation	Do I use end punctuation after all my sentences?	
	Have I correctly punctuated all direct quotations?	
	Do I use commas in compound sentences?	
Capitalization	Do I start all my sentences with capital letters?	
	Do I capitalize proper nouns and titles?	
Spelling	Do I spell all my words correctly?	
	Have I double-checked the spelling of names in my report?	
Grammar	Do I use the correct form of verbs?	
	Do my subjects and verbs agree in number?	
	Do I use the right words (e.g., *to, too, two*)?	

Editing Stage

6 + 1 Traits	Checking Points	Note
Ideas	Have I written a clear thesis statement?	
	Do I include one main idea in each topic sentence?	
	Have I accurately quoted or paraphrased my sources?	
Organization	Do I have an effective beginning, middle, and ending?	
	Have I put my middle paragraphs in the best order?	
	Do I use transitions?	
Voice	Does my writing show any knowledge and interest?	
	Does my voice sound formal?	
Word Choice	Do I define or explain any unfamiliar words?	
	Do I use specific nouns or active verbs?	
Sentence Fluency	Do I vary the lengths and beginnings of my sentences?	
	Do I avoid rambling sentences?	

As students' writing skills progress, teachers guide the students to express their thoughts and intentions in writing, being mindful of their communication purposes and paying specific attention to the size of the audience as well as to their audience's background so that they can adjust their writing to appeal to and engage that audience. For young learners, this skill begins with observing other people's way of writing—for example from different storybooks or nonfiction books. After that, students learn to identify their writing purpose—whether they want to communicate information, reflect on their thoughts, retell a story, or persuade someone to adopt a certain point of view or take a certain action, and so on. Then students learn to adjust their writing style and supporting visuals based on their understanding of the audience's background and belief, employing increasingly sophisticated strategies as they progress.

How Is Audience-Centered Communication Measured and Assessed?

Like the other essential skills, the Audience-Centered Communication skill gradually gets more comprehensive as students move to higher continuum levels. As previously stated, this skill has four elements. The rubric in Figure 5.8 identifies *active listening* as ACC.1; *effective speaking* as ACC.2; *strategic reading* as ACC.3; and *impactful writing* as ACC.4.

The rubric also describes three stages of performance:

- Stage 1: Student performs a task somewhat accurately with consistent guidance from others (teachers and peers).
- Stage 2: Student performs a task accurately with little guidance and redirection from others (teachers and peers).
- Stage 3: Student independently performs a task with ease, speed, and accuracy.

The following descriptions of the continuum levels focus on the second key element, *strategic reading,* which we defined earlier as the ability to apply the best strategies to critically comprehend essential information based on a reading goal. We provide examples of settings that can be designed to assess this element, along with examples of acceptable evidence.

FIGURE 5.8
Rubric for Audience-Centered Communication

	Early (Preschool–K)	Beginning (K–3)	Transition (3–6)	Developing (6–9)	Expert (9–12)
ACC.1 **Active Listening**	• Understands information and follows directions to show listening skills. • Gives comments and/or asks questions. Stage 1 2 3	• Obtains information with emphasis on the identification or clarification of the basic ideas by asking questions related to topics and taking notes in graphic organizers. Stage 1 2 3	• Interprets key messages of the information with some details as shown in note-taking tools (e.g., graphic organizer) and asks questions to confirm or clarify. Stage 1 2 3	• Summarizes the information as shown in note-taking tools (e.g., graphic organizer) and asks good questions to clarify, evaluate, check for understanding, and to decide whether to agree or disagree from own perspectives. Stage 1 2 3	• Develops understanding of the presented information as shown in note-taking tools (e.g., graphic organizer) and asks more complex questions to evaluate information in an unbiased way, based on multiple perspectives. Stage 1 2 3
ACC.2 **Strategic Reading**	• Expresses ideas, information, or emotions in small and larger groups clearly (sometimes with the use of drawings or concrete objects to clarify the message). Stage 1 2 3	• Expresses ideas, information, or emotions in small or larger groups with logical sequence and relevant facts or details. Stage 1 2 3	• Expresses ideas, information, or emotions in small or larger groups with logical sequence and better sentence structures and intonation by considering the audience's educational backgrounds or beliefs. Stage 1 2 3	• Communicates key messages or essential ideas in small and larger groups with logical sequence, effective sentence structures, word choice, and gestures by considering the audience's educational backgrounds or beliefs. Stage 1 2 3	• Communicates key messages or essential ideas in small or larger groups clearly (logically and uses effective sentences), persuasively (uses strong word choice and paralanguage), and enthusiastically by considering the audience's educational backgrounds, beliefs, and roles. Stage 1 2 3

Audience-Centered Communication   109

	Early (Preschool–K)	Beginning (K–3)	Transition (3–6)	Developing (6–9)	Expert (9–12)
ACC.3 **Effective Speaking**	• Chooses books based on interest and starts reading a few words. • Uses picture clues, recognized words, and a number of strategies to comprehend a text (predicting, questioning, visualizing, making connections). • Retells the message in their own words (orally, in drawing, or simple writing).	• Plans to choose reading materials based on identified goals. • Uses context cues to understand new vocabulary and a number of strategies fluently to comprehend a text based on the reading level while using appropriate graphic organizers. • Retells the message sequentially in detail.	• Plans and sets a reading goal based on the understanding of learning objectives and multiple perspectives. • Uses pattern and text structures using appropriate graphic organizers to comprehend a text based on the reading level and applies comprehension-monitoring strategies (rereading, adjusting pace). • Creates reading responses using summarization and other strategies.	• Plans and sets a purposeful reading goal while connecting to resources of other disciplines. • Applies more complex strategies (inferring, determining importance, and synthesizing) and independently monitors to comprehend a text based on the reading level while using appropriate graphic organizers. • Creates more elaborated reading responses that include summarized essential ideas.	• Plans and sets critical and purposeful reading goals to corroborate or to challenge information. • Automatically applies relevant strategies fluently to achieve the reading goals and independently monitors to comprehend challenging texts, whether for information or pleasure. • Creates sophisticated reading responses based on multiple perspectives and applicable in different contexts.
	Stage 1 2 3	Stage 1 2 3	Stage 1 2 3	Stage 1 2 3	Stage 1 2 3
ACC.4 **Impactful Writing**	• Expresses thoughts, feelings, ideas, or information based on interest by writing a combination of words, usually accompanied with their own drawing showing the sequence of events.	• Expresses thoughts, feelings, ideas, or information based on a communication purpose—e.g., informing, reflecting, retelling, maintaining a relationship.	• Expresses thoughts, feelings, ideas, or information based on communication purposes (e.g., informing, persuading) learning objectives, and interest, and understands how these goals affect the writing.	• Expresses insights based on multiple communication purposes (e.g., informing, persuading, collaborating, instructing), in an engaging way.	• Expresses insights purposefully and contextually based on complex communication purposes, in a powerful and engaging way, with a specific audience's background in mind.
	Stage 1 2 3	Stage 1 2 3	Stage 1 2 3	Stage 1 2 3	Stage 1 2 3

(continued)

FIGURE 5.8
Rubric for Audience-Centered Communication—*(continued)*

ACC.4 *(cont.)*	Early (Preschool–K)	Beginning (K–3)	Transition (3–6)	Developing (6–9)	Expert (9–12)
Impactful Writing	• Observes other people's way of writing and begins to jot down his/her words.	• Uses writing strategies (e.g., observation and clustering). • Begins to write simple paragraphs with a clear main idea and relevant supporting details, ordered sequentially, using graphics to support the message delivery (e.g., illustration, photographs, or charts).	• Uses more varied writing strategies (e.g., brainstorming, journalist questions, and self-edit rubrics). • Writes paragraphs that reflect multiple perspectives, with a clear main idea, elaborated supporting details (explanations, examples, evidence, graphics), ordered in a logical way, and by considering the audience's educational backgrounds or beliefs. • Uses word choices that include figurative language and specific terminology based on the writing purposes.	• Uses more varied writing strategies (e.g., outlining and double-entry journal). • Writes paragraphs that reflect multiple perspectives, with engaging openings and closings and with elaborated key messages supported by reliable data. The paragraphs are cohesive and coherent, with the audience or readers in mind. • Chooses words that engage readers' interest. • Includes more varied literary devices (e.g., figurative language, analogy) and relevant terminology based on the writing purposes.	• Uses various writing strategies skillfully and effectively to accentuate the message and personal writing style. • Writes paragraphs with engaging openings and closings, with elaborated key messages supported with reliable data, clearly and persuasively to counter readers' biases and appeal emotionally and scientifically, in consideration of their backgrounds, beliefs, and roles. Maintains strong perspectives throughout the entire writing piece. • Chooses a variety of words, phrases, and varied syntax that can convey a message in an impactful way.
	Stage 1 2 3	Stage 1 2 3	Stage 1 2 3	Stage 1 2 3	Stage 1 2 3

Stage 1: Student performs a task somewhat accurately with consistent guidance from others (teachers and peers).

Stage 2: Student performs a task accurately with little guidance and redirection from others (teachers and peers).

Stage 3: Student independently performs a task with ease, speed, and accuracy.

Early (Preschool–K)

Students at the Early level rely mostly on pictures or illustrations to comprehend a text. Many also rely on words they are already familiar with. Teachers can assess students' strategic-reading skills during any reading activities, whether student- or teacher-initiated.

An example of a student-initiated reading activity in our preschool occurs during what we call "work time"—a period when students choose an activity based on the plan they made during a Plan-Do-Review activity (Hohmann et al., 2008); "reading books" is a popular choice. Teachers take note of students' literacy skill—can they read a few words? many words?—and of any use of reading comprehension strategies such as predicting, questioning, visualizing, and making connections. If a student invites the teacher to join the reading or comment on the story, the teacher can ask the student to retell the story in their own words.

In an example of a teacher-initiated activity, teachers can give each student two or three storybooks and have them choose one to retell during small-group time. Finger puppets can serve as props for their retelling.

Beginning (Grades K–3)

Young students can reflect on their experience from reading books—ones they've read alone, with the teacher or classmates, and with their parents at home. Teachers can interview students who are not writing yet by using a reading-response recording sheet such as the one shown in Figure 5.9 (see p. 112).

Students at the Beginning level are able to choose what they want to read based on their reading goal (determined by a teacher-informed learning objective) and depending on their reading ability. Let's consider the example of Julia, a Grade 2–3 student.

Julia's class was beginning a social studies project on the topic "interaction in communities." To collect information, the students had to read various relevant texts. The teacher provided several suitable books within the reading-level range for Grade 2–3. Julia picked a book titled *Firefighters*, written by Katie Knight.

To assess comprehension, the teacher gave the students a "herringbone technique" graphic organizer, modified from Margaret Bouchard's *Comprehension Strategies for English Language Learners* (2005). This graphic organizer prompts students to identify their reading goal and to select and use appropriate strategies, such as determining the importance of information from a body text to achieve the reading goal, and guides the student in retelling the information in the reading material using the prompts of *who, what, when, where, how,* and *why.* After reading the text, Julia completed her graphic organizer, as shown in Figure 5.10.

FIGURE 5.9
Template for Weekly Reading Response

Weekly Reading Response

Name: _____ **Date Due:** _____

Fill out the table.

Title of Book: Date: _____ Minutes: _____	What do you like most about the book?
Title of Book: Date: _____ Minutes: _____	One interesting word from today's reading is:
Title of Book: Date: _____ Minutes: _____	I have a question for the author:

When the teacher asked Julia to share what she understood from the text, Julia replied,

> My reading goal is to find information about firefighters. They put out fires and rescue people from big and dangerous fires. Sometimes it can happen in buildings, houses, or forests. They use equipment like a large hose, ax, and fire extinguisher. Firefighters are community helpers. It is their job to help keep the community safe from fire.

Based on Julia's response, we can conclude that she is at Stage 3 for the element of *strategic reading* because she is able to select reading materials based on her goal and use the strategy of determining important information to understand the text. She is also able to retell important information cohesively based on the text structure.

FIGURE 5.10
Example of a Student's "Herringbone" Graphic Organizer

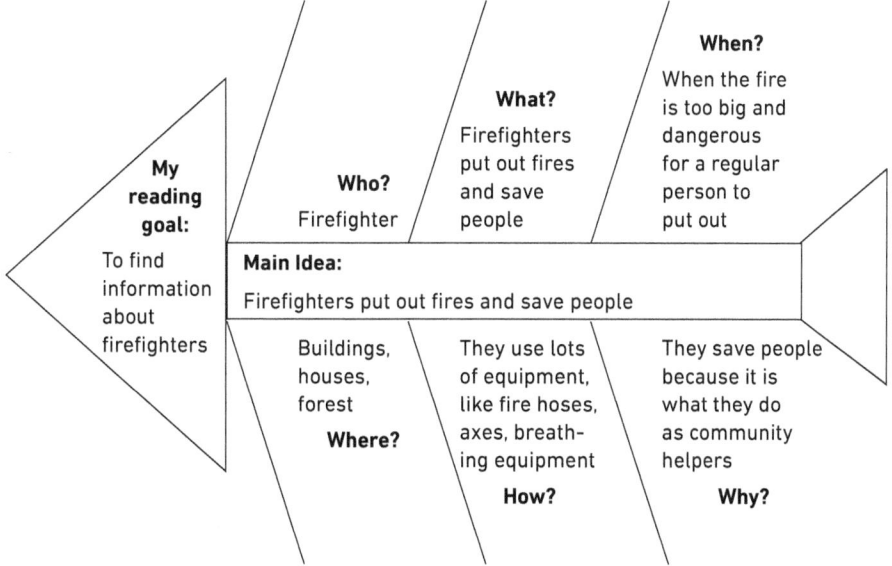

Now let's look at Aaron. He chose to read *Carlos's Family Celebration*, by Lorena F. Di Bello. As he was reading, he asked the teacher what a piñata is. Looking at the book, the teacher read aloud the sentence, "The third thing we can do is to fill the piñata." She continued, "We're trying to figure out the meaning of the word *piñata*. Let's see if there are any clues before or after the sentence." She turned to the first page and read, "It's Mexican Independence Day! Carlos and Selena are getting ready for a big party." Then she said, "So *piñata* is related to a celebration or party. Hmm. That's helpful, but we need more information. Let's look at the next sentences and pictures that might help us identify the meaning."

After collecting the information, and guided by his teacher, Aaron filled in a "spider web" graphic organizer that made the information more visual and helped him understand the meaning of the word *piñata* (see Figure 5.11, p. 114). He showed his understanding by saying, "It's a decoration filled with candies. We hang it, and people use a stick to break the piñata."

FIGURE 5.11
Example of a Student's "Spider Web" Graphic Organizer

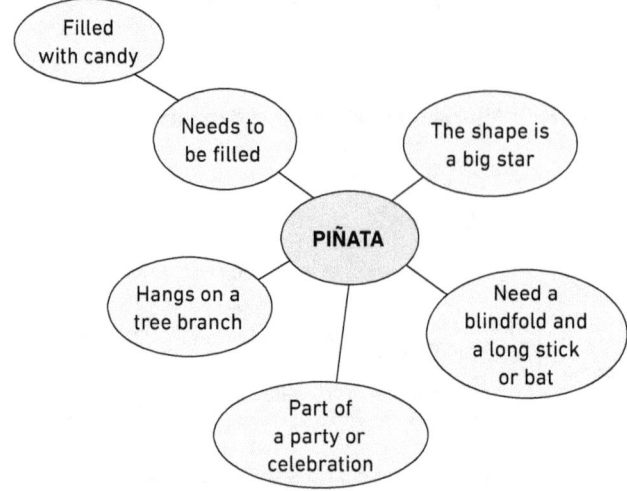

The teacher then asked Aaron to retell the story. Aaron said, "The story is about Carlos and his sister. They have a lot of things to do for a big party. One of them is a piñata." The teacher then prompted him with several questions to help him retell the story with more details, such as "What day do Carlos and Selena celebrate?" "What are the five things Carlos and Selena are doing for the party?" "How do Carlos and Selena prepare the piñata?" "What can we find at their home for the party?" and "Who came to the party?"

Aaron exemplifies Stage 1 for the element of strategic reading because he still needs guidance from the teacher to use the strategy of making connections to understand the reading, including the context clues. He also needed teacher prompts to retell the story more completely and in sequence.

Transition (Grades 3–6)

Compared to students at the Beginning level, who still need teachers to provide them with books that fit the learning objectives, students at the Transition level are more aware of their learning objectives and can pick books without a teacher's guidance. They also begin to search for multiple resources so they can read about a topic from multiple perspectives.

Students at this level are more capable of recognizing a wider variety of text structures, such as descriptive, chronological, compare-contrast, cause-and-effect, and problem-solution. Figure 5.12 shows graphic organizers that students can use to demonstrate their understanding of the patterns of these

FIGURE 5.12
Graphic Organizers Based on Text Structure

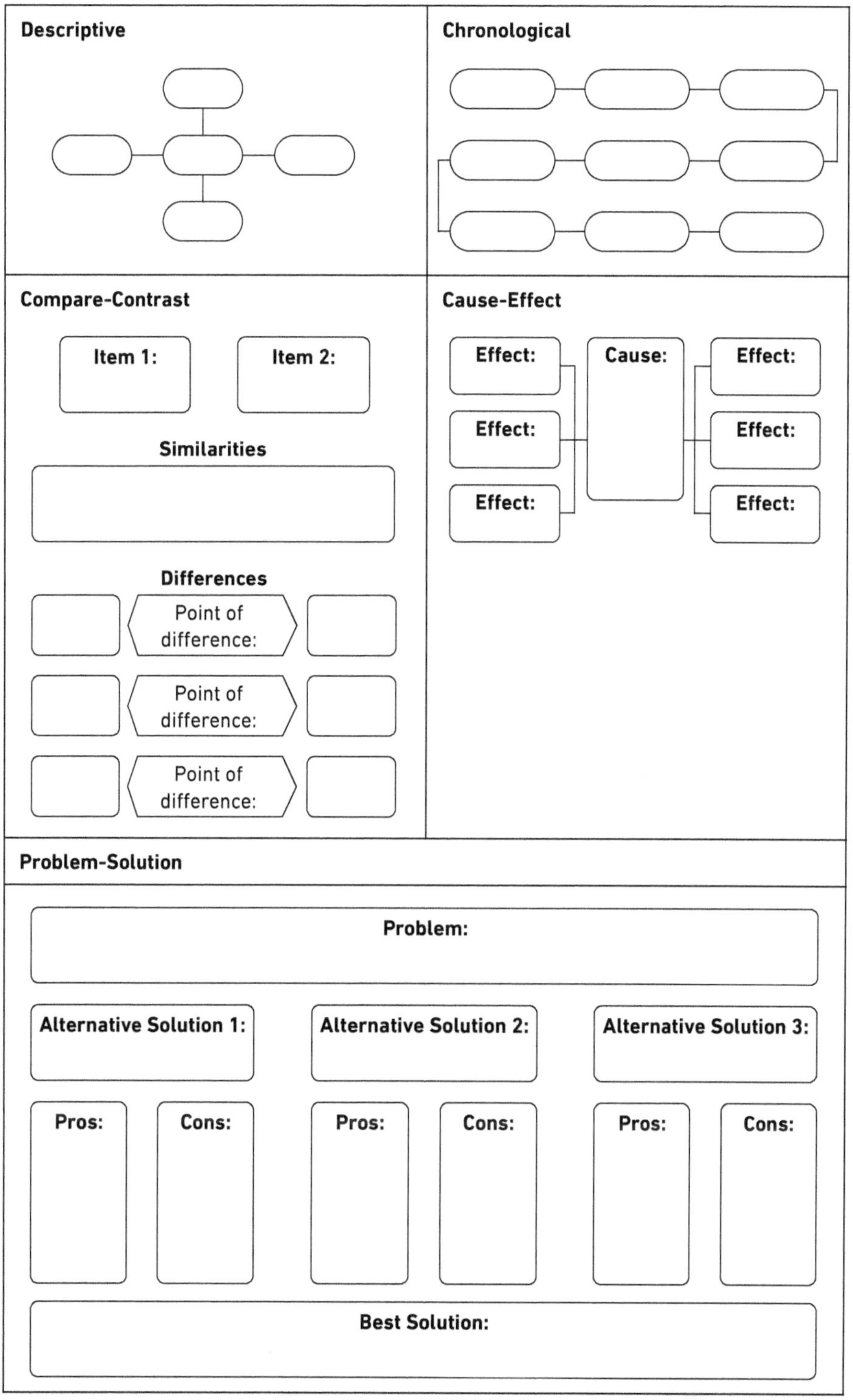

Descriptive

Chronological

Compare-Contrast

Item 1:   Item 2:

Similarities

Differences

Point of difference:

Point of difference:

Point of difference:

Cause-Effect

Effect: Cause: Effect:

Effect: Effect:

Effect: Effect:

Problem-Solution

Problem:

Alternative Solution 1:   Alternative Solution 2:   Alternative Solution 3:

Pros: Cons: Pros: Cons: Pros: Cons:

Best Solution:

structures, and they are able to decide for themselves which tools will best help them organize their thinking.

In addition to the strategies learned in previous levels, students at the Transition level are expected to use strategies to monitor their comprehension—for example, by rereading and adjusting their reading pace. As evidence for comprehension, Transition-level students are expected to create reading responses in the form of summarizations, synopses, or book recommendations.

Developing (Grades 6–9)

Students at the Developing level are able to use more complex strategies to comprehend literal and nonliteral meaning by inferring, determining importance (essential and nonessential information) based on the reading goal, and synthesizing. They use appropriate graphic organizers to map the information and write a comprehensive reading response.

Let's refer back to Reuben, the Grade 8–9 student who was working on a science project to solve the problem of waste management in his school cafeteria. During his research, he read various articles about different types of automated trash bins and possible solutions to increase awareness of waste-related problems in schools. He focused on finding technology-based solutions that could address his goal of increasing the use of trash bins. He began by using the *questioning* strategy and listed the following questions to guide him in comprehending the resources he read:

- What is my reading goal?
- What valid and reliable resources should I use?
- Which reading strategies can I use?
- How can I categorize the important features of a trash bin?
- What do people look for in an automated trash bin?
- What are the important features of automated trash bins?
- Which line supports the information?
- What are the similarities and differences of automated trash bins in those resources?
- What can I conclude from the information?

He then used a graphic organizer (see Figure 5.13) to summarize the results of his reading result (reading response).

Reuben's approach to his research indicates he is at Level 3 in the element of *strategic reading*. He was able to apply a reading strategy—in this case, questioning—without a teacher's help.

FIGURE 5.13
Summarization of a Reading Response

My reading goal: Finding different features of technology that can upgrade the use of automated trash bins Reading strategies: Determining importance and questioning			
Title: Best Motion Sensor Trash Can **Resource:** https://www.popsci.com/story/reviews/best-motion-sensor-trash-can/	**Title:** Smart Trash Disposal Choice for Your Home **Resource:** https://www.vitarecycles.com/blog/sensor-trash-bins-smart-trash-disposal-choice-for-your-home/	**Title:** Best Kitchen Trash Can **Resource:** https://www.apartmenttherapy.com/best-kitchen-trash-cans-36762370
• Design: Square, oval, and rectangle • Functionality and features: eliminate germs, futuristic with sensor • Materials: Durable type 430 stainless steel	• Design: Tall and cylindrical • Functionality: Reduces the filth around us by its monitoring solution • Materials: Stainless steel, automatic lid	• Design: Rectangular type and round type. • Functionality: Touch-top cans open by touching the lid or a nearby button. Automated cans; open either by waving your hand near a sensor or by using voice activation. • Materials: Stainless. Automatic lid with sensor and voice activation.
Conclusions: All the trash bins have automated features such as sensors, automatic lid, voice activation. They are made of stainless steel which is durable and easy to clean.			

On the other hand, Catherine also worked on the use of reading strategies while looking for information about automated trash bins, but when she tried to comprehend the articles, she needed guidance from the teacher. Consider the following dialogue:

Teacher: What is your reading goal?

Catherine: I have to find the features of automated trash bins.

Teacher: What strategies can you use?

Catherine: Determining the importance of information.

Teacher: Why is that a good choice?

Catherine: Because I need to extract essential information about the features of an automated trash bin.

Teacher: So, what question would you ask yourself to guide you to find that information?

Catherine: "What are the important features of an automated trash bin?"

Teacher: OK. What will you do after you find the information?

Catherine: I'll look for more details that can show how good the automated trash bin is.

Teacher: How good it is compared to…?

Catherine: The manual trash bin.

Teacher: OK. That means you're going to compare-contrast the features of automated and manual trash bins. Which graphic organizer should you select?

Catherine: Well, I should select a graphic organizer where I can compare and contrast them.

Teacher: Do you think it is enough to compare-contrast only those features, or do you need more information?

Catherine: Um… I think I want to find out about design… and… function, I guess.

Teacher: So, you're going to compare and contrast both types of trash bins using the three categories: features, design, and function. And, to help you focus on your reading goal, what other questions would you ask yourself?

Catherine: "What are the similarities and differences of the design, materials, and features?"

Teacher: All right. Go ahead and start reading. Let me know when you're ready to discuss your progress, OK?

Catherine is at the Developing level for the element of *strategic reading* because she is well aware of her reading goal and is familiar with some reading strategies and graphic organizers. That said, she needed a lot of help to decide on specific things to do to complete her work. For that reason, she is still at Stage 1.

Expert (Grades 9–12)

At the Expert level, students are critical readers capable of setting their own reading goals and pursuing them. They continuously think, question, and assess the rationality of the material and their reliability as a source. They can read to find information and confirm or corroborate a statement.

They are comfortable with challenging a particular statement or piece of information.

At this point, reading strategies should be a natural part of the reading process. Students at the Expert level are more capable of choosing the best strategies to fit their needs as they seek to comprehend particular texts.

When writing their reading responses, students provide deeper content than students at other levels because they are armed with multiple and varied resources that enrich their background knowledge and thus their perspectives. Also, with richer background knowledge, they are now ready to tackle wider and challenging topics.

As an example, when learning about the art of persuasion in rhetoric, Grade 11 students were asked to identify an article, a speech, or an advertisement that they believed was manipulative or deceptive and one that was civil and effective. They had to write a short response explaining their reasons for choosing each example. They used the strategy of SOAPS analysis (**S**ubject, **O**ccasion, **A**udience, **P**urpose, **S**peaker (adapted from the "SOAPSTONE" strategy developed by the College Board) to help determine the purpose of the author or creator. Figure 5.14 (see p. 120) shows an example of how a student used the strategy to reach her conclusions about the two advertisements she had chosen for the assignment.

The development of strategic reading skills plays a critical role in equipping students to navigate the intricate world of texts. By intentionally selecting appropriate reading strategies, students can identify valuable information and critically analyze the materials. These skills will also help them develop their own unique perspective and improve their comprehension.

Suggestions for Integrating Audience-Centered Communication into Curriculum and Classroom Practice

- Include an Audience-Centered Communication rubric into the curriculum standards.
- Gradually introduce the concept of understanding audience needs by asking students first to share their ideas in front of others, then to analyze the characteristics of their audience (background and needs), and finally to match the key message with the most appropriate delivery method. Have them sharpen this skill by practicing with audiences that have different perspectives and backgrounds.

FIGURE 5.14
Example of a SOAPS Analysis

Advertisement 1	
Subject	Camel cigarettes *"More Doctors Smoke Camels Than Any Other Cigarettes."*
Occasion	America, 1946 *"In America today, thanks to the intrepid spirit of these pioneers..."* *"1946 Version"*
Audience	Existing Camel smokers and smokers of other tobacco products *"If you are a Camel smoker, this preference among doctors will hardly surprise you. If you're not—well, try Camels now."*
Purpose	To persuade consumers to buy their tobacco products by convincing them that even doctors prefer to smoke Camels compared to other cigarette products. They claimed that it was supported by research without actually naming the resource. *"According to a recent nationwide survey..."*
Speaker (or Author/ Creator)	R. J. Reynolds Tobacco Company *(printed on the right bottom of the ads)*
Conclusion	The advertisement can be categorized as a deceptive or manipulative advertisement due to lack of reliability and misleading statements about health care professionals' preference for their products.

Advertisement 2	
Subject	Blood Donor *"Share life give blood"* *"World Blood Donor Day"*
Occasion	World Blood Donor Day *(printed on the left bottom of the ads)*
Audience	The world citizens *"World Blood Donor Day"*
Purpose	To raise awareness of the society to donate their blood on the World Blood Donor Day to save people's lives. *"Share life give blood"*
Speaker (or Author/ Creator)	World Health Organization *(printed on the right bottom of the ads)*
Conclusion	It is a civil and effective advertisement because it is for a good cause to save people's lives, released on the right moment of World Blood Donor Day by a trustworthy nonprofit organization of WHO.

- Design activities for students to become active listeners who are confident and tactful in responding to verbal and nonverbal cues. Try read-alouds, shared readings, and peer discussion of students' written work.
- Model and design practices on how to set reading goals and to apply reading strategies accordingly. Provide tools such as reading strategies cards and graphic organizers.
- Get students to practice crafting the content of their presentation using the PREP structure (Point-Reasoning-Example-Point).
- Provide plenty of opportunities for students to present their work and reflect on their own presentation skills based on the aspects of poise, voice, passion, eye contact, gestures, and speed.
- Model and have students practice what to do in each stage of the writing process and how to maximize the use of writing strategies. Provide graphic organizers for each writing stage.

6

Synergistic Collaboration

Coming together is a beginning, keeping together is progress, working together is success.
—Henry Ford—

In Chapter 5 we discussed Audience-Centered Communication—how students practice the ability to communicate and adapt their communication strategies based on their understanding of the audience. In this chapter, we explore how Audience-Centered Communication skills are practiced in group settings, particularly during collaborative work. Collaboration is communication experienced and practiced in a group setting with a shared goal (Meyer, 1994).

Today we live in a world that is better connected than ever, yet more volatile, uncertain, complex, and ambiguous. To keep up, individuals must be able to collaborate with each other in meaningful and purposeful ways. We define *Synergistic Collaboration* as the ability to work effectively on a team in which each member commits to a personal role to accomplish a common goal through face-to-face or technology-mediated coordination, or both.

We included the word *synergistic* to emphasize the combined power of working together, which is greater than the power achieved by working separately (Cambridge Dictionary, n.d.). We believe teachers need to empower their students to collaborate effectively in groups. Instead of simply dividing work within a group and requiring students to cooperate, teachers must build each group member's responsibility for a portion of the work to reach a shared goal through collaboration.

Why Is Synergistic Collaboration Important?

Synergistic Collaboration helps students commit to a shared group goal during collaborative work and then work hard in whatever role they have within the group. In most instances, learning is a social endeavor. The process of collaborative problem solving, for example, involves sharing ideas to enrich our thinking and help add more alternative solutions.

Synergistic Collaboration is important for two reasons. First, it helps students practice the notion of a shared goal and shared responsibility to achieve a better result. Second, it helps students develop strategies to maintain positive interaction.

Shared Goal and Shared Responsibility

It is important to begin any group work with a clearly defined goal that all group members share. A clearly defined, shared goal helps increase group members' sense of ownership of the work. It also heightens everyone's sense of responsibility to contribute ideas so the group can succeed in achieving the shared goal.

Our preschool teachers nurture a sense of shared goal and responsibility by providing opportunities for students to take charge of learning activities and various daily routines, which also helps them understand how to work collaboratively. For example, during snack time, preschool teachers frequently allow students to choose an activity from a list of responsibility options (e.g., passing plates, forks, or cups), showing that we need to share responsibilities to achieve the shared goal of having a snack together.

Starting from the elementary level up to high school, teachers begin having students discuss and negotiate shared goals, gradually increasing the complexity of the goal as students advance in grade levels. While negotiating the goal, each group member comes up with a problem definition and strategies for realizing the goal in order to strengthen all students' knowledge related to the problem (Springer et al., 1999). Teachers need to teach students the importance of group work—not only splitting the work, working with others, and getting the job done, but also understanding the significance of contributing ideas in collaborative work and consolidating the ideas into compromise solutions. For example, as middle school students collaborate on a community service project, they should begin by discussing whom they will be serving and what kinds of activities would be most helpful to that group.

Strategies to Maintain Positive Interaction

Throughout the collaboration process, team members must have strategies to maintain positive interaction and communication with each other.

They need to feel comfortable sharing opinions and communicating their ideas, even when they have disagreements. They also must maintain their motivation so that everyone on the team is committed to achieving the group goal.

For students to feel comfortable sharing opinions in their group, everyone must agree to listen carefully to one another. Teachers should develop a secure environment where everyone's ideas are appreciated, and they should help students practice the strategies of *active listening* and *effective speaking*, which are elements of the skill of Audience-Centered Communication.

Teaching collaboration begins with designing an educational program. A multiage program helps build a learning atmosphere in which students see differences as normal, and it teaches them to collaborate with students at different levels and with diverse backgrounds. Phyllis Blumenfeld and her colleagues emphasize that successful collaboration requires knowledge and understanding to avoid negative stereotypes and to create spaces for effective communication among participants (Blumenfeld et al., 1996).

Our elementary schools' multiage structure creates numerous opportunities for students to practice interacting with classmates of different ages and to see differences as normal. For example, kindergarten and Grade 1 students are grouped together in a K–1 class, and Grades 6 and 7 are grouped together as a Grade 6–7 class. The older students readily understand that many of their younger classmates may need more help in reading or writing. In other instances, however, younger students may excel. In this way, students take turns being leaders and followers as they help each other.

If a multiage setting is not possible, teachers can rely on flexible grouping to help students become more comfortable interacting with anyone and expressing their ideas. Flexible grouping must accommodate both homogeneous and heterogeneous levels of readiness, interest, or learning profiles so that students can work with a diverse range of classmates. Heterogeneous grouping based on readiness or preferred ways of expressing their learning is a way to cultivate students' respect for differences, as well as their comfort sharing their opinions. It's a practice that helps create an atmosphere where positive interaction is expected and valued.

Key Elements of Synergistic Collaboration

As shown in Figure 6.1, our approach to Synergistic Collaboration combines four elements: (1) *individual accountability*, (2) *group cohesiveness*, (3) *critical opinion*, and (4) *virtual collaboration*. Let's take a closer look at each of them.

FIGURE 6.1
The Key Elements of Synergistic Collaboration

Individual Accountability	Group Cohesiveness	Critical Opinion	Virtual Collaboration
The ability to understand one's personal role and be fully responsible in achieving the team's goal	The ability to contribute to a team's solidity	The ability to speak up and express a critical opinion based on reliable and analytic data or evidence-based arguments in order to find the best solution	The ability to work together effectively using technology without having to meet face-to-face

All arrows point to: **Synergistic Collaboration**

Individual Accountability

Individual accountability means every group member has a specific role, explicit responsibilities, and contributes to achieving the group's overall goal. All group members understand the expectations for the role they hold and contribute to the best of their ability to fulfill that role. They also take responsibility for the consequences of their actions and decisions. Specifically, we define *individual accountability* as the ability to understand one's personal role and be fully responsible in achieving the team's goal. To successfully fulfill the expectations of *individual accountability*, students must learn and understand the concept of a shared goal, the procedures to reach the goal, and each group member's role and task description.

> To successfully fulfill the expectations of *individual accountability*, students must learn and understand the concept of a shared goal, the procedures to reach the goal, and each group member's role and task description.

Nurturing the concept of a shared goal

The shared goal is what directs the work of the team. In project-based learning, students have a project mission to accomplish. The mission can serve as a starting point for students to provide their personal perspective on the group goal, which will direct their collective work. In all collaborative projects, students take on different responsibilities and roles to accomplish the group goal; some might do deeper research, some might provide analysis, and some might gather different perspectives on a challenge in order to generate alternative solutions.

Teachers can provide a project mission that is open-ended enough for students to choose their own angle of interest (see the example in Figure 6.2). Students discuss the project mission together in a group. Each team member provides a perspective regarding the project mission, sharing personal insights, passions, and related interests. Then, as a group, students discuss and analyze the pros and cons of several topics to propose one focus or topic for their group project. This becomes their shared goal. The process of creating this shared goal ensures that all team members are heard, considered, and have equal say in the group decision, which is the essence of the *synergistic* in Synergistic Collaboration. Students learn how different perspectives can add value to their goals and solutions.

For example, one group working on the mission shown in Figure 6.2 chose to focus on how simple machines could help their mothers cook more easily. Another group decided to explore how to help parents who transport their babies in strollers move with minimum effort from elevated platforms to the grass areas in the public park, using a simple machine. The shared goal follows the chosen focus—for example, "To create a simple machine to help our moms cook faster" or "To create a simple machine to move baby strollers smoothly in a public park." The process of choosing the shared goal takes place through discussion and voting. Each member of the group shares a problem in their daily life that they would like to solve, and they discuss and vote to determine the focus for the shared goal. This process continues to high school. For example, in a global citizenship class, students decided on their shared goal stemming from a project mission related to global issues (see Figure 6.3).

Nurturing the concept of procedures to reach the group goal

After the group comes up with a shared goal, they need to generate procedures to reach the goal. For lower-elementary students, we begin by introducing the concept of procedures in concrete ways, using analogies. For example, one teacher showed a figurine and a staircase made of wooden blocks. She explained how the figurine could reach the top of the staircase (the goal) by moving from one step to the next (the procedure). To check the students' understanding, she had them work in small groups to draw their own staircases and write down the procedural steps needed to reach the top.

FIGURE 6.2
Example of a Project Mission for Grade 2–3

> Dear Students,
>
> Everyone has needs and wants. Needs and wants are the reasons that make people in any community interact with each other and the environment because interactions help them get the things they need and want.
>
> In fulfilling our needs and wants, people invented simple machines to help us do our work easily. These simple machines are the lever, pulley, wheel and axle, wedge, inclined plane, and screw. However, we need to modify those simple machines so that they can be functional objects to fulfill our needs and wants.
>
> As an SHI school student, how can we do this? How do we fulfill a need or want in our community using simple machines?
>
> Observe your environment to find a problem that you care about and think is important to solve. Your project should offer a beneficial contribution to your community.
>
> Warm regards,
>
> Grade 2–3 teachers

FIGURE 6.3
Example of a Project Mission for a High School Global Citizenship Course

> Dear High School Students,
>
> In this course, we aim to reach the global community and promote positive change through education, leadership, and collaboration.
>
> In order to truly put our school on the map and create widespread positive change in a number of areas, we need your help. Each of you is an emerging leader, within the school, your community, and the world at large. You have the power to ignite sparks of change. Those sparks can become an enduring flame of action if your efforts are well-planned, widespread, and carefully executed. One way to do this is to utilize technology as a tool to reach more people. Create a digital application focused on solving a global issue that will educate, inspire, and connect members of the larger community.
>
> To carry out your mission, you will be working collaboratively with your peers to conduct research, develop a proposal, find a solution, develop a prototype/blueprint, and write an individual report on how you executed the mission.
>
> Your application represents the steps in starting to build a foundation that will lead our school to become more global, more connected, and more effective in finding solutions through working beyond borders to address the critical issues that affect us all. We need your help, and we value your contribution.

Depending on students' readiness, their versions of procedures can vary. Some may be as simple as (1) discuss the goal and (2) do the task. Others may come up with more complex procedures, such as (1) each team member comes up with ideas and reasons; (2) team discusses and votes on the alternatives; (3) team determines the group goal; (4) team discusses roles; (5) team members do the tasks; (6) team checks the tasks; and (7) team submits the tasks.

Upper-elementary students and beyond should be able to describe more detailed procedures. To do that, they must be able to break down their learning outcomes and reframe them into specific procedures for reaching the goal. For example, the group goal for a Grade 8–9 class was to "create a more effective waste management system for the school cafeteria." Here is how they broke down their goal into specific procedures:

1. Elect a leader.
2. Each team member shares ideas and reasons.
3. Vote for the shared goals.
4. Discuss the shared goal related to the Big Question to ensure everyone's understanding of the expectation.
5. Discuss each team member's point of view to answer the Big Question and achieve the shared goal.
6. Listen actively and respectfully to each opinion.
7. List the tasks.
8. Assign the roles for each team member.
9. Have the leader delegate the work.
10. Create a timeline.
11. Create a communication plan for the team members.
12. Gather resources.
13. Do research to gather reliable information about the problems.
14. Develop hypotheses.
15. Analyze and draw conclusion.
16. Present proposed ideas and test proposed solutions.
17. Write the report and create a presentation to the whole group.
18. Give feedback and offer critical opinions during the process.
19. Discuss and decide the solution.
20. Implement the solution and measure the results.

Nurturing the concept of roles and task descriptions

In the preschool and lower-elementary level, students are introduced to the concept of roles through daily routines. For example, preschool teachers use visual charts to help students remember who is responsible for a certain classroom task each day, such as watering classroom plants or moving the pointer from one daily schedule to another. In the elementary grades, after teachers share the visual analogy, they can explain more about shared roles, tasks, and responsibility and provide graphic organizers, such as the one shown in Figure 6.4, to help students be aware of their contribution to the group goal. Visual charts are used through high school as a tool to introduce the concept of shared responsibilities.

FIGURE 6.4
Example of a Log for Individual Accountability at the Early-Elementary Levels

In this group work, my role is _____.

My responsibilities in this role are:

★ _____
★ _____
★ _____
★ _____
★ _____
★ _____

Date	What did I do to achieve the group goal?

Teachers empower students to uphold their individual accountability by monitoring progress throughout the working process. They can provide a group logbook for students to keep track of their work and conduct Meta-Level Reflection as a group. Students must inform their teacher and teammates if they are behind in their working schedule and will not be able to meet the deadlines. As they progress, teachers expect students to be able to explain their roles objectively, describe where they contributed to the group goal, and share what they learned from others' contributions.

As students move into higher grade levels, the complexity of role divisions and the level of responsibility for each group member increases. Figure 6.5 is an example of possible group project roles and tasks that can be used starting in Grade 4–5. Students can select different perspectives on a topic (the economics of school waste management, for example, or technological solutions to school waste management challenges) and become experts in those perspectives.

FIGURE 6.5
Example of Roles in a Collaborative Task

Tasks	Roles		
	Leader (Ron)	Economic Expert (Jenny)	Technology Expert (Reuben)
Delegate the work and resources; monitor timeline and progress.	✓		
Research reliable information.	✓	✓	✓
Develop hypothesis.	✓	✓	✓
Analyze and reach conclusion.	✓	✓	✓
Present proposed ideas and test out proposed solutions.	✓	✓	✓
Write report and create presentation to the whole group.	✓	✓	✓
Give feedback and critical opinions during the process.	✓	✓	✓
Lead discussion to decide on solution.	✓		

As the figure shows, successful group work is based on the premise that individuals can work on the same project from different perspectives and be equally responsible for achieving the project's goal. In addition, it helps avoid dividing tasks into "researcher," "writer," "illustrator," and so on. This type of task division is not equal, and an approach like this will not allow team members to develop the same kind of well-rounded, big-picture understanding of the project.

Teachers can foster students' equal and synergistic contributions to achieving the shared goal by following five steps:

1. Ensure that everyone feels responsible for achieving the group goal and has made a conscious effort to understand the expectations of the project. This might be accomplished, for example, by having all group members read specific resources to enhance their understanding of the problem.
2. Have students share their research-based knowledge with the rest of their project group (keeping the goal in mind) and convey their points and perspectives clearly.
3. Remind students that they must listen attentively to other group members' perspectives in order to successfully combine the various perspectives on the problem into a big-picture understanding.
4. Have students in each group write or record their understanding of the problem discussed and brainstorm possible solutions.
5. Give students time to decide on a solution together but, for accountability, require each member of every group to submit an individual product, such as an essay or a report on the group's solution.

All of these steps involve Audience-Centered Communication, Expert Thinking, and Meta-Level Reflection skills. Students also need to have an agile mindset (Adaptability and Agility) when listening to others' perspectives. Furthermore, collaborative tasks provide a medium for students to practice decision-making skills along with Ethical Leadership. Collaborative work projects are specifically designed to empower students and encourage participation in decision making (Meyer, 1994).

Group Cohesiveness

Working well in a group of individuals with different personalities, work habits, and temperament requires effort and strategy. Crucial in this process is that groups maintain their cohesiveness. We define *group cohesiveness* as the ability to maintain a team's solidity.

One of the simplest ways to examine group cohesiveness is to determine if the student group has regular meetings along with a specific schedule and timeline for achieving the group goal. Each team member keeps track of the meeting schedule and notes progress toward the goal. Because all are equally invested in achieving the group goal, they work together to solve any problems encountered along the way. Teachers can conduct formative assessments to check for group cohesiveness by observing the group's working process, how organized the team is, and how they make progress together toward the group goal. Another formative assessment method involves asking students to keep a logbook of their meeting schedules and minutes of the meeting. By looking at the log, teachers can get a good sense of how well the team members work together. To assess individual progress in this element, teachers can create opportunities for individual self-reflection, during which each team member describes their experiences and insights related to working in a group. Teachers can also conduct peer assessment in which all the team members rate their other team members on how well each one works together in the group.

To maintain *group cohesiveness*, students must understand the concepts of caring and communication. To be able to reach a common goal, they need to take care of one another as a team by acknowledging their teammates' strengths and areas for improvement and by motivating them. They also must be able to listen to others and speak to one another in a positive manner. In this way, group cohesiveness is closely related to other life skills, especially Audience-Centered Communication.

> To maintain *group cohesiveness*, students must understand the concepts of caring and communication.

Nurturing the concept of caring

Students can be exposed to the concept of group cohesiveness from an early age. Although preschool and lower-elementary students are still characterized by their egocentrism, teachers can introduce the concept of "caring" as a foundation for group cohesiveness. For example, a teacher can read aloud a story about compassion and caring, such as E. B. White's *Charlotte's Web*, discussing with the students how Charlotte and the animals in the barnyard worked together to save the piglet.

For practice and formative assessment, "clean-up time" provides another practical example. In our preschool, after students finish their play during the child-initiated routine called Plan-Do-Review, they must clean up the classroom together. As the students work, teachers observe how readily they engage and how they show respect for one another. In a particular class, for example, the teacher noticed one student who sat alone, continuing his play while others were cleaning. So, during the next clean-up time, the teacher used a more interactive activity called "relay basket cleaning" to ensure this student's engagement. This activity felt like a game to this student, and he began to join in by putting his toys into a basket and then "relaying" them to the next basket.

Another way teachers help younger students learn to develop empathy and caring for others and get beyond their ecocentrism is to have them practice adaptive social problem-solving skills when conflicts arise. Under the guidance of teachers, students discuss their problems, listen to one another's point of view, and come up with solutions. This process helps students see that there can be different perspectives related to problems, as they listen to the other students' points of view. Although it takes time for students to be able to accept different perspectives, conflict-resolution practice serves as an important starting point. In Chapter 7 on Empathetic Social Skills, we describe this process in greater detail.

As students grow older, "caring" can be practiced through the habits of doing and saying kind things and motivating others. For example, a Grade 6–7 teacher regularly shares motivational quotes and engages students in a practice of caring by showing a short clip from the movie *Pay It Forward* and discussing the moral message. To assess how her students apply caring during collaborative work, this teacher asks students to reflect on how they took care of other members of the team and to then record these reflections on a card such as the one shown in Figure 6.6.

FIGURE 6.6
Self-Reflection Card for Group Cohesiveness

Another way to check students' understanding about caring is to use a case study. Multiple-choice questions can ask students what they think about the case and how they care for others.

Nurturing the skill of Audience-Centered Communication

We discussed Audience-Centered Communication at length in Chapter 5. Its components are transferable in many other life skills, including group cohesiveness in Synergistic Collaboration. To maintain the cohesiveness of the group, students need to practice active listening and communicating their thoughts in a positive manner. Many teachers facilitate this by engaging students in team-building activities that require them to communicate effectively with one another. Grade 6–7 teachers use a game called "Moving the Bottle," in which students must move a bottle from one end of a sheet of cloth to the other while making sure the bottle stands upright the entire time. The difficulty of the game overwhelms students at first. But eventually they begin to share an idea, ask others to communicate their ideas, and coordinate their efforts.

In other instances, students practice acknowledging their classmate's strengths using Constructive Friends Protocols in collaborative tasks. These protocols are procedures students use to elicit positive responses from others while attentively listening and being agile while receiving constructive feedback. Using this protocol, each student is given the opportunity to express a critical opinion and, in turn, accept constructive feedback from classmates. Students learn to practice this skill as early as Grade 1, as it is integrated within the Problem-Based Learning cycle. It is done after students complete each part of their task, such as the planning or product-prototype phases. It helps students see the value of and accept constructive feedback.

Critical Opinion

A common challenge in collaboration is ensuring that every group member feels free to offer constructive criticism and has the courage to speak their mind rather than simply agreeing with the majority opinions. Everyone needs to be aware when conversations get off track and understand that honest evaluations don't harm group cohesiveness. We define *critical opinion* as the ability to speak up and express a critical opinion based on reliable and analytic data or evidence-based arguments to find the best solution.

Of course, students must be able to balance group cohesiveness with expressing critical opinions. Being a tight-knit group does not mean allowing "groupthink," where the entire team agrees with one opinion even though some team members realize critical flaws. For this reason, to develop *critical opinion*, it is important that students learn and understand the concepts of "courage to speak up" and "giving suggestions with sound arguments."

> **To develop *critical opinion*, it is important that students learn and understand the concepts of "courage to speak up" and "giving suggestions with sound arguments."**

Nurturing the courage to speak up

In preschool and early-elementary grades, students tend to focus on only their own work and may not be accustomed to offering critical opinions in a collaborative setting. Nevertheless, they are able to express their feelings, as well as their likes and dislikes. To support these behaviors, preschool teachers can model appropriate ways to calmly express dislikes, such as expressing feelings verbally instead of through physical actions like hitting or frowning. In most Asian countries, students are afraid to speak up, as a result of being punished when they did not say the "right thing." But we want students at our school to feel safe when expressing their thoughts and opinions, so we accept all ideas and discuss them together.

One preschool teacher has found that an effective way to model and practice such courtesy is through story discussions, either when reading a book or when watching a short video clip. She encourages students to use an "I" statement to share what they like and dislike about the characters and then to explain their reasons. For example, one student said, "I'm sad when I see the baby bear's porridge is eaten by Goldilocks." The teacher conducts informal formative assessments throughout the story discussion by observing students and writing anecdotal notes on whether students are able to use the "I" statement.

As they grow older, students can practice expressing critical opinions through various means of communication. One common strategy is to provide students with sentence frames to express agreement and disagreement during group discussions and debates. This approach gives students a model for how critical opinions can be presented in tactful ways.

Many teachers use the Constructive Friends Protocol to show students how to give constructive feedback on other students' presentations of their work (project results), as well as on individual results. The protocol also helps students who are presenting learn to accept constructive feedback positively. A Grade 2–3 student, for example, asked a friend to give her feedback while practicing her presentation. Using the Constructive Friends Protocol, the friend recommended that she "make more eye contact during the presentation." The student included this feedback in the improvement plan in her logbook and then applied the feedback to her initial plan. Accordingly, she worked to improve that aspect during the actual performance.

In this example, the students learned to express feedback in a constructive way, avoiding judgments and harsh criticism. The student receiving the feedback learned to develop an agile mindset, an element of Adaptability and Agility. She learned to be open-minded when listening to other students' opinions. In collaborative settings, these discussions become all the richer when everyone is willing to help and has the courage to speak up.

Nurturing the ability to give suggestions with sound arguments

As we noted earlier, preschoolers and early-elementary students still focused on their own interests can practice expressing dislikes or disagreements using "I" statements. As students mature, they become more capable of expressing clear opinions. Grade 4–5 teachers can begin with a collaborative task that requires students to express their critical opinions through short essays or journal entries. The problems may involve everyday situations, such as traffic jams or littering. The essays or journal entries provide evidence for formative assessments.

Based on the assessment, the teacher may find out that some students need more guidance in expressing an opinion clearly and with a strong supporting argument. The teacher can provide a minilesson for a skill for better communication using the PREP (Point-Reason-Example-Point) strategy, which we mentioned in Chapter 5 on Audience-Centered Communication. In this strategy, students first state their point or premise, then provide the reason (e.g., "Based on my analysis and research, I suggest..."), then continue with examples to illustrate the point and the reason, and end by restating the point.

Virtual Collaboration

Earlier in this chapter we touched on how advances in technology have created a borderless world that enables people from all over the globe to work together with the support of digital-meeting platforms and other digital tools. The impact has been so massive—not only during the COVID-19 pandemic but also during normal times—that we think it is important to address the specific skill of *virtual collaboration*. We define *virtual collaboration* as the ability to work together effectively using technology without having to meet face-to-face.

To perform effectively in this element, students need to understand how various technologies work and apply the appropriate netiquette (the agreed-upon, informal set of rules for how to behave appropriately when communicating via the internet). In turn, they should be able to apply their knowledge to choose technological tools or features to upgrade the quality of their virtual-collaboration process. The two important concepts students need to learn and understand are (1) netiquette and (2) technology application.

> The two important concepts students need to learn and understand for *virtual collaboration* are (1) netiquette and (2) technology application.

Nurturing the use of netiquette

The use of technology as a tool for communication presents certain challenges. Some of the most common are disengagement—minimal participation attributable to a lack of in-person interaction and accountability—and misunderstanding compounded by limited access to others' facial cues or body language. Netiquette is key here. To empower students to grasp the nuances of online communication and successfully navigate its nuances, we teach them to pay extra attention when choosing their words and to be mindful of various ways in which their intent might be correctly and incorrectly communicated and understood.

Preschool students understand better when new information is introduced in conjunction with concrete materials. What students see in class *always* matters, but it matters even more when they are preliterate. Staying focused for a synchronous learning session when the teacher is present only on a screen is not easy at this level. Likewise, collaborative small-group activities may be a huge challenge. For preschool students, we focus more on the second concept, technology application (discussed in the next section), than on netiquette.

Beginning in elementary school and continuing through high school, teachers at our school allocate time at the beginning of the academic year to get students familiar with the concept of netiquette and how to work collaboratively in a virtual setting. In K–3, teachers can tell a story about people working together using technology as a means of communication. Teachers introduce and remind students about simple netiquette rules, such as (1) keep the camera on, (2) mute the mic except when talking, (3) show your whole face on camera, and (4) use the "raise hand" button to ask questions or share your opinion.

Starting in Grade 4–5 and through high school, the discussion gets richer, depending on the expectations in the Synergistic Collaboration rubric for different continuum levels. With teacher guidance, students may read the descriptions of the expectations and choose a number of keywords and phrases, such as *complex digital tools, netiquette,* and *initiate virtual collaborations* for further exploration. Engaging students in a vocabulary activity such as semantic mapping helps them break down definitions and come up with examples (see Figure 6.7). They can then personalize the concepts and vocabulary by writing about which digital tools they believe they would use the most and in what contexts and by recording a list of behavioral do's and don'ts they would follow to conform with the tools' netiquette.

FIGURE 6.7
Semantic Mapping of "Netiquette"

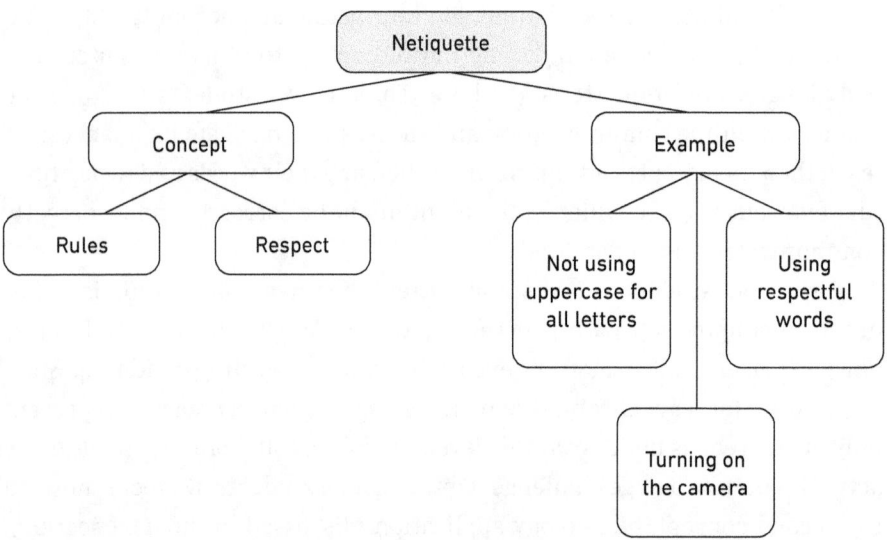

The teacher and students can also discuss why the element of *virtual collaboration* needs to be part of the Synergistic Collaboration skill. If possible, the discussion can be done virtually to practice netiquette. The students can be asked to work virtually from different spots within the school. Clear instructions and graphic organizers can help students gradually become more independent as they collaborate virtually. To check their understanding, teachers can create a netiquette quiz.

Nurturing technology application

For preschoolers and early-elementary students, the focus is not on using technology for communication but on getting them to explore various technologies as tools to supplement their learning. Guided by their teachers, students at this level can explore educational games or try to type letters using word-processing tools.

From Grade 4–5 through high school, informational videos can lead to class discussions about how digital skills are among today's most sought-after competencies. With teacher guidance, discussion can include specific examples of technology-dependent occupations such as operating online conference platforms, digital design, and coding.

Providing a list of digital tools (for example, MindMup, MindMeister, Jamboard, Kleki, and Canva) for students to explore can help them decide which ones are best to use for a specific purpose. Students can do a compare-contrast of the tools to specify their functions. Teachers can also model specific skills for using digital brainstorming tools, such as MindMeister or MindMup, or project management software, such as Asana or monday.com.

As students progress, they gradually learn to use collaborative tools independently and eventually no longer need a teacher's presence to facilitate their virtual collaboration. At the highest level, they are able to participate in a global collaboration, working together virtually with people around the world.

During the progression in student competency, it's important for teachers to point out that although tech-based collaboration is important, there has to be a balance between technology usage and face-to-face interaction. They should lead discussions of the negative impact of excessive usage of technology and the positive value of face-to-face interaction.

How Is Synergistic Collaboration Measured and Assessed?

As for the other essential life skills, we have created and use a developmental rubric to measure and assess students' progress and achievement in the essential skill of Synergistic Collaboration (see Figure 6.8, p. 141).

It describes the behaviors we expect to see at each developmental level. As previously stated, Synergistic Collaboration comprises four elements: (1) *individual accountability*, (2) *group cohesiveness*, (3) *critical opinion*, and (4) *virtual collaboration*. These are represented in the rubric in Figure 6.8 as SC.1, SC.2, SC.3, and SC.4, respectively.

Although the assessment of collaborative work applies equally to all group members, it is only fair to differentiate between the quality of the product and the quality of the process (Guskey & Brookhart, 2019). For that reason, teachers need to differentiate between the assessment of group products and the assessment of students' contributions to collaborative work. Each team member's contribution and individual product will be part of the assessment of the element of *individual accountability*. The evidence of Synergistic Collaboration should be gathered during activities that are purposefully designed as a collaborative task, when the key elements of the skills are more likely to appear.

An example would be students working collaboratively on a project. As discussed earlier, in such a setting, students decide on their roles within the group, so teachers can collect evidence of *individual accountability*. While working in their own role, students need to make a conscious effort to keep everyone in the group working harmoniously—to demonstrate the element of *group cohesiveness*. They need to meet regularly to check one another's progress and see whether they are on the right track. Teachers can assess group cohesiveness when they see students showing effort in taking care of one another. To check understanding, they can ask students to write one-minute essays on how to care for the others in their group. Teachers can assess the third key element, *critical opinion*, through observation or asking students to brainstorm what "critical opinion" means to them when they begin to share their ideas—for example, "I think my opinion for our next action plan is sound and valid because I back it up with sufficient evidence."

As we have noted, the fourth key element, *virtual collaboration*, is about the ability to use technology to increase the effectiveness of collaboration (to enhance connectivity and accessibility) by using digital meeting platforms and various digital tools such as smartphones, smart tablets, PCs, and laptops. Students should know how to use digital content resources such as Brainpop, PBSKids, and Epic, and digital collaborative tools such as Padlet and MindMup, to name a few. The goal is for students to be able to use their technology-related knowledge and skills to enrich their collaboration in the classroom. For example, when a videoconference is needed, students must be familiar with features of digital meeting platforms such as Google Meet, Zoom, Microsoft Teams, or Webex.

FIGURE 6.8
Rubric for Synergistic Collaboration

		Early (Preschool–K)				Beginning (K–3)				Transition (3–6)				Developing (6–9)				Expert (9–12)			
SC.1	Individual Accountability	• Works on a task assigned by teammates, unaware of her/his own goal or the group's goal.				• Knows the "title" of her/his own role with the role description (i.e., what to do) as defined by teammates or teacher. Completes the role with responsibility.				• Knows her/his own role description and the group's goal and completes her/his roles with responsibility to ensure efficient approaches toward the group goal.				• Understands the expectation of her/his own role and completes the task with a full sense of responsibility to ensure effective and efficient approaches toward the group goal.				• Understands the expectation of her/his own role in achieving the group's goal, completes the task with responsibility and excellence, and contributes ideas to ensure efficiency, effectiveness, and productivity toward surpassing the expectation of the group's goal.			
		Stage	1	2	3	Stage	1	2	3	Stage	1	2	3	Stage	1	2	3	Stage	1	2	3
SC.2	Group Cohesiveness	• Focuses on her/his own task during teamwork activity.				• Shows caring toward others by asking or talking about what other team members are doing during group tasks.				• Shows caring toward others by asking or talking about the progress of what other team members are doing during group tasks.				• Shows caring toward others by asking or talking about not only what they are doing but also how it affects the team's goal.				• Acts as the "glue" of the team by acknowledging that every team member is a valuable asset for the team and by motivating others to achieve the group's goal.			
		Stage	1	2	3	Stage	1	2	3	Stage	1	2	3	Stage	1	2	3	Stage	1	2	3

(continued)

FIGURE 6.8
Rubric for Synergistic Collaboration—*(continued)*

		Early (Preschool–K)	Beginning (K–3)	Transition (3–6)	Developing (6–9)	Expert (9–12)
SC.3	Critical Opinion	• When doing a group task, s/he works based on personal interest.	• When doing a group task, s/he listens to the opinions of others and follows them, but in a way that still favors her/his interest.	• When doing a group task, s/he follows the most popular opinion, but begins to spot flaws in the group's opinion and shares a personal opinion.	• When finding a flaw in the group's decision or work process, s/he points out the flaw along with the reason and offers a simple suggestion.	• When finding a flaw in the group's decision or work process, s/he tactfully points out the flaws and gives elaborate constructive suggestions that best serve the interest of the group's goal.
		Stage 1 2 3	Stage 1 2 3	Stage 1 2 3	Stage 1 2 3	Stage 1 2 3
SC.4	Virtual Collaboration	• Explores technology as a learning tool and explains how it works.	• Understands the functions of simple digital tools and the netiquette for virtual collaboration (e.g., shows entire face instead of just the forehead). • Use technology to learn in collaborative settings, as have been set up by the teachers (e.g., teachers create links and provide templates for collaboration) to achieve the group goal.	• Understands the benefits of using more complex digital tools and the netiquette for virtual collaboration (e.g., shows entire face instead of just the forehead). • Purposefully initiates virtual collaboration with classmates using digital tools to conduct virtual collaboration (e.g., creates a meeting link for Google Meet, Zoom).	• Understands the distinctions of multiple digital tools and consistently applies the netiquette for virtual collaboration. • Purposefully selects and uses digital tools to enhance the process of virtual collaboration with the school community using additional tools (e.g., visualizes ideas using Jamboard, MindMup, Padlet).	• Understands and bridges the limitations of virtual collaboration and adapts the netiquette to deal with the limitation. • Takes an active role as a global citizen by initiating globally distributed collaboration using a purposeful and sophisticated integration of digital tools.
		Stage 1 2 3	Stage 1 2 3	Stage 1 2 3	Stage 1 2 3	Stage 1 2 3

Stage 1: Student performs a task somewhat accurately with consistent guidance from others (teachers and peers).

Stage 2: Student performs a task accurately with little guidance and redirection from others (teachers and peers).

Stage 3: Student independently performs a task with ease, speed, and accuracy.

The element of *virtual collaboration* is the focus of the following descriptions of the continuum levels in the rubric for Synergistic Collaboration. We provide examples of settings that can be designed to assess the element and samples of acceptable evidence.

Early (Preschool–K)

At the Early level, the focus is on getting students to explore various technologies—smartphones, smart tablets, PCs, and laptops—as learning tools so that eventually they can explain how such tools are used. To assess their understanding, teachers may ask questions such as "What is this tool for?" "How do you use it?" and "Could you give examples?"

Understandably, a number of developmental issues may prevent students from using certain digital tools, especially those that require typing long sentences or drawing digitally using a mouse or a trackpad. For that reason, the expectation for children at this level is only for them to be able to use the tools' basic features to do the following:

- To access and use educational websites or content resources as assigned by the teacher
- To use education software/games on their PCs or laptops
- To participate in a virtual class (in an online classroom setting)

Beginning (Grades K–3)

At the Beginning level, students start to better understand the functions of digital tools that the teachers use in class and can demonstrate basic netiquette. Teachers can conduct formative assessments such as a netiquette quiz to assess students' current understanding of this skill; they can create digital templates for the students to use when working collaboratively and observe their process; they can also observe students' netiquette during an online meeting.

Transition (Grades 3–6)

At the Transition level, students have been exposed to more complex digital tools or more complex functions of a familiar digital tool. They know how to use virtual collaboration tools designed for creating mind maps, digital art, stories, or games, and they understand how these various tools can benefit them.

Students at this level are able to demonstrate netiquette skills that show both respect and familiarity with how digital tools work, as well as other technical skills. For example, they use lowercase letters appropriately when commenting in a chat box, knowing that the use of all uppercase letters might signify anger or impoliteness. In addition, they choose words carefully and apply appropriate punctuation, knowing that careless choices may cause misunderstandings. Students also understand that complex issues need to be discussed orally instead of through the simplified sentences that characterize chat box exchanges, to avoid misunderstanding.

Compared to their peers at the Beginning level, Transition-level students are more independent in executing their collaborative tasks. They can create their own meeting link when the teacher signifies that it is time for a collaborative workshop. They work collaboratively in separate breakout rooms without the need for a teacher to provide a detailed template for the collaboration. Teachers can collect evidence of students' competency by observing them during their group work and taking anecdotal notes. Of course, throughout the process some students are more independent than others —hence, Stages 1, 2, and 3.

Let's look at the example of Olive, a Grade 6 student. Olive's class was exploring a number of works by famous artists. Students were divided into groups to create a piece of collaborative artwork inspired by an assigned artist. They could use the digital whiteboard Google Jamboard or the collaborative painting tool Aggie.io.

Olive's group decided to try to recreate the style of Edvard Munch, a Norwegian artist who is famous for his painting *The Scream*, to express emotions through painting. When the teacher checked to see if Olive understood the task, Olive replied, "My group has to observe Edvard Munch's style more closely, discuss the colors and the lines he used to paint emotion, and then collaborate to make our own painting about emotion." Olive then said, "Miss, let me create the Google Meet link for my group to meet. We will draw on Aggie.io. I will share the link with everyone in my group and with you too, Miss." When asked why she chose to work on Aggie.io rather than Google Jamboard, Olive said, "In Aggie.io, we can choose the size of the brush and the opacity level, so it's possible to have color gradation like in Edvard Munch's work."

As the students proceeded, the teacher moved from one link to another to briefly observe their working process. She saw that everyone in Olive's group took turns sharing their ideas using appropriate terms, and they finished the work on time. She noted Olive's ability to use Google Meet independently by creating her own meeting link. Olive was also able to choose the most appropriate technology tool based on her goal, as shown in her choice of Aggie.io over Jamboard to create her product. She understood the benefit of using a more complex digital tool that would help her team create a gradation of colors, and she demonstrated appropriate netiquette. Recording these observations as evidence in anecdotal notes, the teacher assessed Olive as being at Stage 3 for the element of *virtual collaboration*.

Developing (Grades 6–9)

As students move to the Developing level, they should clearly understand the characteristics of various digital tools, especially in terms of how each tool affects collaborative work and which ones enhance the process. Students at this level are consistent in applying the rules of netiquette.

For formative assessment, teachers can use the methods described earlier—for example, observation of the virtual collaboration process and a quiz to check for understanding of netiquette expectations. Other options are exit cards or discussion of a hypothetical scenario, followed by students writing about how they would apply their netiquette skills and knowledge to address the situation described in the scenario. Teachers may also ask students how and why they choose specific digital tools to facilitate their projects and observe their consistencies in applying netiquette.

Let's look at the example of Reuben, the Grade 8–9 student working on a waste management project involving trash in the school cafeteria, as discussed in previous chapters. When collaborating, he and his team members used Jamboard, a virtual whiteboard, for their discussions. Reuben created a virtual-meet link for himself and the others.

The team shared their ideas by using sticky notes on the virtual whiteboard. When the teacher visited their link and observed the collaboration process, she suggested they use a mind-mapping digital tool to make the brainstorming process easier. Reuben then tried using MindMeister, and the team was able to create more solutions related to the specific types of trash in the cafeteria. Reuben explained to his team members, "This is much better than using sticky notes on a virtual whiteboard. It's easier to see what solutions [work] for which waste and the number of possible solutions for each waste.... Based on this mind map, we can choose which solution is best for each type of waste." The teacher used a screenshot of Reuben's mindmap as evidence of his developing understanding.

Reuben acknowledged different opinions from his team members and discussed each idea they had offered in the mind-mapping digital tool. A digital recording of the group's conversation during class provides evidence of some aspects of his developing netiquette skills. In addition, Reuben's teacher asked him and the other students to write a one-minute essay about the importance of using netiquette.

Reuben's activity and behavior indicate he is at Stage 2. He was able to choose a tech tool that could facilitate Synergistic Collaboration, but he needed some guidance from his teacher, who suggested a better tech tool to improve the process. Reuben also needed a reminder from his teacher to consistently perform certain netiquette requirements, such as turning on his camera during the virtual collaboration session.

Let's compare Reuben's performance with that of Jenna, a Stage 3 student whose class was working on a project to address problems related to illegal fishing in various world regions. Jenna and her teammates chose to work on illegal fishing in the seas around Southeast Asia. As they began to brainstorm, they first used Jamboard; but halfway through the process, Jenna notified her teacher that they would use MindMeister instead. When asked how MindMeister would better help them reach their group goal, Jenna explained:

> We need a larger space to brainstorm ideas from different aspects, like the location and possible reasons why the location is prone to illegal fishing; the perpetrators and how they usually commit the crime; and the country who owns the ocean—how they handle the problem; and, of course, our ideas for a solution. MindMeister is a specific tool for mind mapping, so it is easier for us to classify the ideas based on the aspect that we want to focus on. Also, we just need to click the plus sign on the main bubble to add new sub-bubbles, whereas in Jamboard we need to manually create the bubbles and link them.

Because Jenna had been using MindMeister for multiple projects, she was able to explain the benefit of MindMeister compared to Jamboard. When observing Jenna's group, the teacher could see that Jenna had her camera on throughout the session and her whole face was visible on the screen. She also used her time effectively to work on the task. She occasionally did share jokes with her teammates, but only ones that were related to the case being discussed, and she was careful not to say anything potentially offensive. The evidence the teacher used for assessment was the group's submitted digital work and the timestamp of submission (as evidence of the group's time management).

The evidence showed that Jenna was at Stage 3 for the element of *virtual collaboration*. She, not the teacher, initiated the choice of a virtual collaboration tool that would help the team work more efficiently than the original tool. Also, she met the expectations for appropriate netiquette behavior without her teacher needing to remind her to do so.

Expert (Grades 9–12)

Ultimately, students at the Expert continuum level are expected to understand that there are limitations to working collaboratively in a virtual setting, such as a greater likelihood of miscommunication due to limited interaction or text-based communication that leads to miscommunication. With that understanding, they manage to bridge or minimize such limitations by using their skills and knowledge of digital tools' various features.

What makes students at this level more advanced than others is their ability to use the platform of virtual collaboration. They can digitize content and create prompts that generate automated solutions to the world's problems, collaborating with far-away peers. Also, with their advanced knowledge of digital tools, which may include coding skills, they can take a sophisticated approach to integrating the use of one digital tool with another to help reach the group's common goal. To assess this skill, teachers observe students as they collaborate with people around the world to complete their projects, paying particular attention to their use of online communication tools.

An example comes from a virtual collaboration for a Business Challenge Competition, in which students from different countries worked together to create an idea for a business that would be both environmentally friendly and socially empowering. They decided to empower single mothers in rural areas to create sellable products that could be promoted worldwide and that could elevate women's economic condition. With a knowledge of multimedia coding, the group members collaborated to create a landing page and a homepage that were linked to a marketplace account. Their effort created a technology-supported solution that emerged from their collaborative work with other citizens of the world.

Suggestions for Integrating Synergistic Collaboration into Curriculum and Classroom Practice

- Incorporate elements of a Synergistic Collaboration rubric in the curriculum. For example, include the element of *virtual collaboration* in a

digital literacy curriculum, and the element of *individual accountability* in a physical education curriculum.
- Design learning activities that allow students to collaborate with not only their classmates but also other community members.
- Establish a respectful and caring learning culture that nurtures collaboration and student confidence in speaking up.
- Assist students in comprehending their role in a group to help them monitor their contribution and achievement.
- Instill the habit of supporting arguments with reliable resources or evidence.

7

Empathetic Social Skills

Anyone can become angry—that is easy. But to be angry with the right person, to the right degree, at the right time, for the right purpose, and in the right way—this is not easy.

—Aristotle—

As global citizens, we interact with others with diverse backgrounds, needs, and purposes. As such, conflicts are bound to occur. Having said that, it's possible to maintain an environment in which everyone feels safe and respected during interactions. Empathy is the key. Empathy is about understanding how certain situations or factors influence other people's feelings and behavior. Our students, as future leaders, need to learn how to practice empathy as soon as they are ready to view situations from others' perspectives. They should be able to resolve conflicts and respond effectively to complex social issues.

For these reasons, our students need to learn *Empathetic Social Skills*, which we define as the ability to function adaptively in the community by regulating one's own feelings and behavior to interact positively and develop a culture of respecting differences as a part of digital and global citizenship. Please note that throughout the chapter, we discuss examples from the field; names used are not real names.

Why Are Empathetic Social Skills Important?

During the learning process, students have to interact with teachers, classmates, and others—to collaborate on group projects, for example—and they have to do so in a safe and respectful manner in both online and offline settings. They also need to establish and maintain healthy relationships. In addition, they need to manage their emotions so they can resolve conflicts that may occur and grow from the experience. Let's explore each of these points in greater detail.

Interacting Safely in Online and Offline Settings

Interaction plays a crucial role in the classroom. Learning is a social endeavor that requires students to collaborate with their peers and teachers and to engage with other members of the school community and communities outside school. When teachers allow and encourage plenty of interaction, students are more likely to enjoy learning.

Nowadays, technology-based tools are an important means for students to interact with one another, gather information, and create products. Students can easily share knowledge and collaborate with other students—even those in other parts of the world—to work on a project. But first, they have to learn certain social skills and develop the ability to be empathetic.

The key behaviors in Empathetic Social Skills are to interact positively by respecting differences and diverse backgrounds. In some cases, this can be translated into acts of kindness and friendliness. That said, students need to know that friendliness has limits and that they cannot always accept "kindness" offered by others. They must be aware that in social settings, there are always possibilities of danger, especially when it comes to interacting with unfamiliar people or people who are behaving in a questionable manner. To introduce preschoolers and lower-elementary students to the concept of "taking charge of one's own safety," teachers can start by reading storybooks in which the character meets with strangers or people with strange behaviors and explore the situation via a discussion. As an example, what might students do if they were playing in a park and realized they had strayed far away from their mom or dad and were in an unfamiliar place, out of sight of anyone they know? What if a nice-seeming stranger approached and offered to help them find their parents? During the discussion of this particular example, the teacher might advise students to decline the offer and instead find a person wearing a uniform, like a police officer, or a person at an information desk nearby and explain the situation and need for assistance.

In upper grades, the context of the discussion can be expanded to the case of interactions in a teenager's world, in which peer pressure becomes more apparent. They need to be able to differentiate empathy with feelings of wanting to be accepted by others by doing dangerous actions. They also must learn how to build positive interactions in virtual settings (as in collaborative work through online tools), while at the same time taking care of their own safety by not sharing private information, pictures, or documents that may risk one's privacy and safety.

Establishing and Maintaining Healthy Relationships

Cultivating the core values of respect, responsibility, integrity, and excellence is an important aspect of developing healthy relationships. Students need to understand what these core values look, sound, and feel like. In the inclusive, multiage settings of our school, our students are used to interacting with others of different ages, with different underlying conditions, and at different levels of readiness. They learn to empathize with those who are different from themselves, creating an atmosphere that is an important foundation for building healthy relationships in school and elsewhere.

In preschool and the lower-elementary grades, one way to teach respect is through storytelling, using what we call "persona dolls." Teachers create these dolls with a variety of skin colors, hair types, and facial features. Each doll gets a name and an age, as well as a birth date, family members, and likes and dislikes. The dolls go through life experiences throughout the year, just as the students do, and the students learn about respect and empathy by expressing feelings about what's happening in the dolls' lives.

Stories are another way to teach the values necessary for healthy relationships. For example, when a preschooler did not want to wear his glasses because he was afraid others would mock him, his teacher read a book called *Arthur's Eyes*, by Marc Brown, to the class. Arthur, the main character, was being teased by his classmates because he wore glasses. The story related how much Arthur really needed his glasses to navigate his way around the school. The teacher described the problem the character was facing and discussed with her students what Arthur should do and how his classmates should treat him. The preschoolers offered various ideas about how they could help Arthur be comfortable wearing his glasses at school.

To develop Empathetic Social Skills related to healthy relationships, teachers need to engage students in discussions and provide activities that involve respect for differences. Differences among peers should be highlighted and celebrated. In upper grades at our school, an activity called "Get to Know More and You'll Respect" has students working in pairs and asking each other this question: "Describe a tradition in your family that relates to the way you treat other people and draws from a value shared within your family or community." Students take turns interviewing each other and then retelling what they learned to another pair of students.

Managing Emotions and Growing from Conflicts

Conflicts are natural parts of social life. Teachers and students need to understand that conflicts, when managed well, can be a catalyst for improving emotional management. Teachers need to consider what students might gain as a result of conflict and help them to believe that "conflict" is an opportunity to learn. In collaborative settings, conflicts require that teams put their heads together to tackle even the most challenging situations by coordinating the various perspectives of everyone involved and ensuring that the proposed solutions can mitigate the problems at hand (Gallo, 2018).

This aspect of managing emotions and resolving conflict is closely related to another life skill, Audience-Centered Communication, which we discussed in Chapter 5. Problem solvers, at heart, are excellent communicators and mediators of feelings, after all; they are able to effectively manage the emotions and drivers of themselves and others through both verbal and nonverbal communication.

We can facilitate the development of managing emotions and conflicts from an early age by familiarizing students with specific steps for resolving any conflicts. Our preschool and elementary school apply HighScope's Steps in Resolving Conflicts, developed by Hohmann and colleagues (2008):

- Approach calmly. Stop any hurtful actions.
- Acknowledge children's feelings.
- Gather information.
- Restate the problem.
- Ask for ideas for solutions and choose one together.
- Be prepared to give follow-up support.

At this level, teachers are the ones who mediate the conflicts. Although they encourage children in conflicts to share their own ideas for solutions, teachers may propose or suggest ideas students could use to resolve the conflict or that they need to learn to help them better understand others' perspectives.

One of the most important steps is the second one—to acknowledge each student's feelings (e.g., "I can see that you're feeling upset, Nadine. I can see you're feeling upset, too, Aimee"). This step de-escalates the tension and helps students manage their emotions so the next steps will go more smoothly. At the same time, this action also models for students how to describe their feelings properly without resorting to physical actions.

Similar concepts continue throughout middle school and high school. Synthesized from several underpinning theories, we use *adaptive problem solving* (which we describe in the next section of this chapter) in the upper grades. Unlike students in preschool and elementary grades, students at these levels learn to mediate conflicts between peers.

Let's go back to seeing how students are able to solve their conflicts, build emotional intelligence, and respect different perspectives, with or without guidance. In preschool, the teachers' approach is obviously crucial in the effort to grow a mindset in young children that they, too, can solve problems. Teachers must maintain a positive attitude when dealing with students' social conflicts; they must be consistent in holding themselves back from solving the problem for the students; and they must provide space for children to share their ideas for solutions. Of course, teachers must also incorporate activities specifically designed to help students identify emotions.

Preschool teachers can create "eggmotions"—plastic eggs printed with faces showing different emotions—to help students be more aware of their feelings and articulate those feelings without having to resort to physical actions, such as hitting or kicking. The eggmotions represent different feelings: *scared, happy, angry, disgusted,* and *sad.* The teacher uses them during small-group time. Each student gets a set of eggmotions and is free to engage in "pretend" play using them as props. As the students are busy making up stories with the eggmotions, the teacher moves from one child to another, restating what the student said or did, using specific words to enhance their vocabulary, and sometimes asking them to say more about the stories.

Key Elements of Empathetic Social Skills

Empathetic Social Skills comprise both intrapersonal and interpersonal skills. More specifically, they have three elements: (1) *taking charge of personal safety*, (2) *developing healthy relationships*, and (3) *adaptive social problem solving* (see Figure 7.1, p. 154). Let's look more closely at each of these.

Taking Charge of Personal Safety

The first element of Empathetic Social Skills is *taking charge of personal safety,* which we define as the ability to understand the need to be aware and alert, avoid unnecessary risk, and find appropriate

> The important concepts in *taking charge of personal safety* are (1) recognizing safe and unsafe situations and (2) creating safety plans.

and effective approaches to prevail in perilous situations originating from and caused by others. The important concepts in *taking charge of personal safety* are (1) recognizing safe and unsafe situations and (2) creating safety plans.

FIGURE 7.1
The Key Elements of Empathetic Social Skills

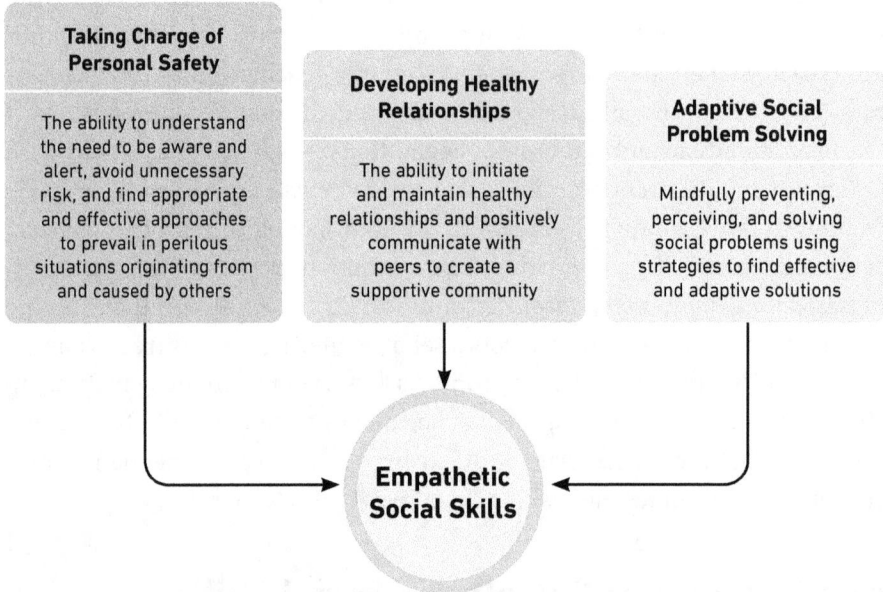

Nurturing the ability to "recognize safe and unsafe situations" and "create safety plans"

Before students can make their own safety plan, teachers need to discuss with them how to recognize safe and potentially unsafe or dangerous situations in both online and offline settings. Above all, the school's learning atmosphere must provide a sense of security. A clear sign of this is when students are able to voice their feelings and opinions confidently and politely and to make choices responsibly. Following up, students should have designated time to learn to identify what safe versus unsafe situations look like, sound like, and feel like in both offline and online settings.

In preschool, teachers can use storytelling (whether through reading aloud or watching short video clips) to discuss social problems. These are concrete ways to introduce safe and unsafe situations to young children. Unsafe situations in an offline setting can include being alone in a new place or risky places (e.g., busy streets, lakes, dark alleys) or interacting with strangers and "tricky" people—people who seem nice and familiar but have bad intentions. Through this storytelling activity, teachers can introduce the basic rules of how to stay safe during such situations (the safety plan). The two posters shown in Figure 7.2 present the rules for young children and teens.

FIGURE 7.2
Posters for Basic Safety Rules

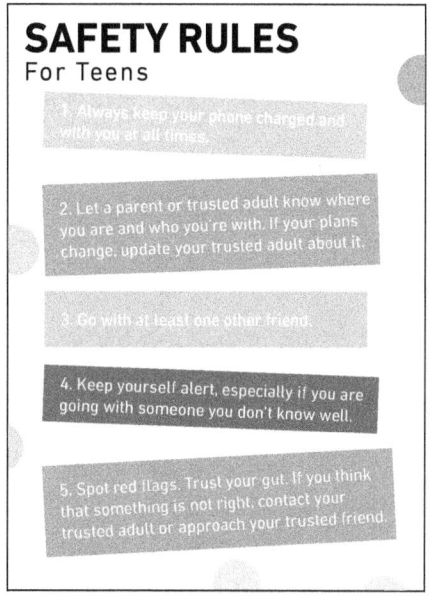

A preschool teacher in our school used storytelling during small-group time (which we abbreviate as "SGT") to introduce the topic of safety. In our school, SGT is a teacher-initiated activity that is designed and carefully planned to meet an objective in a curriculum. There are two teachers in the classroom, and each leads half of the class. In this case, the teacher opened the SGT by retelling the gist of a story she had created called "Stay Safe from Strangers and Tricky People." The story includes a number of potentially unsafe situations, such as strangers offering us snacks, strangers asking for our help to get something from a car, or familiar people other than Mom and Dad offering to give kisses and hugs. The students can choose one situation and draw the next part of the story—namely, what to do when facing such situations—using the graphic organizer shown in Figure 7.3 (see p. 156).

FIGURE 7.3
Graphic Organizer for Preschool Safety Activity

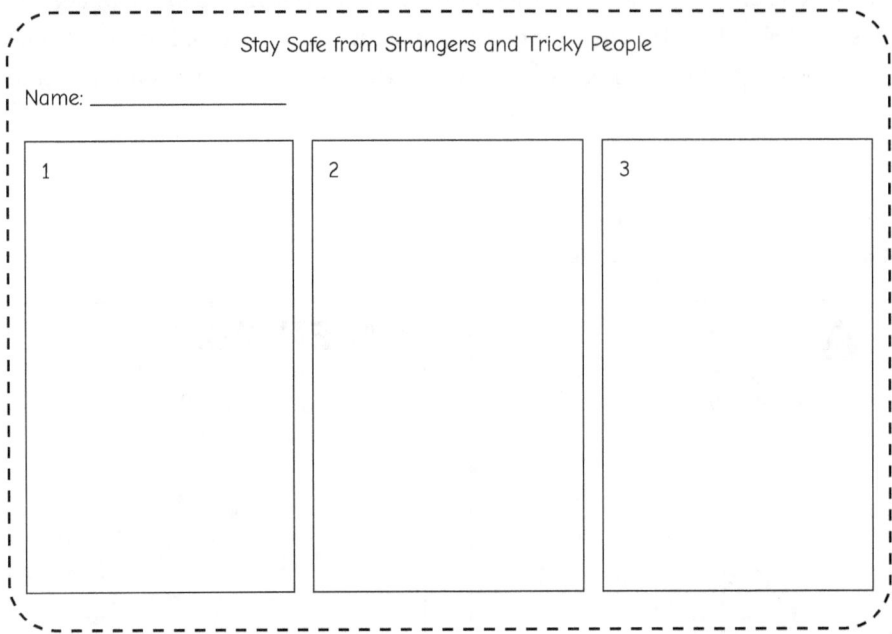

For exposure to potentially unsafe situations in the online setting, as previously explained in Chapter 6 on Synergistic Collaboration, preschool and early-elementary students begin to explore technology as a tool to supplement their learning, but at this age, their focus is not yet on using technology for communication. Discussion of potentially unsafe online behavior or situations can be appropriate in Grade 2–3, depending on the students' readiness. Examples of unsafe online behaviors include setting up a social media account before the required minimum age (if such a requirement is in effect) or sharing photos or videos that expose personal information (e.g., taking a picture in front of one's own house and unintentionally showing the address).

In another example of teaching young children about safety in offline settings, a K–1 teacher invited her students to explore vocabulary words related to the topic, such as *danger* versus *safety*, *healthy* versus *sick*. The day after reading aloud a storybook she had created titled "Stranger Danger and Tricky People," the teacher conducted an extension activity in which she showed the storybook through a projector so students could see it in a larger format. The students get green and red sticky notes and were asked to raise a hand and volunteer to paste a green one on the screen when they spotted an illustration or phrase that indicated safe situations, and a red one on the screen when they spotted unsafe situations. At the end of the session, the students did a movement-based classification activity. The teacher wrote *safe* with a green check mark and *unsafe* with a red cross mark on separate, large pieces of colored paper. Students moved to any of the marks as they heard the teacher describe a situation. The same activity can be done in the upper grades while incorporating the case of unsafe situations in online settings.

At our middle and high schools, teachers do similar activities to discuss safe and unsafe situations, using the "group activity" or "message of the day" segments during advisory times. Students discuss recent news and social phenomena occurring in the real world, identifying the big issue and narrowing it down to the school environment. Teachers can also use subject time as an opportunity to read resources regarding the matter and do what we call a "social action" to enhance comprehension and students' voice in the learning process. Here's an example.

A high school sociology teacher incorporated a social action into a reading task. The students were asked to do research regarding making safety plans to deal with potentially unsafe situations, in either real-world or online settings. The students worked in groups to come up with a final product. One group did research on dating violence. They read a number of reliable resources from places such as the Centers for Disease Control and Prevention and other government websites, as well as academic journals. After some brainstorming sessions and discussions, they decided to raise awareness on this matter by creating a short video and a series of social media posts on what to do to prevent physical, sexual, and even emotional violence when dating.

Developing Healthy Relationships

In line with *Social and Emotional Skills Training for Children* (Bierman et al., 2017), we believe that positive peer interactions support the development of social skills, as well as foster the development of feelings of self-competence and self-esteem. We refer to positive peer interactions as *healthy friendship*, which we define as the ability to initiate and maintain

Developing healthy relationships involves two important concepts: (1) respect for differences and (2) healthy versus unhealthy relationships.

healthy relationships and positively communicate with peers to create a supportive community.

One of our biggest causes for concern that led to the creation of this element of Empathetic Social Skills is bullying. We like the definition of bullying that describes it as a specific type of aggression caused by repeated systematic abuses of power (Olweus, 1994). Bullying often goes beyond deliberate physical, in-person harm to cyber-aggression. In the digital world, it includes spreading false rumors, sending offensive messages, and coercing peers.

Developing healthy relationships involves two important concepts: (1) respect for differences and (2) healthy versus unhealthy relationships.

Nurturing respect for differences

Respect is nurtured through culture. Teachers need to model respect not only among their colleagues but also toward students. Because our school uses multiage class grouping (e.g., prekindergarten combines 4- and 5-year-olds in the same class) and is inclusive of students from multiple countries and different regions of Indonesia, our students are used to interacting with classmates of different ages, levels of readiness, and abilities and needs, including students with exceptional needs.

Let's look at an example from a prekindergarten that included two students with special conditions. One child, whom we will refer to as "Seth," was diagnosed with mild autism. The other child, "Darryl," had a diagnosis of Pervasive Developmental Disorder Not Otherwise Specified (PDD-NOS). Every day, during small-group time, when other students were focusing on their task at hand, Seth moved around the classroom while taking down all the area signs pasted on the wall, one by one. When this happened, one or two of his friends would try to call Seth back to the group activity. Occasionally, one of them even came to him and held his hand gently to get him back to his seats. At the same time, Darryl would sometimes scream when something overwhelmed him.

The other children were adjusting to the situation. Sometimes they would look at the teacher and sigh. Once, a student asked the teacher what Darryl was doing, and the teacher replied that Darryl was probably feeling uncomfortable. Then the teacher suggested to the student that he might find out more by trying to talk to Darryl, which he did, but Darryl did not respond. Darryl generally played well with the other children in the classroom during most routines. When either he or Seth seemed to be playing by themselves, the teacher stepped in to play with them briefly before connecting them with other children who were playing in parallel.

The same multiage and inclusive approach applies in middle and high school as well. For example, a new student in a Grade 6–7 classroom did not speak Indonesian fluently. During Indonesian language class, the teacher always gave her the basic-level texts or vocabulary activities for Indonesian language learners. The student grumbled quite loudly whenever she was feeling frustrated with a task. When the teacher was helping other students, a friend often volunteered to help this student understand the task.

Teachers can note all of these behaviors as evidence of respect. As mentioned earlier, it is part of our school culture to respect differences, and teachers use multiple activities to encourage this behavior. For example, students discuss their own differences and uniqueness, and teachers highlight the unique characteristics of each individual child. Then they discuss how these differences should not influence students' friendships and how they should try to be friends with everyone.

Teachers also nurture respect through the use of storytelling, movie clips, and social stories—a strategy for discussing a problem that is occurring in the classroom (e.g., students arguing over a toy or resource or not cleaning up after project work) and then visualizing and discussing possible solutions by drawing on empathetic responses (e.g., What are the children feeling as they argue? How can they deal with these feelings? What should they do next time they face the same conflict?). These approaches help to make the abstract concept of respect more concrete for younger students so they can implement it in their daily life.

In upper grades, discussions and activities related to respect can be part of various daily routines, such as morning advisory time, as well as integrated within the content and learning processes. Teachers can also facilitate exploration of respect through special events. During a Multicultural Week or United Nations Day, for example, a teacher might lead a discussion of how to navigate cultural differences to sustain a positive atmosphere in a diverse community.

Nurturing "healthy versus unhealthy relationships"

Healthy relationships need to be modeled and experienced from an early age. In preschool, this means developing students' ability to interact comfortably in parallel play situations and gradually moving toward cooperative play.

A preschool teacher had a student, whom we will refer to as Ken, who did not seem comfortable playing with other students. At first, he stayed in one corner of the classroom observing others as the teacher sat next to him trying to initiate conversation. As Ken gradually began to choose some toys to play with by himself, the teacher played along, following Ken's ideas. After a couple of days, the teacher sat between Ken and some other students and tried to prompt a conversation and play among them. The teacher said, "Vincent, Jess, look! Ken is moving his dinosaur so fast, it's almost flying. I wonder where it's going." The effort did not work the first time, but as the students became more aware of each other's existence, Vincent began to ask Ken questions, and Ken began to sit closer to his two friends.

Young children often resort to physical actions if they are not yet able to articulate their feelings. Although this is a natural developmental problem, if left unmanaged, it could potentially become a behavioral problem. This is where storytelling comes in handy. A K–1 teacher created a scenario, based on an actual recent incident, in which children in the class were fighting over wooden blocks and began to hit each other. The teacher made the storytelling interactive and asked the students to suggest ideas on how to solve the problems. They replied with statements such as "Just say, 'I don't like it!'" and "Take turns!"

Teachers also model the use of "I" statements by saying, for example, "I feel really angry right now. I want to play with the blocks, but Andrea is using all of them." Teachers also label the emotions of the children by saying, for example, "I can see that you're really angry right now. Let's say it with our words and keep our hands to ourselves." Very young children can practice empathy and healthy relationships through parallel play before continuing to develop these capacities through associative and cooperative play and then formal collaborative activities.

To create healthy relationships, teachers also need to be aware of the possibilities of unsafe atmospheres that might be different for each individual. These unsafe atmospheres create a sense of insecurity and negative feelings in general. The causes or triggers of these feelings can also be different for each individual; for example, one student may feel uncomfortable when having to speak in public, and others may feel insecure when walking around the school by themselves, feeling judged by their peers. It is important to recognize these potential unsafe atmospheres and, in response, to create a healthy learning atmosphere where students feel safe.

A Grade 4–5 teacher used an activity called "Random Acts of Kindness" to build healthy relationships and empathy. The teacher prepared a large board with multiple colorful envelopes (one for each student), written notes on cards describing random acts of kindness, and instruction steps written on large paper. (Figure 7.4 shows examples of the "random acts of kindness" cards.)

FIGURE 7.4
Random Acts of Kindness Cards

Ask someone if they need help.	Do good things when no one is watching.	Share your snack with someone.	"Thank you"—Say it at least five times a day.
Entertain someone, sing someone a song, share a joke.	Inspire! Your act of kindness will make others be kind.	Use your words to help others.	Volunteer to help your teacher.
Join others you see doing a kind deed.	Greet everyone you see with a smile.	Write a note to someone to make them smile.	Make new friends.
Mentor a younger student in school.	Notice acts of kindness around you.	Apologize.	Be nice.
Show love to others.	Open the door for others.	Make someone happy.	Cheer up someone who is sad.
Pick up trash that you see.	Read a book to someone.	Make someone laugh with you.	Show that you care.

The teacher put a card in each envelope and stuck the envelopes onto the large board. Using morning-meeting time to launch this activity for the first time, the teacher wrote this quote from author Martin Kornfeld on the whiteboard: "If we all do one random act of kindness daily, we just might set the world in the right direction." Then the teacher asked the students what they thought the quote meant, pointed out that there is a lot of negativity in the world today, and asked the students to give some examples. The teacher then said, "We are going to do something to change it," and explained the purpose of the board:

> In each envelope I have a small act of kindness that we can do to other people, like opening the door for them, or offering to share our snack, or giving someone a nice note to brighten up their day. You may think that this is a small act, it won't mean anything, but you never know. This small act might make a difference in the world. So now, I want all of you to pick a card, and do the act that is written on the card. You can do it

during recess or transition time. You don't have to tell me when you do, but I want you to write just a small reflection on how you feel after you do it. Write the reflection on a small piece of paper and put it inside the envelope [you picked], along with the kindness act card so that someone else can also pick that card later.

The teacher continues to encourage the students to perform as many random acts of kindness as possible, "because who knows? You might actually make a difference."

In middle school and high school, students typically develop closer and more intimate friendships, cement their social reputations, make decisions more collaboratively, and have more intense conversations with peers. As such, a great focus must be placed on managing social pressures, as well as on broadening students' understanding and recognition of varying perspectives, in order to minimize conflicts arising from an inability to deal with differences.

A high school teacher can use advisory time to promote the concept of healthy versus unhealthy relationships, using the "group activity" segment to talk about the balance between rights and responsibilities in a relationship. For example, the teacher might begin the discussion by asking the students to identify how competing rights and responsibilities can cause conflicts and pressures, then asking them what they think "compromise" means in the context of building a healthy relationship and why compromise is important. Asking for examples of compromise can ensure that students know what the word means.

Teachers can have students in large groups brainstorm the rights and responsibilities people have in relationships, encouraging them to think about how these apply to themselves and to others. Using the graphic organizer shown in Figure 7.5, students can record their responses in the "My Rights" and "My Responsibilities" columns. Examples of rights might include to be told the truth, to have your opinions and feelings respected, to be listened to, to be spoken to respectfully, and not to be pressured to do things you are not comfortable doing. Responsibilities correspond with these rights. Then, in small groups, teachers can ask students to reflect on the rights and responsibilities they have in relationships with their parents, siblings, and friends.

Teachers can also implement peer mediation with middle and high school students, empowering them to use their strong relationships with their peers to mediate conflicts that occur among them. Students can volunteer to join a peer mediation program and become certified to become neutral mediators in resolving conflicts. The mediators facilitate the problem-solving process and ensure that the root causes are uncovered and addressed; they also facilitate the decision-making process to achieve fair ways to resolve the conflict. Peer mediation is voluntary, and all parties must agree to take part. This process helps the conflicting students to use communication, negotiation, and problem-solving skills to resolve conflicts and reach a mutually beneficial decision. At the same time, the mediating students are gaining a deeper understanding of conflict resolution. Peer mediation consists of the following steps:

1. Use active listening—Be impartial. Listen without judgment.
2. Identify issues—What was the problem that led to the conflict?
3. Elaborate—Restate positions and reasons.
4. Brainstorm solutions—Come up with different possible solutions.
5. Discuss pros and cons—Discuss why a particular solution would or wouldn't work.
6. Decide—Decide on a mutually beneficial solution.
7. Review—Set a time to review and renegotiate, if necessary,

FIGURE 7.5
Graphic Organizer for Rights and Responsibilities

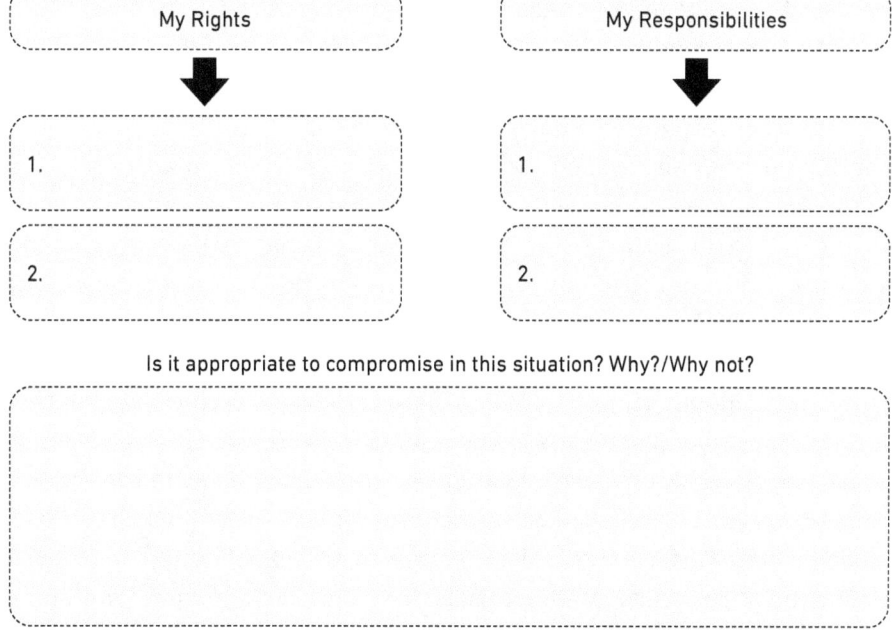

Adaptive Social Problem Solving

Psychology defines *social problems* as issues that obstruct humans' adaptive functioning in the social world (D'Zurilla et al., 2004). Studies on social-problem-solving skills, then, aim to learn how broad problem-solving concepts can be adapted and adjusted to applications in our social spheres, thereby resolving complications that hamper our ability to assimilate and perform well in society. We define *adaptive social problem solving* as mindfully preventing, perceiving, and solving social problems using strategies to find effective and adaptive solutions. The aim is for students to have the mindset that every conflict is an opportunity to reflect, and the solution to each conflict must always fit the specific context. It involves the process of solving problems that occur in our "real world," or "natural environment."

Teachers should teach this skill at all grade levels. The skill involves addressing the variety of problems that may influence people's functioning, including interpersonal issues (for example, family disputes and conflicts in the workplace), intrapersonal problems (for example, behavioral, cognitive, health, and emotional issues), impersonal conundrums (for example, financial stability and property ownership), as well as societal and communal predicaments (for example, racial injustice and incarceration) (D'Zurilla & Goldfried, 1971). Beginning in preschool, teachers can help students understand social norms and expectations and solve related problems. Students progress until, at the highest level, they can see problems as opportunities.

Teachers of younger students can begin discussing the concept and vocabulary of adaptive social problem solving during the first weeks of the academic year, as they introduce the various essential life skills. For example, a teacher introduced Empathetic Social Skills by reading books about conflicts among children and asking the students to come up with a solution to the conflicts. As the students turned and shared their ideas with a friend sitting next to them, the teacher moved around the class to listen to what the students had to say. After a while, some of the students shared their ideas with the whole class.

The next introductory activity for the concept of Empathetic Social Skills involved important vocabulary words related to each element of this life skill. For example, for the element *adaptive social problem solving*, relevant words include *problem*, *feeling*, and *solution*. The teacher did an activity called "Hop and Solve," a game modified from the classic hopscotch that had students jumping from a "problem" square to a "feeling" square to a "solution" square. The students were divided into four small groups to minimize waiting time. The teacher modeled the game by hopping to each square while using the following sentence frame, which students could copy:

- *Problem* square: "If I fight with...."
- *Feeling* square: "I feel...."
- *Solution* square: "I solve the problem by...."

After all the students had their turns, the last activity was to create a visual reminder of what to do when a social problem (a conflict) happens. The teacher prompted students to recall the key vocabulary words they had used during the earlier activities—for example, "What were the words that we used when we did Hop and Solve?" When an expected word was not mentioned, the teacher offered a prompt to help the students guess the word—for example, "The word on the last square—we need it so the problem is solved." The teacher helped students write the key words on a large piece of poster paper and then asked them to add drawings to visualize the words on their own sheets of paper. At the end, all the sheets were collected and pasted onto the large poster, which the teacher displayed on the wall to remind everyone of what to do when conflict arises.

Teachers at upper grade levels guide students through similar activities that are increasingly complex.

- *Problem* square: "If I have conflict with...."
- *Feeling* square: "When I calm down and think more clearly and less emotionally, I feel...."
- *Solution* square: "I approach the conflict by...."

Teachers can also provide a vocabulary activity like the one shown in Figure 7.6 (see p. 166) to emphasize and help with understanding of important words and concepts, such as *mindfulness, adaptive solutions,* and *conflict as an opportunity*. After these activities, the teacher distributes and asks students to review the rubric for Empathetic Social Skills (described later in this chapter). Students then demonstrate their understanding of the expectations for Empathetic Social Skills by creating a poster reminder, such as the one shown in Figure 7.7 (see p. 167).

Once students understand the Empathetic Social Skills, they are expected to practice using them throughout their school day. Opportunities frequently occur during

There are two important concepts in *adaptive social problem solving*: (1) conflict and (2) problem solving. These concepts go hand-in-hand.

166 *Life Skills for All Learners*

FIGURE 7.6
Example of an Upper-Grade Vocabulary Activity

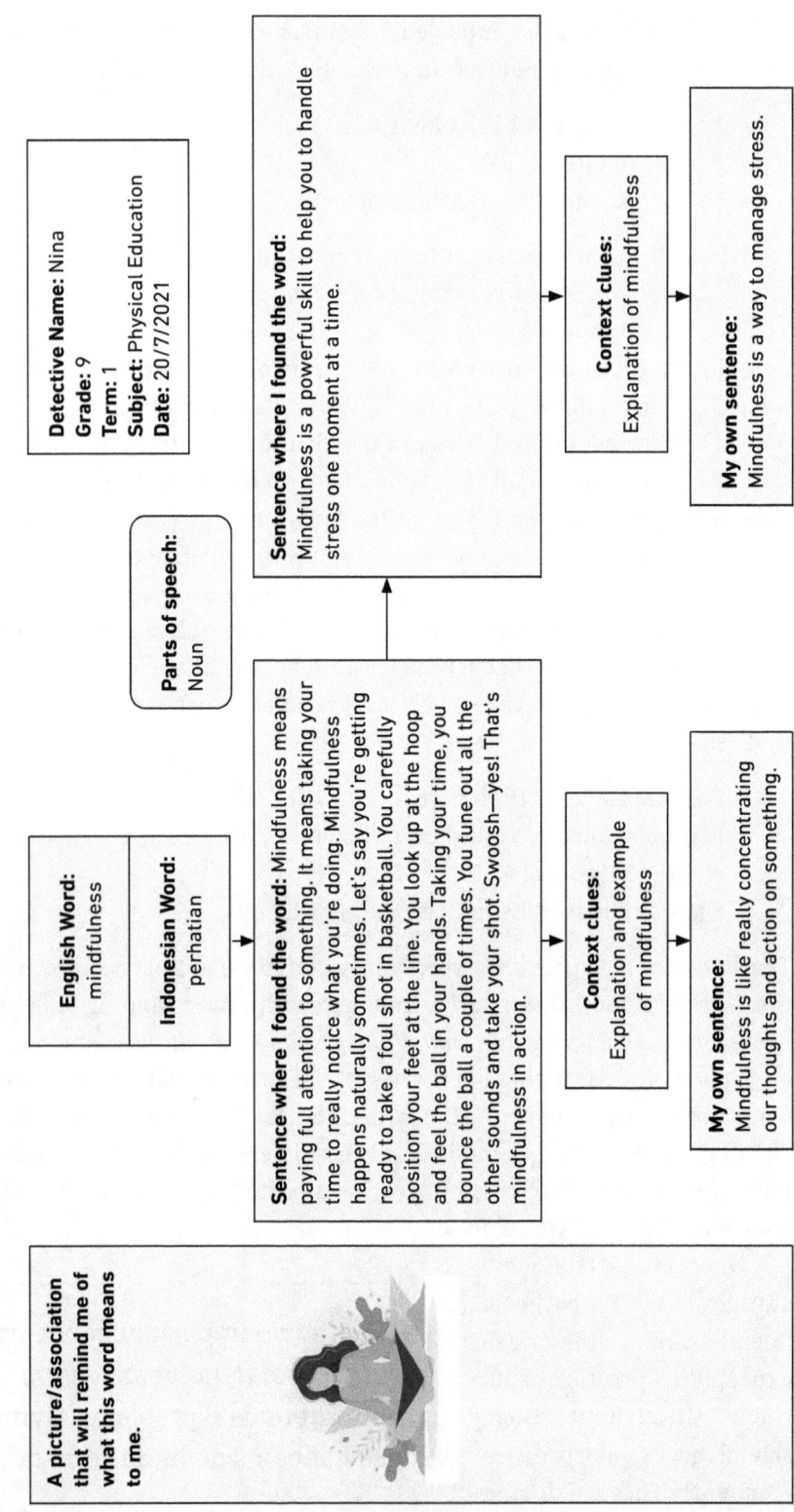

routines such as morning-meeting time, when the skills might be a topic for sharing, the focus of a group activity, or part of the message of the day.

There are two important concepts in Adaptive Social Problem Solving: (1) conflict and (2) problem solving. These concepts go hand-in-hand, and so the next section discusses them together.

FIGURE 7.7
Example of an Upper Grade Poster Reminder for Empathetic Social Skills

Taking Charge of Personal Safety	Healthy Relationship	Adaptive Problem Solving
Be aware and careful of the surroundings, be aware of the dangers of illegal goods and the consequences for the body, and also maintain privacy from strangers.	Be respectful to your friends by keeping their secrets. Support them when they're having conflicts by giving your honest opinion about what they should do to solve their conflict and understand other people's perspectives. Compromise to find solutions. See if there are areas for us to improve.	Express emotions in an honest, clear way and avoid using hurtful expressions by keeping a positive mindset. Understand a person's verbal and nonverbal signs and understand the steps on resolving conflicts such as actions/consequences and being a mediator.

Nurturing the concepts of conflict and problem solving

As we have said, both teachers and students need to see conflict as part of normal life and an opportunity to grow. Conflict is not something to endorse; it's something to manage and mediate effectively when it inevitably arises. Students need to learn to face conflict with a positive mindset and a willingness to seek a solution.

Earlier, in the section titled "Why Empathetic Social Skills Are Important," we mentioned that our preschool and elementary schools use High-Scope's Steps in Resolving Conflicts (Hohmann et al., 2008) to guide teachers when social conflicts happen among their students. Recall that the steps are the following:

- Approach calmly. Stop any hurtful actions.
- Acknowledge children's feelings.
- Gather information.
- Restate the problem.
- Ask for ideas for solutions and choose one together.
- Be prepared to give follow-up support.

At their developmental level, younger students may not be able to accurately describe their feelings. This is where the Steps in Resolving Conflicts (Hohmann et al., 2008) can play a part. One of the steps is for teachers to acknowledge students' feelings and to make sure students notice this acknowledgment—with the intent of helping them gradually become more aware of their emotions and learn to express these emotions verbally instead of using physical actions, like hitting or kicking.

In terms of solutions, the egocentrism characteristic of young children means that the first solution they propose may incline toward personal interest, as in "I go first. They can go after me." With consistent application of the Steps in Resolving Conflicts (Hohmann et al., 2008), students learn to face conflicts with positivity and to produce win-win solutions. They learn there are perspectives other than theirs, and they begin to demonstrate less egocentrism. The teacher's role is to be the mediator and show the children that other kids have different opinions.

As an example, a conflict over the use of wooden blocks happened during work time in a preschool class. The teacher gathered the students involved and spoke with all of them at the same time. First, the teacher acknowledged the students' feelings to make them feel heard and valued and asked each student to share their views of the problems. One student, Nadine, said, "Aimee took my blocks. I was still using it." Aimee said, "I want to make a castle, too. Nadine took all the blocks." The teacher then prompted the children to think of a solution. Nadine said, "I use the blocks first, then Aimee can use them." Aimee said the same thing, with herself "first." Being familiar with such "me-first" solutions, the teacher shared an idea: "Both of you want to play first, but we only have this many blocks. What should we do?" The negotiation process ended when Nadine and Aimee agreed to build their castles together.

In middle school and high school, students learn to mediate conflicts among their peers. Teachers can guide students in using the Adaptive Problem-Solving Steps, as displayed in the poster shown in Figure 7.8. The word *adaptive* is added to emphasize the message that students need to be able to use this strategy for resolving conflicts in different contexts.

Although a teacher may begin by working with certain students who seem to be ready to mediate conflicts, after a while, all students learn the necessary skills. The teacher can model the process and have the students work in groups to role-play the conflicting students and the mediator, referring to the poster showing the steps of adaptive problem solving. With teacher-provided, hypothetical scenarios and guidance, the students

Empathetic Social Skills   169

FIGURE 7.8
Adaptive Problem-Solving Steps for Middle and High School

STEP 1: MINDFULNESS
Stop, engage students in mindfulness strategies.

STEP 2: ACKNOWLEDGMENT
Acknowledge feelings and perspectives from each party.

STEP 3: PROBLEM DEFINITION
Identify problems based on the conflicting perspective to see the gap.

STEP 4: SOLUTIONS
Look at the gap and generate alternative solutions and consequences for each alternative to determine mutually agreed-upon decision.

STEP 5: SUPPORT
Monitor and follow up the implementation.

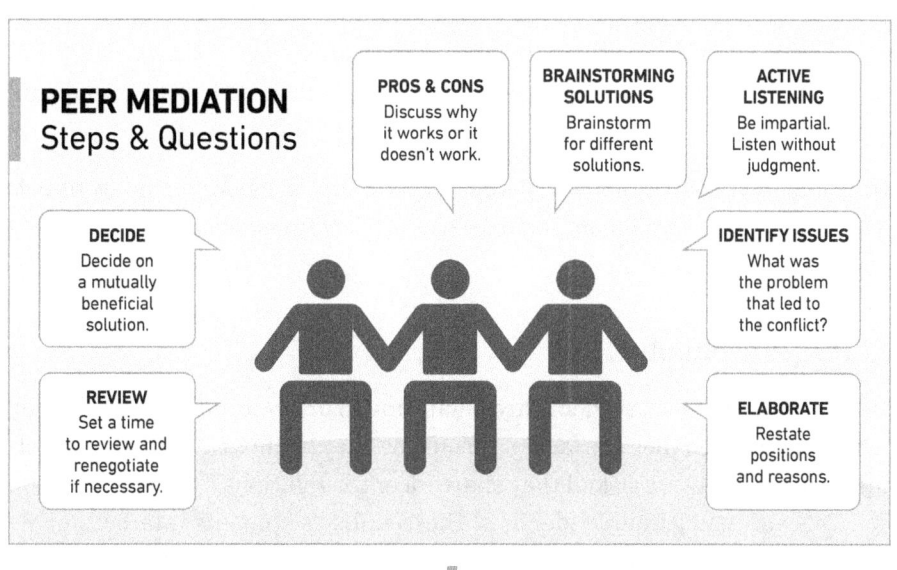

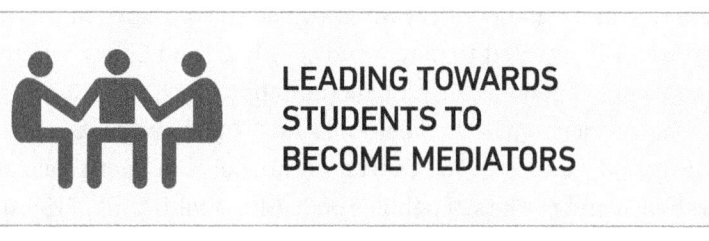

LEADING TOWARDS STUDENTS TO BECOME MEDIATORS

practice the steps. Following the role-play, teachers ask the students to self-reflect on how well they resolved the conflict and how they could improve, and to identify particular statements or keywords they might use to help them resolve conflicts in a real-life situation. After reflecting independently, students share the result with the whole class.

How Are Empathetic Social Skills Measured and Assessed?

The Empathetic Social Skills gradually become more comprehensive as students move to higher continuum levels. As previously stated, Empathetic Social Skills comprise three elements: (1) *taking charge of personal safety*, (2) *healthy relationships*, and (3) *adaptive social problem solving*. In the rubric for this skill set (Figure 7.9), these are represented as ESS.1, ESS.2, and ESS.3, respectively. The rubric also describes three stages of performance:

- Stage 1: Student performs a task somewhat accurately with consistent guidance from others (teachers and peers).
- Stage 2: Student performs a task accurately with little guidance and redirection from others (teachers and peers).
- Stage 3: Student independently performs a task with ease, speed, and accuracy.

In the following sections we further explain and provide examples of evidence for the third element, *adaptive social problem solving*, at the various continuum levels.

Early (Preschool–K)

At the Early level, students are beginning to understand the actions they need to take when they are facing a problem. They begin to identify their feelings and the problem(s), and they share ideas for solutions.

Teachers can gather evidence of these skills as students interact during their learning process—specifically, by observing students' interactions as they play with their peers. For example, during outside time in a preschool class, Elly and Shona both wanted to use the workbench, but for different purposes. Elly wanted to play "mud cooking," and Shona wanted to make a mandala out of pebbles. Elly looked unhappy.

The teacher approached her and said, "You look upset."

Elly said, "I want to cook at the workbench, but Shona has taken over the workbench and put lots of pebbles on it. She is taking all of the space."

FIGURE 7.9
Rubric for Empathetic Social Skills

	Early (Preschool–K)	Beginning (K–3)	Transition (3–6)	Developing (6–9)	Expert (9–12)
ESS.1 Taking Charge of Personal Safety	• Identifies a dangerous situation and knows how to react by screaming for attention/help if needed. • Understands how to say "No" to unwanted or inappropriate behavior using clear words, eye contact, and assertive body language.	• Understands that there are different safety rules (e.g., do not leave with/eat something from a stranger) when on their own and knows how to verbalize a dangerous situation to a caregiver/authority figure. • Uses technology responsibly and safely to get reliable information by showing understanding of personal data (e.g., home address, phone number, etc.) and keeping the data private.	• Understands that s/he has to have a self-made safety plan for how to get help anywhere and in any situation (e.g., when going out with friends, s/he needs to provide the driver's phone number to her/his parents). • Uses digital communication tools responsibly and safely by understanding the positive and negative effects of the tools and uses them to build positive relationships in the community.	• Understands that there are actions, circumstances, and relationships that have considerable risks and knows how to improvise when the safety plan does not work (e.g., rejects when s/he is asked to drink alcohol, smoke, have sexual interaction) OR explains why her/his safety plans work. • Understands the rights and responsibilities of living, learning, and working as a digital citizen and applies legal and ethical practices in using digital tools to keep her/himself safe and respected in the global community.	• Understands that there are places, actions, and relationships that have considerable risks and is able to take charge of personal safety by mitigating the risks when unexpected problems occur, with consideration for others. • Understands the rights and responsibilities of living, learning, and working as a digital citizen and advocates ethical practices in the global community with consideration for others to ensure everyone's safety.
	Stage 1 2 3	Stage 1 2 3	Stage 1 2 3	Stage 1 2 3	Stage 1 2 3

(*continued*)

172   Life Skills for All Learners

FIGURE 7.9
Rubric for Empathetic Social Skills—*(continued)*

	Early (Preschool–K)	Beginning (K–3)	Transition (3–6)	Developing (6–9)	Expert (9–12)
ESS.2 *Developing Healthy Relationships*	• Develops and maintains friendships with peers in class. Understands the do's and don'ts in friendship.	• Understands that people are different (e.g., race, religion, hobbies) and s/he has to be kind and show respect to everyone, including those who are different from her/him. • Understands signs of unhealthy friendships (e.g., name calling, exclusion) and is able to listen, communicate, and discuss the issues in the community (friends/teachers).	• Understands and respects that people can have different opinions and that disagreements may happen. • Understands signs of unhealthy friendships (e.g., name calling, exclusion, bullying) and is able to stop the issues and show empathy by listening, comforting the victim, and befriending her/him.	• Understands and respects that people have different perspectives. • Maintains healthy relationships in his/her community by listening attentively, communicating respectfully when addressing the issues, and managing social pressure.	• Empathizes when people have different perspectives. • Takes an active role as a global citizen in cultivating the culture of respecting the differences within the global community with positive interaction and intention.
	Stage 1 2 3	Stage 1 2 3	Stage 1 2 3	Stage 1 2 3	Stage 1 2 3
ESS.3 *Adaptive Social Problem Solving*	• Understands what to do when facing a problem with support from adults. • When facing a problem, refrains from physical action and tries to label own feelings.	• Understands what to do when facing a problem and shows motivation to solve it. • When facing a problem, s/he describes own feelings and gives a reason for the feelings.	• Views the situation as changeable, identifies the difficulty, and decides what to do about it. • When facing a problem, acknowledges own feelings.	• Shows a positive attitude by believing that problems are solvable and is curious to find solutions. • Begins to conduct mindfulness strategies to pause and acknowledge own feelings.	• Shows a mindset of seeing problems/conflicts as challenges or opportunities to grow by committing to solve the problems rather than avoiding them. • Consciously conducts mindfulness strategies and acknowledges own feelings.
	Stage 1 2 3	Stage 1 2 3	Stage 1 2 3	Stage 1 2 3	Stage 1 2 3

Empathetic Social Skills

	Early (Preschool–K)	Beginning (K–3)	Transition (3–6)	Developing (6–9)	Expert (9–12)
ESS.3 (cont.) Adaptive Social Problem Solving	• Identifies the problem and shares how s/he wants the problem to be solved.	• Identifies the problems and the cause of the problems. • Gives a solution that achieves the problem-solving goals.	• Defines the problems and generates acceptable/satisfactory solutions for all parties involved. • Makes sure the solution is implemented to prevent recurrence in the future.	• Analyzes the problems (uses "I" statements) and generates solutions and consequences (pros and cons) for each solution. • When witnessing a conflict, s/he helps mediate the conflict.	• Analyzes problems (uses "I" statements) and generates solutions that maximize positive consequences while minimizing the negative consequences. • Ensures the solution is implemented effectively and identifies the pattern in the problem/conflict to prevent recurrence in the future. • When witnessing a conflict, s/he helps mediate the conflict and volunteers to monitor the progress.
	Stage 1 2 3	Stage 1 2 3	Stage 1 2 3	Stage 1 2 3	Stage 1 2 3

Stage 1: Student performs a task somewhat accurately with consistent guidance from others (teachers and peers).

Stage 2: Student performs a task accurately with little guidance and redirection from others (teachers and peers).

Stage 3: Student independently performs a task with ease, speed, and accuracy.

The teacher restated the problem: "So the problem is both of you want to play on the workbench. What can we do to solve the problem?"

Elly, stomping her foot, said, "I don't know! The workbench is full of her pebbles."

Anasha, a classmate, noticed the conflict and came over with a suggestion: "Why don't you use the workbench together?"

The teacher restated the suggestion: "Elly and Shona, Anasha has an idea that you use the workbench together. Do you think Anasha's idea will work for you?"

Elly answered, "OK, but I need bigger space for my cooking table! Can you scoot over the corner so I can put my cooking stuff on the table?"

Shona replied, "I only use small pebbles. You can use some space for cooking."

The teacher wrapped up this conflict resolution process by saying, "Looks like both of you have solved the problem. Both of you have agreed to use the workbench together, and Shona, you've agreed to give bigger space to Elly."

The teacher continued to observe the two students for some time and checked back to see how they were feeling after the discussion. She saw evidence of Stage 1 behavior for Elly and Shona; both of them needed a lot of support from the teacher in terms of stating feelings and—with the help of Anasha—finding solutions for the problem.

Now let's look at an example of Stage 3 evidence involving K–1 students Jackie and Shawn. Jackie was using blocks to build a "city" of tall structures. Nearby, Shawn was assembling train tracks and putting animals next to them. Accidentally, one of Jackie's blocks fell off, breaking part of Shawn's track assembly and knocking over some of his animals.

Shawn frowned and said, "Jackie, you destroyed my train tracks and animals! I don't like it! I'm angry!"

Jackie apologized and offered to put the animals back in their original positions. "I'm sorry, Shawn," he said. "I think my buildings are too close to your train tracks. They're tall so they get wobbly." He reached out toward Shawn to shake hands.

Shawn shook Jackie's hand and said, "OK, but don't build it too close to mine."

Jackie then asked Shawn what he was playing and also shared that he was building a city. After a while, Jackie suggested to Shawn that they play together. Shawn agreed. They both then added roads for cars, toy houses, and more animals. They built "a city zoo."

After closely observing the entire interaction, the teacher checked on how they were doing. Jackie filled the teacher in, who acknowledged the work they had done, saying, "You had a problem and you solved it!"

From this illustration, we can conclude that Jackie is able to solve a social conflict independently; hence, he is at Stage 3. He was able to identify and describe the problem, understood what to do when facing a problem, and solved it with his own ideas.

Beginning (Grades K–3)

Students at the Beginning level already show motivation to solve problems. They understand the actions they need to take when they are faced with social problems, and they are able to identify, describe, and justify their feelings.

For example, when a student has difficulties in completing his work because his classmates are noisy, he can say "I'm feeling very frustrated right now. I can't focus and do my work because my friends are very loud. I can't think." Students at the Beginning level are also capable of correctly identifying the cause of the problems, building upon the skill of identifying problems mastered at the Early level. Based on their understanding of the causes, they are able to propose solutions. Teachers at this level still use and model the Steps in Resolving Conflicts to help mediate students' conflicts.

Transition (Grades 3–6)

At the Transition level, students are able to adopt a different point of view when facing problems. They see the problematic situation as something that can be changed, which motivates them to identify the difficulties and improve the situation. They can acknowledge their own feelings and begin to see how their emotions affect their problem-solving ability.

Students at this level also learn to define the problem and generate solutions. For example, when a student realizes his group will not be ready to meet their project deadline, he is able to define the problem based on its causes and effects. He might say something like this:

> Our project was unfinished because one of our group members did not finish his task. He was supposed to go to the printing place and print our poster that we designed together. But he did not tell us that he could not do it until this morning, and we were all already at school, so none of us could go to the printing place. I feel so upset with him. We need to talk to him about this.

This student can then propose a solution for all parties, as he explains to his teacher:

> We already discussed this issue in our group, and we decided to present the poster using the digital version by projecting it from the class computer to the big screen. We also talked about the unfinished task with our group members, and we came up with an action plan to better communicate next time and not be afraid of sharing our problems so that all of us could help each other. We need better time management, and a project schedule.

We also expect students at this level to be able to follow up on the action plan to ensure correct and consistent implementation.

Developing (Grades 6–9)

As students progress to the Developing level, they are able to have a positive mindset and attitude about problems. They do not become discouraged when facing a problem; instead, they view problems as something that can be changed and solved, and they're curious about finding solutions. However, at this age, students' emotional development is proceeding faster than their ability to regulate those emotions. This state often results in impulsive decision making. Teachers need to be aware that students at this level need guidance in managing their emotions and reactions to situations.

To prevent students' inappropriate expression of emotions and impulsive behavior when facing a problem, a teacher can engage them in using mindfulness strategies that are best suited for their individual needs. Teachers can help students practice sound decision making, including taking the time to analyze the situation. After pausing and calming themselves, the students can use "I" statements to analyze the problems and brainstorm solutions. They should consider both the positive and the negative aspects of each solution before deciding together on the best option. They take the extra step to create strategies to ensure the effective implementation of their solution.

Students at the Developing level also begin to engage in the role of mediator when their peers are in a conflict. They ensure that when a conflict occurs, they do not become a bystander but instead take on the role of helping to mediate the conflict. The following example describes a situation experienced by Reuben, the Grade 8–9 student we have featured in other chapters.

During science class, Reuben shared with his teacher that he felt angry at his teammates. He said that there were some "free riders" in his group. He didn't want to vent his emotions to his teammates, but he also didn't want to feel angry during every group work time. The teacher gave him some prompts, in the form of reflection questions, to help him to solve the problem. Reuben answered the prompts and showed the teacher what he had written (see Figure 7.10).

FIGURE 7.10
Example of a Student's Reflection on Problem Solving

Describe the problem:
There are some free riders in my group. I got to do all of the work, and those free riders get credits for something that they didn't do.

How do I feel?
I feel angry and miserable.

How do I think the other people involved feel?
I don't know, seems like they're just OK.

What can I choose to do?
I can share my feelings with my friends and ask them what we can do to solve this problem.

What are the consequences of my choices?
I can tell my friends my feelings, and maybe we can work together to solve the problem.

My final plan is...
To talk about how I feel with the free riders and solve the problem with my friends. I need for us to do our work equally and for them to understand how I feel.

The teacher acknowledged that Reuben now had a plan to solve his problem. She suggested he follow the Adaptive Problem-Solving Steps in addressing it, and she asked whether he wanted her to be there during the problem solving. He said no, he wanted to do it by himself first. He had a discussion with his teammates about solving the problem, as planned in his reflection notes. The teacher observed how Reuben executed his plan and took some observational notes. To make sure that both parties involved in the conflict solved the problem successfully, the teacher also interviewed Reuben's teammates and asked for their opinion on how successful the problem solving was and how they felt as a result. His teammates said that Reuben was very clear when describing the problem and proposing the solution. They felt relieved that they talked it out and believed that their team's solidarity would improve.

The evidence showed that Reuben still needed help from his teacher to be able to solve his problem. However, he was able to use the question prompts independently and wanted to try to solve the problem by himself. These factors identified him as a Stage 2 student.

Expert (Grades 9–12)

At the Expert level, students are expected to adopt the perspective of viewing problems as growth opportunities. They embrace problems as challenges and are intrinsically motivated to do their best in solving these problems.

Similar to the students at the Developing level, students at this level also find ways to calm themselves before engaging in problem-solving strategies. They are able to choose mindfulness strategies that work for them and engage in mindfulness activities consciously as they acknowledge their own feelings. When faced with conflict, they consciously take the time to calm themselves down before engaging in problem solving. They say to their peers, "I need time to calm down." Students are equipped with a mindfulness toolkit at the beginning of the academic year, and they continuously practice mindfulness exercises during advisory time.

After the various individuals engage in mindfulness activities, they analyze the problem and come up with solutions that are well-thought-out and aim to maximize positive outcomes and decrease negative consequences. Students at this level are also able to use their Expert Thinking skills to identify patterns in the problems and to design implementation strategies for their solutions to ensure that the same problems don't arise in the future. Furthermore, building upon their skills as mediators, they volunteer to monitor the progress of the implementation of the solution among their classmates.

Teachers can assess understanding of *adaptive social problem solving* by giving students hypothetical cases to analyze. Complex cases will demonstrate the student's ability to have the perspective of viewing problems as growth opportunities, to analyze the problem and generate effective solutions, and to explain how they might mediate the conflict. Furthermore, students can be asked to write their plan for using specific mindfulness strategies and how they will monitor the implementation of the solution.

Suggestions for Integrating Empathetic Social Skills into Curriculum and Classroom Practice

- Infuse Empathetic Social Skills into the curriculum standards in the "physical education and mental well-being" subject area to design learning that builds students' ability to manage their emotions and feelings.
- Infuse Empathetic Social Skills into the curriculum standards in the "digital literacy" subject area so that students can learn how to use technology and interact with others safely.
- Nurture a safe and respectful culture in the classroom, ensuring that differences are encouraged and celebrated.
- Use mindfulness activities in the beginning of the lessons, such as belly breathing or mindful observation of the surroundings.
- Allow students to regularly reflect on and regulate their feelings.
- Create specific steps for problem solving that are increasingly complex as students get older. Familiarize students with these steps to create a habit of solving their interpersonal problems independently.
- Encourage plenty of interaction among students. Engage them in group work and group discussion to provide them with opportunities to use their Empathetic Social Skills.
- Discuss and explicitly teach the norms and safety plans that students need to know to navigate in both the offline and online worlds. Doing so is especially important for younger students as they begin to explore their environment independently and experience increased exposure to online interactions.
- Acknowledge the reality that identifying and understanding emotions are the basis of Empathetic Social Skills by engaging students in activities to identify and regulate their emotions. Use dolls, books, and other everyday objects to introduce younger students to different kinds of emotions. Follow up with activities to introduce students to multiple ways of regulating their emotions, such as mindfulness strategies, an emotions log, or talking to a trusted adult.
- Treat conflict as an opportunity to learn. If conflict arises, involve other students to act as mediators and remind them of the steps to resolve conflict that were previously agreed upon.
- Nurture the development of a kindness mindset by integrating the practice of kindness into the students' daily routine.

8

Ethical Leadership

Nearly all men can stand adversity, but if you want to test a man's character, give him power.

—Abraham Lincoln—

Destruction of habitat, loss of biodiversity, and climate change are just a few of the crises facing the modern world. Our society is well aware of these problems, and efforts have been made to mitigate them. Nevertheless, achieving a better future demands a strong commitment and sustained and systemic efforts led by highly capable leaders.

Most important, we need leaders who are not only able to persuade and motivate others, but also capable of making wise decisions by embodying values such as responsibility, respect, excellence, and integrity. This is why we added the word *ethical* before *leadership* when naming this essential life skill. We define *Ethical Leadership* as the ability to influence, motivate, and lead others based on responsibility, respect, excellence, and integrity.

Why Is Ethical Leadership Important?

We argue that Ethical Leadership is essential for three reasons. Specifically, it (1) sharpens the ability to make self-thought and adaptive decisions, (2) helps to develop good character, and (3) fosters respect for and responsibility toward others and the sustainability of the environment.

Self-Thought and Adaptive Decisions

We believe that the ultimate goal of learning is for students to be able to do their own analysis and make sound decisions—"self-thought and adaptive decisions." We want them to be decision makers who are thoughtful and reflective. Students make self-thought and adaptive decisions by asking questions that are guided by conscious planning and aimed at benefiting themselves or their community. The capacity to make self-thought, or "actor-centered" (Goldberg & Podell, 1999) adaptive decisions, is determined by the brain's *executive function* and *executive skills*. Experts describe *executive function* as a cognitive process involved in planning, prioritizing, and organizing (Center on the Developing Child, 2019; McCloskey et al., 2009; Meltzer, 2018). The cognitive process is about organizing information and making connections. *Executive skills* help individuals engage or focus, process working memory, be agile and flexible, and think analytically and at a higher-order level. They support metacognitive processing required for making decisions, finding solutions, and setting long-term goals.

We believe that choice is an important component of developing students' executive function. The principles of a democratic learning atmosphere—achieved by means such as developing classroom rules with students and implementing logical consequences—drive classroom activities. Teachers act as motivator, facilitator, advisor, and evaluator.

In our school, students practice making decisions through structures for learning such as Plan-Do-Review (PDR), Making Good Choices (MGC), and Project-Based Cycle (PBC). Making decisions also entails a great deal of communication. For example, in certain stages of the PBC, students need to work on their project collaboratively, proposing their own ideas for the best solution. As developing leaders, they must be able to see the big picture, use reliable sources, and engage in effective analysis to capitalize on their team members' ideas as a basis to make decisions to reach the common goal.

Good Character

To cultivate good character and the principles of ethics in every student, schools need to provide lots of opportunities for each student to apply empathetic social skills, share their opinions, respect different perspectives, and practice being ethical leaders, along with clear expectations and opportunities to learn from their mistakes.

The concept of "good character" encompasses a lot of different behaviors. Travis Bradberry and Jean Greaves (2012) define character as "a cohesive approach to conducting yourself, interacting with others, and representing the organization" (pp. 205–206). The character traits that are specifically related to leadership are "integrity, credibility, and valuing differences (acting on the belief that everyone has something to offer)" (p. 41).

Developing character obviously takes a lot of time, modeling, experience, and reflection. What's more, "character" is a complex concept. In the lower-elementary grades, the concept can be clarified by using language younger children are more likely to understand—"honesty" in place of "integrity," for example, or "respecting differences" rather than "valuing differences." It's true that these concepts are also fairly abstract; K–1 teachers can make them more concrete by weaving them into read-aloud activities or games in morning meeting's group activity. Regarding "valuing differences," as we have mentioned before, students at our school are exposed to lots of differences in our multiage classrooms, with many different cultures represented. Students recite a pledge every morning—"Respect myself, everyone, and everything"—which reinforces the importance of respecting differences.

In upper grades, the discussion can get deeper and take more forms. An example from an 11th grade English language arts class involved a project in which students were asked to create poems under the topic of various values, one of which was integrity. A student wrote a poem (see Figure 8.1) describing what integrity means using key phrases from the rubric.

FIGURE 8.1
Example of a Student's Written Work on Integrity

> Integrity, a priceless treasure,
> Valuable beyond measure.
> Integrity stands up for what they believe is right and builds trust
> A virtue that's a must.
>
> A person with integrity has a strong sense of self
> And behaves with conscience and consideration
> Towards ethical values in the community.
>
> A person with integrity dares to express concern about any wrongdoing
> And make an effort to correct them.
> Integrity creates harmony.

Respect and Responsibility Toward Others and the Sustainability of the Environment

The ability and conscious effort to behave responsibly is said to be one of the major reasons why a person excels in life (Zenger, 2015). The value of respect and responsibility underlies the major qualities any individual needs in order to be successful and thrive in any situation. In our school, we explicitly teach about values, specifically respect and responsibility toward others. Students have opportunities, tailored to their developmental levels, to discuss and create their own insights regarding these values.

Our students begin to practice self-respect and responsibility in preschool. Teachers use concrete examples, such as being responsible by cleaning up materials we have used. Then the concept moves to a broader realm, away from self and into the community. In leadership roles, students practice respecting their team members' opinions and ideas and fulfilling their responsibilities as a leader. We instill the mindset of "I am responsible for helping my team to succeed."

The recent acceleration of the climate change crisis, with its global impact, places an even greater importance on the need for future leaders to be respectful of the environment and responsible in creating a sustainable future. At our school, we instill a love of the earth at every grade level, from early childhood through high school. We encourage students to use found materials from nature or recycled items to create their products. Elementary students are given the choice to create a sustainable project for their Making Good Choices project, and middle school students are required to create a project as a solution for one of their chosen Sustainable Development Goals. High school students create projects that have a wider impact, such as creating an online source of learning materials for children in remote areas.

Key Elements of Ethical Leadership

As shown in Figure 8.2 (see p. 184), the essential skill of Ethical Leadership has three elements: (1) *sound decision making*, (2) *personal integrity*, and (3) *developing oneself and others with a growth mindset*. Let's examine each of these in turn.

Sound Decision Making

Essentially, all decisions made by leaders must focus on problem solving. For this reason, it is crucial for leaders to have analytical and systematic thinking skills, as well as conceptual knowledge. This ability is indispensable, especially for making difficult decisions at the right time. We define *sound decision making* as the ability to determine the right decision from alternative solutions based on complex argument and systematic, valid, and well-supported generalization, considering the team

Sound decision making involves two important concepts: (1) Expert Thinking (one of the essential life skills) in making decisions and (2) respecting different perspectives.

members' perspectives and multiple factors surrounding the issue. *Sound decision making* involves two important concepts: (1) Expert Thinking (one of the essential life skills) in developing the ability to make sound decisions and (2) respecting different perspectives.

FIGURE 8.2
The Key Elements of Ethical Leadership

To make the right decisions, leaders must have both conceptual and practical knowledge of areas related to the world in which they are involved. At the same time, leaders must consider the issues from multiple perspectives and interests and have empathy, which is important for understanding the emotional aspects of others in the decision-making process.

Nurturing expert thinking

Sound decision making requires the ability to make decisions that are analytical, systematic, critical, creative, and ethical. From the concept of leadership to its practical application, "decisiveness" is the key to becoming a good leader. Leaders are required to understand "what needs to be done" and "the right thing to do." We aim to develop ethical leaders who know how to control disruptive impulses and moods, avoid premature judgment, and think thoroughly before deciding on a course of action (Emmerling & Goleman, (2003).

In preschool, students need to have hands-on and minds-on experiences, with opportunities throughout the learning process to make decisions. The students do this with the support of their teachers to arrive at the best solution. Research has shown that preschoolers are capable of making simple decisions for themselves (Schweinhart et al., 2005). As students are able to focus on a goal (Berk, 2017), we expect them to make simple decisions for themselves regarding daily matters, such as what activities to do during a certain routine or which area they want to play in, or even to find a solution for a social conflict they are facing. However, because of their natural egocentrism, we are not expecting them to make these decisions in consideration of others. An example of a student-initiated decision-making routine in our preschool is the Plan-Do-Review, a 50- to 65-minute period in which the children decide what they want to do, how they want to do it, and with whom they will be working.

Students in the elementary grades are able to decide on a simple solution based on comparison of concrete objects and experiences, after listening to team members' opinions, though the decision reached still favors the individual student's opinion. As students are able to express their opinions, teachers should provide a choice of activities in which the options are meaningful and beneficial. Students make sound decisions, based on alternative good choices facilitated by the teachers. Teachers can start the learning activities by designing games or role-plays. They should emphasize the vocabulary being used (as appropriate to the grade level), such as *decision*, *solution*, and *opinion*. These words are then posted on the wall, so students will remember them and understand what they mean.

Leaders are called on to solve complex problems. They must make the necessary decisions fluently, through analytical and systematic thinking—a process we call "Expert Thinking." It is similar to what Bob Iger, CEO of the Walt Disney Company, described as "decisiveness," when we wrote that "all decisions, no matter how difficult, can and should be made in a timely way" (quoted in Scipioni, 2019, para. 18). At the same time, leaders must also make *informed* decisions. They must have both conceptual knowledge and, in a business environment, practical knowledge about the marketplace and its changing dynamics. It is also critical to align the perspectives and interests of the stakeholders after consulting reliable sources.

Teachers can facilitate the nurturing of sound decision making by providing choice-based activities, projects, and events. In our school, we hold Conscious Business Day, an event that asks students to plan and initiate their own sustainable business by considering not just profit but also the planet, people, and purpose. Through this event, we aim to create self-regulated leaders who can envision their purpose in solving problems related to social and natural phenomena. They develop an entrepreneurial spirit dedicated to a sustainable economy, establish a pattern of mindful social and economic behavior, find a purpose to support economic growth, exercise a sense of responsibility toward the environment, and apply math, financial literacy, art, and digital literacy in a real-life situation.

Nurturing the ability to respect different perspectives

Decision-making ability is indeed the key trait of a leader. It is the capacity to know and decide the right thing to do, and in the process of doing so, ethical leaders consider other perspectives and have empathy for people. It is important to understand the emotional aspect of every person they are dealing with. Leaders need to implement organizational justice (Bradberry & Greaves, 2012), which enables them to always be transparent and act based on the truth.

Leaders must be able to convince and inspire their team members. People need to feel that their ideas and efforts are valued and respected. Each team member should be asked for their ideas and opinions and to contribute toward achieving the group goal. This approach encourages a constructive classroom environment and school culture that are conducive to achieving the goals of Ethical Leadership.

In nurturing respect for different perspectives, students need to understand that it is normal for people to have different perspectives on the same matter. This understanding enables them to be open to the idea of listening to different opinions and responding without any resentment.

In preschool and the lower-elementary grades, where, as we've noted, egocentrism may hinder students from accepting different perspectives, they can be exposed to routines that require them to listen to others and to follow. Consider, for example, a K–1 class in which students are about to transition from the main classroom to another classroom, such as art, and one student stands at the front of the line as the leader. The teacher may ask the leader to decide on a new way to walk to the other classroom, such as walking while waving. As the students walk, the teacher sings, "Follow, follow, follow Laqeesha. She is the leader now!" As a prerequisite to this activity, younger students need to be exposed to the word *leader*. Teachers can provide this exposure through various methods, including reading books about leaders, discussing the concept, and using tools such as the Vocabulary Detective Graphic Organizer we mentioned in Chapter 2.

Another example for elementary students (Grade 4–5) would be Vocabulary Bingo, which can be done as an exploratory activity at the beginning of the academic year or as fluency practice during transition times. The targeted vocabulary terms are taken from the rubric (e.g., *decision, solution, generalization, comparison, data, consideration, opinion, represent, majority*). The teacher presents the targeted vocabulary words in a grid and prepares the definitions of each vocabulary term. Students draw their own grid and place the words in any columns on their own grid. The teacher then reads the definition aloud and students get to cross the mentioned word. When students have crossed out the whole line across, diagonally, or vertically, they yell out "Bingo!" (see Figure 8.3).

FIGURE 8.3
Example of a Vocabulary Bingo Game

decision	solution	generalization
comparison	data	consideration
opinion	represent	majority

By middle school and high school, students have the developmental readiness they need to accept different perspectives. Students in middle school need to know how to determine the best solution by considering alternatives, team members' perspectives, and the surrounding factors. A teacher might introduce the word *perspective* by showing an optical-illusion image literally depicting multiple perceptions. When the teacher asks students to interpret the picture, they soon realize that they interpret it differently from other classmates, depending on how they see and process the information. Teachers can also create games based on current issues that involve multiple perspectives, giving students another way to practice this ability. An example might be preparing "case cards" featuring specific examples of world problems (e.g., hunger, war, climate change events) and asking students to share their opinion about a particular case while paying attention to the perspectives of others. At the end of the sharing, the class reconfirms their understanding of what "perspectives" means and what to do when dealing with different perspectives.

Another way to engage students in practicing Ethical Leadership is by questioning. During collaborative activities, for example, teachers might prompt students to consider multiple perspectives ("What might another take on this topic be?" "What factors might influence how someone sees this issue?"), sound decision-making practice ("What factors do we need to consider before making a decision?" "What *else* might you take into account?"), personal integrity ("What is the basis for your decision?" "How can you respect your values and norms and still find the best solution?"), and the development of a growth mindset ("How might you approach this task next time?" "How could you apply your strengths to reach a new goal?").

As part of the exposure to the skill of Ethical Leadership, including the need to consider various perspectives, a high school teacher conducted an activity on the topic of "Great Leaders in History." Students came up with a list of names of famous leaders from all over the world, including Nelson Mandela, Mahatma Gandhi, Cleopatra, and Napoleon Bonaparte. Students then divided themselves into groups of four, and each group chose a name for a debate on whether that person had enough traits to be called an "ethical leader." Each group had an affirmative team and an opposition team that came up with arguments to support their position. The arguments gave the students the opportunity to learn to listen to others' perspectives. During the debate, the two sides needed to refute the other's stance, and afterward, they wrote a reflection describing what they learned from the other team.

Personal Integrity

An individual's *personal integrity* is significant because it contributes to the creation of a civilized community. It concerns the overall values that shape one's profile—a combination of honesty, kindness, respect, accountability, and other elements that can establish good character. People with *personal integrity* are committed to their words, actions, and beliefs. We define *personal integrity* as the ability to demonstrate conscience, behaving in

Personal integrity incorporates two important concepts: (1) integrity and (2) responsibility and accountability.

consideration of others and the environment, being responsible and accountable, and standing up for what is right. *Personal integrity* incorporates two important concepts: (1) integrity and (2) responsibility and accountability.

Integrity can be displayed by entities such as an organization and can be a core value of an organization. *Personal integrity,* however, is a quality of an individual. Leaders who have personal integrity are always transparent and act honestly. They have a strong social conscience and live their lives with the aim of contributing to the good of society and the world (responsibility and accountability). In addition, they reflect honestly on their mistakes, and they ask themselves whether the decisions they make benefit only themselves or everyone in the community.

Teachers need to emphasize the notion of "Be Truthful, Do My Best, and Be Accountable" as a guide for students as they practice personal integrity. Teachers should also encourage students to truthfully reflect at the end of each day by self-evaluating their performance—what they were proud of, what they struggled with, whether they have faced challenges, and how they worked to overcome the challenges they faced.

Nurturing integrity

When nurturing integrity in preschool or the early-elementary grades, teachers can simplify the abstract nature of the concept by using the word *honesty* and providing concrete examples through stories, videos, or games. For example, a teacher read aloud the storybook *A Funny Thing Happened on the Way to School* by Benjamin Chaud and Davide Cali. The book is about a boy who is late to school and gives his teacher a series of out-of-this-world excuses. When the reading was complete, the teacher asked the students if they had ever experienced being late to school and what the reasons for their lateness were. She invited everyone to self-reflect: How honest were they with their excuses? Could they have been more honest? Would that have been a better choice?

In an upper-grade example, a high school teacher assigned students, organized in small groups, to read books about famous figures who lived with integrity. Some of the groups read a biography of Aristides, the Athenian leader praised by Socrates and Herodotus as "the best and most honorable man that Athens ever produced." Another group read about Aung San Suu Kyi, the leader of the National League for Democracy in Burma. After reading, the students filled out a Frayer model graphic organizer (Frayer et al., 1969, as cited in Buehl, 2014) to write their insight and understanding of integrity (see Figure 8.4, p. 190).

FIGURE 8.4
Frayer Model Graphic Organizer for Integrity

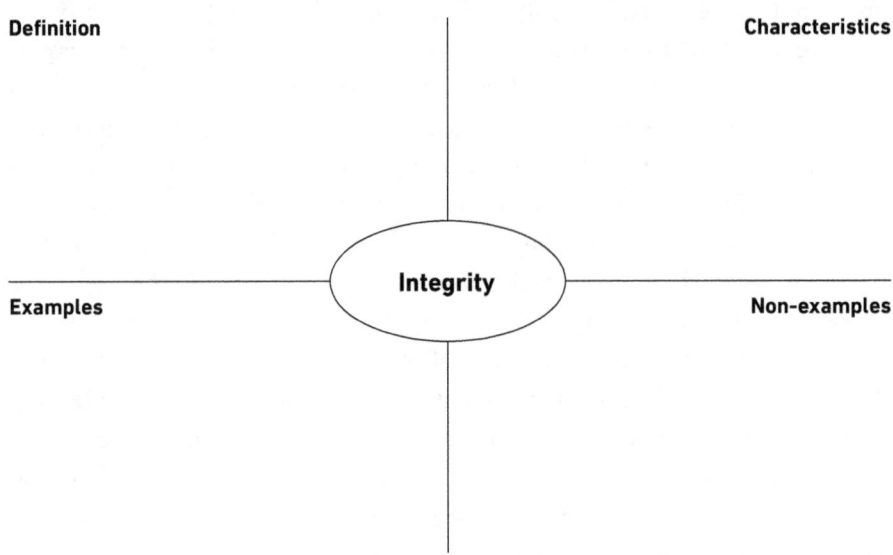

Another high school teacher engaged students in practicing integrity through small-group discussion during advisory time. Students were given cases related to academic integrity issues such as plagiarism and violation of intellectual property. The students used the following questions to guide their discussions:

- What defines an individual's actions as having integrity?
- What role does honesty play in integrity?
- In various situations, how can we ensure that an individual is consistent with his or her moral principles, no matter what?
- In your daily life, when do you think you need to show integrity? How can you show it?
- How important do you think integrity is?
- How important is personal integrity in being a leader?

Nurturing responsibility and accountability

To help students understand and practice the concept of responsibility, teachers at any grade level can assign them simple classroom chores. In a preschool class, a job chart shows students who is responsible for tasks such as watering the plants and feeding the fish. In a Grade 2–3 class, the job chart is titled "Class Responsibility." In addition to the simpler tasks designated for preschool students, the chart also includes roles such as "transition leaders" for students who are responsible for leading others when moving to, for example, art class.

In high school, an English language arts teacher incorporated the concepts of responsibility and accountability as the students learned about rhetoric in advertisements. The students looked at advertisements that could be deemed responsible or irresponsible, and they addressed the question of who should be accountable for the release of those that were irresponsible. After studying different examples, pairs of students discussed the matter of responsibility and accountability using the following questions as a guide:

- What does it mean to be responsible and accountable? How does it translate to the case of advertisements?
- How do we implement responsibility in managing our time and juggling multiple tasks and assignments?
- How can we show that we are being responsible and accountable for our actions?
- How can we ensure that we put the common good above our own interests?
- How do responsibility and accountability relate to integrity?

Developing Oneself and Others with a Growth Mindset

Leaders achieve excellence by developing themselves and others by embracing a growth mindset, in which talents and abilities are developed through consistent effort. Rather than simply looking for talented individuals, leaders build and surround themselves with strong players. They devote time and energy to advancing their performance and that of the team, thereby strengthening the organization. In a school setting,

Developing oneself and others with a growth mindset combines three notions—(1) growth mindset, (2) responsibility, and (3) excellence—under a single umbrella.

a supportive environment is designed to provide children with the opportunity to grow, to make mistakes, and to learn from their experience. We make room for mistakes and, therefore, for improvement. We also engage students in self-reflection about how they have helped others, using questions such as "Who did you help today? What kind of help did you offer?"

We define *developing oneself and others with a growth mindset* as the ability to identify the areas of improvement that oneself and others require and grow with a positive attitude and persistence in achieving the common goal. The overarching concept combines three notions—(1) growth mindset, (2) responsibility, and (3) excellence—under one umbrella.

Nurturing growth mindset, responsibility, and excellence

What is most important to understand about a growth mindset, responsibility, and excellence is that the focus of good leadership is not on controlling team members to simply follow what the leader wants. Leaders need to empower others to embrace the vision, mission, direction, and strategy of an organization to achieve common goals and strive for excellence. Team members need to know the influencing factors in their environment and to understand what contributions are needed for success—and why.

In the school setting, teachers must avoid giving praise, rewards, and punishment to develop students' growth mindset. The HighScope Educational Research Foundation advises against using rewards and punishment to shape behavior, as does psychologist and author Carol Dweck (2006). Teachers who use praise, rewards such as stickers, and punishment should reconsider their approach. A better approach is to acknowledge what the students actually do.

For example, in a preschool classroom, when a student eventually was able to open a bottle lid after a couple of tries, he told his teacher, "I did it!" To acknowledge his effort, the teacher responded, "You worked hard to open the bottle by yourself." In another example, a student accidentally spilled his milk on the table, which led the teacher to say, "We spill our milk sometimes. What can you do to clean it?" The student responded, "I know, Miss—with tissue." When that didn't work, the teacher encouraged the student by saying, "You have tried to wipe it off, yet there is still some left on the floor. That's fine. Sometimes our ideas might not work perfectly. Let's try and find new ways to clean up." In this example, the teacher was teaching the student to be persistent and empowering him to fix his own mistakes. This approach helps to create the perspective of a growth mindset in young students.

As students grow older, they practice this ability when they show persistence in the face of obstacles and find alternatives to reach a goal. Students embody a growth mindset when they believe that they can improve no matter what situation they are in and identify what they can do. The growth mindset becomes a critical concept and the established norm in middle and high school classrooms. Students identify improvements that others could strive for, taking on the role of leader and motivating their team members to do better.

To establish the norm, teachers need to design learning opportunities in which students are able to continuously learn from each other. For example, without asking the teacher for help, a student who is having trouble completing an assignment can ask another student for help. At our school, students can refer to agreed-upon steps to take when they are stuck or facing difficulties: (1) check resources to learn more, (2) discuss and ask your friends, and (3) go to the teachers. Because our school defines "competition" in terms of measuring one's achievement against rubrics, not by competing against each other, this way of thinking is part of our school's atmosphere. We value collaboration in the sense that students should help each other to reach their individual levels of development and achievement.

Teachers should also build students' understanding of the role of feedback from teachers, peers, and others. Students should be able to communicate with team members who make mistakes, without hurting the others' feelings, because an established norm encourages them to actively ask for and provide feedback. Students also are encouraged to influence others to have a growth mindset by identifying and informing their peers about areas that need improvement. They provide suggestions and help their peers learn from constructive feedback to ensure that everyone fulfills their responsibility to achieve the group goal. When students are able to understand their team members' strengths, they can motivate them to accomplish the goal.

Teachers can infuse *developing oneself and others with a growth mindset* in the learning process in various ways. When organizing group activities, teachers can assign a leader in each group, recording and tracking leader assignments in a log so that all students have opportunities to be the leader in various contexts and for different lengths of time—everything from a leader of the day's morning activity to the leader of an extended, cross-curricular group project.

Once a group activity is organized and all groups have a leader, the teacher should ask all students to reflect on the poster reminder of Ethical Leadership, articulated in the rubric. They should be reminded of the characteristics of an ethical leader, focusing on the element of *developing oneself and others with a growth mindset*.

As the group discussions begin, teachers monitor and take notes on how students implement the leadership skills. Near the end of the lesson, teachers can ask the students to reflect on their group work, prompting them with questions such as these:

- What sound decisions did your group make?
- What process did you follow to make these decisions?
- What were your individual contributions to the group's decisions?
- Did the decisions involve resolving conflicts in values? How did you resolve these conflicts?

Teachers then share the assessment findings with the whole class and provide feedback or acknowledgment to the student leader. They might also ask the leaders to rate themselves on a scale of 1 to 5 on how well they identified their team members' areas of improvement and to self-reflect on who they helped and how. Leaders can share their rating using a show of hands. Finally, to end the lesson, teachers can remind all students to continue practicing these leadership skills.

How Is Ethical Leadership Measured and Assessed?

As with the other essential life skills, we created a rubric to assess students' development in Ethical Leadership (see Figure 8.5). The rubric describes the behaviors at each continuum level, from Early to Expert, and covers the three elements of *sound decision making, personal integrity,* and *developing oneself and others with a growth mindset.* The rubric represents these elements as EL.1, EL.2, and EL.3, respectively. The rubric also describes three stages of development:

- Stage 1: Student performs a task somewhat accurately with consistent guidance from others (teachers and peers).
- Stage 2: Student performs a task accurately with little guidance and redirection from others (teachers and peers).
- Stage 3: Student independently performs a task with ease, speed, and accuracy.

The elements of Ethical Leadership evolve based on students' psychological development as they mature. The behaviors we describe in the following sections represent our indicators for the element of *sound decision making* at each developmental level. Recall that we define *sound decision making* as the ability to determine the right decision from alternative solutions based on complex argument and systematic, valid, and well-supported generalization, considering the team members' perspectives and multiple factors surrounding the issue. To see students' progression in Ethical Leadership, teachers

FIGURE 8.5
Rubric for Ethical Leadership

		Early (Preschool–K)	Beginning (K–3)	Transition (3–6)	Developing (6–9)	Expert 9–12
EL.1	Sound Decision Making	• Makes simple decisions based on concrete objects and experiences, to answer his/her own questions of interest and to take action.	• Decides on a simple solution based on the comparison of concrete objects and experiences, after listening to team members' opinions, although the decision reached still favors her/his opinion.	• Decides on a solution based on the generalization of data comparison and considering team members' opinions that represent the majority of the group.	• Decides on the best solution from several alternatives based on the generalization of data analysis by considering team members' perspectives and surrounding factors.	• Decides on the best solution with consideration of other team members' opinions, using complex arguments, based on systematic, valid, and well-supported generalization.
		Stage 1 2 3	Stage 1 2 3	Stage 1 2 3	Stage 1 2 3	Stage 1 2 3
EL.2	Personal Integrity	• Is honest based on own thinking. • Respects classroom expectations. • Fulfills a set of agreed-upon responsibilities.	• Is truthful (core values: integrity), does their best (core values: excellence). • Explains how their behavior affects others (core values: respect). • Admits mistakes when asked. • Fulfills a set of agreed-upon responsibilities to maintain good relationships (core values: responsibilities).	• Is trustworthy by making the right choice even when no one is watching. • Understands core values (respect, responsibility, integrity, excellence). • Fulfills a set of agreed-upon responsibilities; is accountable for personal actions. • Admits mistakes without being asked based on awareness of heart and mind.	• Upholds core values (respect, responsibility, integrity, excellence) by fulfilling a set of agreed-upon responsibilities. • Is accountable for ethical behavior and/or environment. • Demonstrates flexibility in different contexts. • Expresses concern about any wrongdoing based on heart and mind.	• Has a strong sense of self and high self-esteem. • Behaves by conscience in consideration of ethical values on community and/or environment. • Expresses concern about any wrongdoings and makes an effort to correct them as part of their accountability to create harmony.
		Stage 1 2 3	Stage 1 2 3	Stage 1 2 3	Stage 1 2 3	Stage 1 2 3

(*continued*)

FIGURE 8.5
Rubric for Ethical Leadership—*(continued)*

	Early (Preschool–K)	Beginning (K–3)	Transition (3–6)	Developing (6–9)	Expert 9–12
EL.3 Growth Mindset Development	• Shows enjoyment of learning, based on interest, to improve him/herself to achieve goals.	• Demonstrates responsibility for his/her own learning and begins to notice that others may need help to improve themselves so they can achieve a common goal.	• Takes charge of his/her own learning and shows ability to help others improve when achieving a common goal.	• Models how to take charge of self-improvement to inspire others to improve when achieving a common goal.	• Takes charge of self-empowerment and optimally utilizes his/her own potential to mobilize self and others toward a common goal.
	Stage 1 2 3	Stage 1 2 3	Stage 1 2 3	Stage 1 2 3	Stage 1 2 3

Stage 1: Student performs a task somewhat accurately with consistent guidance from others (teachers and peers).

Stage 2: Student performs a task accurately with little guidance and redirection from others (teachers and peers).

Stage 3: Student independently performs a task with ease, speed, and accuracy.

can collect evidence from sources such as observation, conversation with students, and students' projects and presentations.

Early (Preschool–K)

Children start practicing decision making as early as they can communicate their thoughts. Students in preschool and kindergarten demonstrate an ability for *sound decision making* by making a simple decision for themselves based on concrete objects and experiences, to answer their own question of interest, and to take action.

Let's take a look at Bella, a K–1 student who demonstrated this essential skill by making a simple decision during a group-work session. Students were choosing an activity for a Multicultural Week presentation on facts related to West Java. As a group, they could choose to color batik designs, make traditional clothes for dolls, create models of typical foods, or draw traditional musical instruments. While her group mates were still discussing the choices, Bella raised her hand and said to the teacher, "I want to color batik." When her friends discussed what to choose, Bella raised her hand again and said, "Miss, I just want batik. My mom wears it all the time. I want to see what it's like if I color it myself." The teacher then asked her to discuss the choice with her friends again and come up with a group consensus. After the discussion, the group agreed with the choice of coloring batik designs. They later presented their work in front of the class.

Based on the expectations in the rubric and evidence such as the conversation just described and Bella's presentation, her teacher can conclude that she is at Stage 3 for this element. She is capable of making her own decision in choosing the activity she wants, and the decision was not influenced by her teammates' preferences. She made the decision for herself, not persuaded by others.

Beginning (Grades K–3)

At the Beginning level, students should be able to decide on simple solutions by comparing concrete objects and listening to other team members' opinions. Billy is a Grade 2–3 student who demonstrated this behavior in his group. During a science lesson on living and nonliving things, Billy and his group members worked to create a product that represented one of these two categories. During the initial discussion, Billy asked his group, "What are we going to make?" Charlie, a teammate, responded, "I want to make a robot. It's a nonliving thing." Betsy replied, "No, I want to make paper dolls," and Sally said, "I want to make something about animals." Billy listened and said, "I went to the zoo, and it was very fun! I think we should make a video about animals in the zoo. It will be more interesting because people can watch it and not only look at robots or paper dolls. Guys, your ideas are great. Let's decide by comparing and contrasting our ideas." Billy listened to other ideas, as well as peer feedback. The group members worked together to compare the proposed ideas. After everyone looked at the comparisons, they agreed to Billy's idea to create a video about animals.

This anecdote shows how a Grade 2–3 student like Billy is capable of deciding on a simple solution to the question of choosing a product for his group project. The evidence includes his comparison of the experience of going to the zoo with the objects of robots and paper dolls; his listening to all the team members' opinions; and his deciding on a solution—in this case, a product—based on his personal experience. The teacher might gather other evidence, such as asking him to explain how he arrives at decisions. Based on the observations (anecdotal notes), graphic organizers, and his submitted work, Billy is at Level 3—capable of independently deciding on simple solutions.

Transition (Grades 3–6)

Students at this level are able to decide on a solution by generalizing and comparing data and analyzing the group's majority opinion. Students combine ideas from multiple sources to support their decision making.

Group discussion during a project is one of many opportunities to observe and assess this skill. Consider the following, from a Grade 4–5 class in which students were working on a social studies project under the topic of Rights, Obligations, and Responsibilities. One group, led by their appointed leader, Chase, decided to personalize the topic:

Chase: Why don't brainstorm problems we face every day—problems related to rights, obligations, or responsibilities? For example, my mom always scolds me in the morning for not getting up on time and not getting ready faster. These are my responsibilities, but I'm not really meeting them. So that's a problem I want to solve. You can share your problems too. I'll write them all down so we can find the similarities. Then we can pick the problem that most people experience and make solving it the mission of our project. What do you think?

Sonny: Sounds good. And I also have a problem leaving my house to get to school on time. My mom always yells at me, telling me to hurry up.

Debby: I have the same problem. My mom is just like your mom. She always says I'm going to be late if I don't move faster.

Brian: My problem is that there's so much work to do. I just want to play my games instead of doing all my assignments!

Sara: Well, my problem is my little sister. She always comes into my room, messes things up, and then leaves, or she just randomly presses keys on my laptop. She basically destroys my things.

Chase: Oh, I found a similarity. Let me know what you think. It seems like Sonny, Debby, and Brian, all three of you have problems with time. Sara, you have a problem with your little sister. If we have to make a generalization, then maybe it's that most of us have problems in managing our time. What do you think?

Sara: Actually, I think I have the time problem, too. You know I love singing, right? Once I sing, I can't stop, and then I just get distracted from my homework.

Chase: So, what do you say if we decide that our mission should be "Getting Better at Managing Our Time"?

The group agreed and continued to the next steps: gathering data about how to manage time effectively.

To rate Chase's performance, the teacher considered multiple pieces of evidence, including the notes he took and the graphic organizer the group created, her own observation, a piece of Chase's essay that explained how a leader exhibits essential steps to arrive at a sound decision, and the results of a peer evaluation in which his team members indicated whether they felt their ideas and solutions were appreciated. After examining all the multiple pieces of evidence, the teacher concluded that Chase was at Stage 3, as he was able to independently decide on a solution based on the generalization of problems his teammates were facing.

Developing (Grades 6–9)

At this stage, students develop the ability to decide on the best solution from several alternatives by generalizing the data in a data analysis in a way that considers team members' perspectives and surrounding factors. As an example, let's return again to Reuben, the Grade 8–9 student who was working on a waste management project to solve the problem of trash in the school cafeteria.

As recounted in Chapter 5 on Audience-Centered Communication, Reuben read several articles and, based on data gathered from those resources, came up with a generalized conclusion regarding desirable characteristics of automated trash bins, related to design, materials, and features. He concluded that the best automated trash bins have features such as sensors, automatic lids, and voice activation and are made of stainless steel, which is durable and easy to clean. In reaching his conclusion, however, Reuben had not considered his team members' ideas, including bins made of different materials and having different features. His teacher needed to guide him by asking whether he had considered his team members' ideas and how he would decide on the best solution from several alternatives. Reuben got back to his teammates, and, working together, they analyzed different possibilities, including the pros and cons of each. Figure 8.6 shows a summary of their analysis.

Reuben was able to consider different alternatives and surrounding factors to decide how the alternatives could help the team reach its goal—using the waste management tool (the trash bins) for social campaigns related to the litter problem. He needed only a bit of support in considering his team members' perspectives. Based on the evidence from the conversation between Reuben and the teacher, the graphic organizer, his presentation, and peer feedback, Reuben is still at Stage 2.

In another case, Lisa, a Grade 8–9 student who was working on the same project in a different group, gathered perspectives from her teammates on each idea for a solution. She reminded everyone to focus on their big goal and considered her teammates' perspectives to come up with the best solution. She also was able to summarize how she had used sound decision making. The evidence indicated that Lisa is at Stage 3 because she was able to independently lead the discussion within her team to decide on the best solution out of several alternatives.

Expert (Grades 9–12)

At the Expert level, students decide on the best solution with consideration of other team members' opinions, using complex arguments based on systematic, valid, and well-supported generalization. They are able to evaluate the solutions from several perspectives that best serve the interest of the group.

To assess skills in *sound decision making*, teachers can observe and prompt students with questions about how they decide on the best solutions with consideration of other team members' opinions and how they back up those decisions with valid arguments. Additionally, teachers can consider how students evaluate their solutions through their graphic organizer, project log, and presentation.

FIGURE 8.6
Example of a Team Analysis for a Group Project

Goal	Utilize the waste management tool for social campaigns		
Options	**Automated trash bin**	**Waste segregation**	**Composting system**
Pros	Sensor and coding (with recorded voice) enables social campaign: • Opening trash bin is not disgusting anymore because its sensor detects our hand and opens the lid automatically. • The recorded voice says thank you or other acknowledgment to remind students to put the trash where it belongs.	• Students get to separate waste in different bins. • The classification helps the waste collection officers collect the trash more easily.	Organic waste will be better organized
Cons	Without trash segregator, will not solve waste problem.	Needs to add different types of containers and "glue" them together.	Needs a very complex coding system for automation—not feasible.
Ideas to minimize cons	Place existing trash bins next to each other and put stickers of different colors to inform which bin is for which type of trash.	Place existing trash bins next to each other and put stickers of different colors to inform which bin is for which type of trash.	—
Conclusion	• Automated trash bins with a sensor are a good way to motivate students to put trash in its appropriate place. • Composting system is not feasible and might be more suitable as a separate project.		

Suggestions for Integrating Ethical Leadership into Curriculum and Classroom Practice

- Infuse an Ethical Leadership rubric into the curriculum standards and project-based learning by expecting students to make sound decisions based on multiple perspectives.
- Provide opportunities for students to become leaders.
- Explicitly teach values by teaching vocabulary words and providing opportunities for students to practice and experience values throughout learning.
- Allow students to make choices, to make mistakes and admit them, and to view those mistakes as opportunities to learn and grow.
- Infuse expectations in subject-area rubrics for students to develop a growth mindset, and encourage such development in others by asking questions that clarify expectations and taking action to help themselves and others meet these expectations, through means such as participating in school-based or community-based service projects.

9
Grading and Reporting Systems

*We don't assign grades to students—we assign grades to performance.
And just as performance is always temporary,
grades, too, should always be temporary.*
—Thomas Guskey—

Our focus throughout this book has been on helping students develop, by design, life skills that will support their success in our changing world. An essential component in that development process is grading and reporting—that is, gathering evidence on students' development of these skills to further guide and direct their progress and then reporting that progress to parents and families and to the students themselves.

In a comprehensive review of a century of research on grading, Tom and his colleague Susan Brookhart (Guskey & Brookhart, 2019) point out that most grading and reporting practices are based more on tradition than on established evidence of what benefits students. That evidence indicates that three of the most common problems in grading relate to subjectivity, reliability, and authenticity. *Subjectivity* occurs when teachers' views on particular student characteristics or behaviors influence the grades they assign to students' academic performance. *Reliability* problems arise when teachers don't agree on the purpose of grades, use evidence unrelated to the targeted knowledge or skills, or lack sufficient evidence to justify the grades they assign. *Authenticity* problems result when grades are presented as numbers or letters without a clear explanation of what those symbols represent. Despite these problems, the importance attached to grades often causes students to focus more on attaining high scores and getting good grades than they do on what they're learning and the skills they're developing.

Guskey and Brookhart (2019) further stress that students should never be labeled by grades or made to feel that they are incapable of learning and achieving important learning goals. Grades must always be regarded as a temporary record of students' achievement at a particular point in time as they progress along their learning journey. We want students to recognize that they are always moving forward, that hard work is important, and that they control the conditions of their success.

How can we accurately and reliably describe the development of future-ready, self-regulated leaders on a report card? How can we meaningfully communicate students' achievement of essential life skills across grade levels? Progressive learning calls for a progressive grading and reporting system, but what does that system look like?

Progressive Grading and Reporting

Grading and reporting involve communicating students' assessment results, based on learning standards, to students, parents, and families (Guskey & Brookhart, 2019). They require teachers to judge students' progress in regard to explicit learning goals. We typically express those judgments in terms of grades or numbers that describe different levels of student performance.

Reporting how well students achieve life skills requires documentation when students demonstrate certain behaviors based on developmentally appropriate goals and expectations. After analyzing many different kinds of grading and reporting formats, we decided to use analytic, criterion-referenced rubrics to report on students' progress in developing essential life skills. Our rubrics are two-dimensional, with stages of development and specific behavioral indicators for each essential life skill. The behavioral indicators reflect authentic abilities students are expected to display for each element of the skill. We chose the indicators from a review of the research on each essential life skill, and then refined them based on actual observation data of students across multiple ages, from early childhood to high school.

We developed our analytic, criterion-referenced rubrics to describe the expected behaviors of essential life skills at each developmental level. This allows for monitoring students' skill-development progress over years. These behaviors reflect the authentic capabilities of students and result in grades that meaningfully represent students' abilities in each of the skills.

We next determined the number of levels needed and how to differentiate each level. We began by specifying clear learning goals of what students at each continuum level need to know and be able to do as a result of their learning experiences (Guskey & Bailey, 2001). Clear goals make it easier for teachers to design their learning approach, lesson plans, and accompanying learning activities. To be more precise about how the performance is measured, we then considered what evidence we believe best shows students' mastery of the learning goals.

Criterion-Referenced Standards

Our entire approach focuses on criterion-referenced standards of student performance. We expect students to strive to attain these well-defined performance criteria and not compete against each other in the process. Shared learning goals encourage student collaboration because all students are striving to meet the same performance criteria. Because demonstrations of these life skills differ as students mature, we also need to ensure our standards are developmentally appropriate.

Our efforts led to a continuum rubric design that consists of five levels of life skills development:

- Early (Preschool–Kindergarten)
- Beginning (Kindergarten–Grade 3)
- Transition (Grade 3–6)
- Developing (Grade 6–9)
- Expert (Grade 9–12)

Each level identifies specific target behaviors and skills based on developmental abilities.

The most important aspect of the continuum rubrics is the expectation that each level be clearly communicated to students, as well as to parents and families. We believe when students understand the expectations, they become better judges of their own behavior and continuously self-reflect on what they need to do to improve.

Grade-level expectations overlap from the end of one continuum level to the beginning of the next level. Although we have targeted expectations for each grade level, we recognize that not all students develop at the same pace. Therefore, we allow flexibility in applying the continuum, noting each student's individual progress. Our goal is to ensure students develop a firm foundation at each level before advancing to the next level, based on their personal readiness. As an example, Figure 9.1 (see p. 206) shows part of our continuum rubric for Meta-Level Reflection.

To further clarify each child's level of development, we added stages of support within each level. These identify the amount of support students need to perform the expected behavior. At Stage 1, students can perform the task only with consistent guidance from others (teachers or peers). Students at Stage 2 need some guidance and redirection from others (teachers or

FIGURE 9.1
Excerpt from a Continuum Rubric

		Early (Preschool–K)				Beginning (K–3)				Transition (3–6)				Developing (6–9)				Expert (9–12)			
MLR.1 Conscious Planning		• Creates **plans** based on **self-interest** with detailed description (what, when, with whom) and sticks to the plan.				• Creates plans based on **interest** and **learning goals**. • Identifies information and skills needed and creates steps to achieve plans.				• Sets goals that are beneficial for self and others based on **purposeful interest** and learning goals. • Analyzes learned knowledge and skills needed and creates procedures to achieve the goals.				• Sets **thoughtful and responsible plans** based on **purposeful interest** and learning goals. • Supports the plans with arguments and procedures based on learned knowledge and skills to ensure adaptive approaches to achieve the goals.				• Sets **thoughtful plans** with clear measurement criteria, based on purposeful interest, vision of a sustainable future, and learning goals. • Supports the plans with reasoned arguments and adaptive strategies based on interdisciplinary knowledge and skills to surpass the goals.			
		Stage	1	2	3	Stage	1	2	3	Stage	1	2	3	Stage	1	2	3	Stage	1	2	3

peers) to complete the task. And at Stage 3, students perform the task independently and with ease, speed, and accuracy.

Multiple Sources of Evidence

To ensure reliability, validity, and fairness in grading and reporting, we need to consider multiple sources of evidence related to students' performance (Guskey & Bailey, 2001). *Reliability* refers to consistency in teachers' judgments of assessment results. For example, if three different teachers look at multiple sources of evidence on a student's performance and agree on the grade that level of performance represents, then the grading process can be considered reliable. The key to such consistency is agreement on the purpose of the grade and the authenticity of the evidence; that is, students must be assessed in real situations where they authentically implement or use the essential life skills.

Validity refers to alignment between the selected evidence and the learning goal. For example, if the learning goal requires students to draw appropriate and supportable conclusions based on available data, then the assessment should provide authentic evidence on how well students considered and interpreted data without being influenced by irrelevant factors such as extraneous behaviors, background characteristics, or other elements.

We designed our assessment system to use multiple sources of evidence for rating students on each essential life skill. Teachers may provide evidence from different subjects in any form, including anecdotal notes, students' products, presentation videos, interview notes, and so on, as long as the evidence addresses the goal of the performance standard. In addition, the most recent evidence of improved performance always replaces past evidence because it offers a more accurate portrayal of students' current level of development.

At the end of each academic year, students receive ratings from three different teachers on the development of their life skills. Each teacher is required to provide at least one evidence sample to support their rating. If the ratings are different, the teachers meet to present their evidence and discuss their ratings to reach consensus. Therefore, each student's life skills grades are based on different pieces of evidence from three teachers across three different subjects. (We describe the process in greater detail later in the chapter.)

Let's consider an example of multiple pieces of evidence for Synergistic Collaboration for a Grade 12 student. The following are excerpts from the

Synergistic Collaboration rubric for the Expert Level; they describe what is expected of the students:

- Understands the expectation of their own role in achieving the group's goal, completes the task with responsibility and excellence, and contributes ideas to ensure efficiency, effectiveness, and productivity toward surpassing the expectation of the group's goal.
- Acts as the "glue" of the team by acknowledging that every team member is a valuable asset for the team and by motivating others to achieve the group's goal.
- When finding a flaw in the group's decision or work process, tactfully points out the flaws and gives elaborate constructive suggestions that best serve the interest of the group's goal.
- Understands and bridges the limitations of virtual collaboration and adapts the netiquette to deal with the limitation.
- Takes an active role as a global citizen by initiating globally distributed collaboration using a purposeful and sophisticated integration of digital tools.

Evidence #1. In the beginning of the COVID-19 pandemic, 12th grader Michelle was distressed by the number of healthcare workers who had contracted the virus due to the lack of proper protective equipment. She wanted to do something about it. In talking with her biology teacher, Michelle learned about a global fund-raising movement to buy and distribute personal protective equipment for healthcare workers across the world. With the help of her teacher, Michelle was able to contact the administrator of this global effort and meet virtually with other participants in the movement. At this meeting, Michelle described her idea of making a calendar to be sold online that would include information to educate people about COVID-19 so they would be better able to protect themselves and others (see Figure 9.2). Money from online sales would be used to further fund this global movement.

To make the calendar, Michelle worked with two other students in her biology and literature classes, Tom and Adam. Their first task was to establish the role each would have in the project. Michelle's role was to write the information they wanted to share about the coronavirus. Tom's role was to design the calendar, and Adam took care of the online sales through an Instagram account. As they worked on the project, however, their roles overlapped, with Tom and Adam providing suggestions for content, Michelle and Adam recommending appropriate illustrations, and Michelle and Tom offering ideas on sales strategies.

FIGURE 9.2
Example of a Grade 12 Student's Product

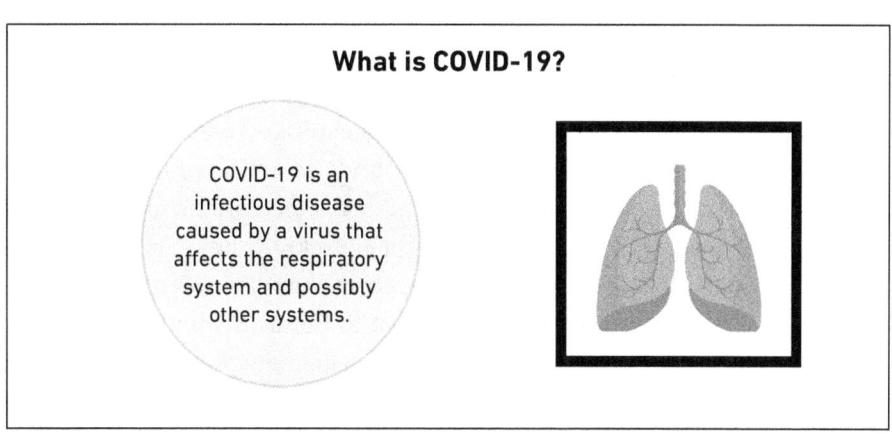

Evidence #2. On another project, Michelle collaborated with students from other countries in an event called a Global Innovation Challenge. Their team goal was to create an app to address the global-warming problem by empowering people to find and purchase environmentally friendly products. In this collaboration, Michelle's role was to develop the storyboard. In approaching their solution, Michelle and her group contacted the Greenpeace community, teachers, an environmental activist, an engineer, and a lawyer.

Evidence #3. Michelle also participated in a different kind of collaborative project, integrating AP psychology and a filmmaking course. She worked collaboratively with Teresa and Sasha to make a short movie on the topic of teenagers and social media. Teresa was interested in exploring social media's role in shaping teens' self-perception, whereas Sasha proposed covering teenagers' strategies for time management. She described how many of her friends miss homework and project deadlines because they spend too much time playing video games. Seeing Teresa and Sasha arguing about the topic of their short movie, Michelle suggested creating a pros-and-cons table to use in making their decision. Teresa and Sasha realized that arguing was not solving their problem, and listing the pros and cons for each option would allow them to make the decision more objectively. After analyzing their pros-and-cons table, the group decided that Teresa's idea of social media's effects on teenagers' views of themselves was the better option.

These three pieces of evidence show that Michelle was at Stage 3 for each element of Synergistic Collaboration. She was able to show *individual accountability*, *group cohesiveness*, *critical opinion*, and *virtual collaboration*.

Assessments for Learning

Grading and reporting depend on a fair and meaningful assessment system, which requires that teachers have a clear understanding of the definition of each essential life skill and the performance expectations for each level, especially the level they teach. They also need to know how the various life skills are linked through connecting elements in the rubrics of each essential life skill. We find that one of the best ways to build this understanding is through collaborative teacher discussions. Teachers work together to study the descriptors for each element and then use brainstorming sessions to consider possibilities for obtaining evidence for each descriptor in the rubric at their level. The procedure is outlined in Figure 9.3.

We believe in a comprehensive assessment approach that allows students to demonstrate their essential life skills in a variety of formats, receive meaningful feedback, and then reflect on their progress. We initiate the assessment process at the beginning of each academic year by having students map their current level for the essential life skills, based on last year's data. In some cases, teachers use skill-based preassessments to ensure the accuracy of the students' mapping. Teachers continually monitor students' progress and update students' mapping based on formative assessment data.

A critical element in the learning process is regular and descriptive feedback from both external and internal sources (for example, self-assessment through the essential life skill of Meta-Level Reflection) that communicates what students have done well and what they need to work on next.

FIGURE 9.3
Essential Life Skills Assessment Procedures

> Each student is assessed on the rubric description of the continuum level that matches the student's current ability. Teachers need to read the rubric description on the current, higher, and lower continuum level for perspective. Below is a general guideline of where to start with each student:
>
> - Grade K: Assess on Early level.
> - Grades 1 and 2–3: Assess on Beginning level.
> - Grade 4–5, 6: Assess on Transition level.
> - Grades 7, 8–9: Assess on Developing level.
> - Grades 10, 11, 12: Assess on Expert level.
>
> 1. Three (3) pieces of evidence from different subjects/sources need to be provided for each descriptor. Evidence can be in the form of anecdotal notes, photos, or videos of students' activity and work, each with detailed annotation. A piece of evidence may be used for more than one element or learner outcome.
>
> 2. Based on the evidence, three teachers will rate independently to decide whether a student is on—
>   - Stage 3: Student independently performs a task with ease, speed, and accuracy.
>   - Stage 2: Student performs a task accurately with little guidance and redirection from others (teachers and peers).
>   - Stage 1: Student performs a task somewhat accurately with consistent guidance from others (teachers and peers).
>
> The rating result for one descriptor from three different teachers will be combined into the final rating result, which determines the bar graph in the essential life skills report. The final rating result will be automatically concluded by the system based on majority rules. If all three teachers rate differently, the final rating will be determined through a discussion based on the evidence.

As mentioned earlier, the continuum rubrics for the essential life skills describe stages of development to be achieved over the span of three years. Because of the complexity of these life skills, we provide students with many opportunities to explore, understand, practice, and internalize them. Our goal is to have these essential life skills become a mindset that students can draw from in various situations.

We use ongoing assessments to check for progress and support learning throughout the school year. Teachers regularly collect evidence on student progress through observations, interviews, student works, and self-reflections not only to document students' current progress but also to modify and adjust the support they offer. All interim evaluations consist of teacher comments shared with students and their families. Then, at the end of the year, we use the most recent and consistent evidence to evaluate students' current standing in life skills development

For example, consider a Grade 4-5 student whose skills in *analytical thinking* (an element of Expert Thinking) in the middle of the term are still at the Beginning stage. He is only able to compare and contrast two concrete objects or experiences. But as the teacher provides support and minilessons to encourage progress, by the end of the term he has progressed to comparing and contrasting three objects and ideas, sorting them into categories and subcategories, and explaining his decisions. We would use the most current evidence for grading, showing he has reached the Transition level.

Because, as the example illustrates, students' life skills development occurs over the long term, we don't grade and report their progress every grading period; we do so only at the end of each academic year. Reporting on students' progress occurs mainly in parent-teacher-student conferences. We call our report card a "Summary of the Learning Journey" to emphasize that learning is a process that never ends. If a student does not meet the learning expectations set for a particular subject or life skill, we assign a grade of "Not Yet" to indicate that although students may not have met a particular goal, we are confident they will get there.

Gathering Evidence

The evidence that teachers gather throughout the school year is based on the rubrics in order to provide support and monitor progress in students' achievement of the expected learning goals. It's worth noting that the best evidence comes from actual behavior in real situations, not imaginary or hypothetical cases, such as asking students to imagine, "What if you...."

Teachers use a variety of sources of evidence, including the following:

- Student portfolios
- Observations in the form of videos, photos, or anecdotal notes
- Student work or products (highlighted to show the specific parts that are relevant)
- Self-reports by students or from their parents
- Conference record forms
- Student interviews
- Reflection essays
- Responses to academic prompts

Let's take a closer look at several of the sources of evidence: portfolios, observations, student products, student reflection essays, and responses to academic prompts.

Student Portfolios

Grading of the essential life skills is accomplished primarily through evaluation of evidence presented in students' portfolios. To be accurate and meaningful, portfolios must show consistent, authentic, reliable, and valid evidence of students' performance. Our student portfolio system is implemented by teachers beginning in grades K–1 and is designed to encourage students to take ownership of their learning. In their portfolio, students assemble evidence that shows their progress in developing the essential life skills. They then reflect on their learning and consider what they did well and what they need to improve.

Teachers explicitly teach students how to organize their portfolio to show learning progress and how to use it to self-assess their learning. Students learn that each life skill needs to be supported by specific evidence. That evidence can come from different contexts and can be cross-referenced for different life skills.

Teachers guide students in preparing their portfolios by asking them to follow these four steps:

1. Read and explain the expectations of each life skill rubric in your own words.
2. Gather evidence on each life skill to include in your working portfolio.
3. Evaluate your performance against the rubrics and select the best evidence that demonstrates your progress. Include this evidence in the final portfolio.
4. Reflect on your work, describe the evidence, and explain the positive aspects of your performance and what needs to be improved.

Teachers continually review the evidence students gather, providing feedback and support as needed.

Observations

Teacher observations in the form of videos, photos, and anecdotal notes take place throughout the school year. Following are two examples of evidence teachers gathered from observations to assess students' development of different essential life skills. The first example represents expectations for the *adaptive social problem solving* element of Empathetic Social Skills for students at the Early level on the continuum rubric. Students are expected to understand what to do when facing a problem with support from adults. They are also expected to refrain from physical action and to recognize their feelings. In addition, they should be able to identify problems and describe how they want to solve the problem.

The second example represents expectations for the *sound decision making* element of Ethical Leadership for students at the Transition level on the continuum rubric. At this level, students are expected to decide on a solution after they have carefully analyzed relevant data. They are also expected to be able to factor in the majority of the team members' opinions in making their decision.

Anecdotal Notes 1
Empathetic Social Skills—Adaptive Social Problem Solving
Name: Dennis
Grade: K–1
Date: October 3, 2023
Context: Science
Time: Math and Science Center

Explanation: Dennis was working on his project about living and non-living things. He worked with a partner (Leo) to observe the environment around school and catalog living and non-living things. When observing some moss, Dennis and his friend got into an argument over whether it was a living thing or non-living thing, with the latter insisting that moss doesn't move so it cannot be a living thing. The argument went on for a while, and Leo began getting angry. At this point, Dennis deescalated the situation. He apologized and said, "I know moss does not move like animals move," he said. "But it breathes and drinks. It needs water to live. So, I think it's a living thing. Based on that, do you agree?" Leo did. With the conflict resolved, they continued their observations.

Conclusion: Dennis was able to solve a social conflict with a friend independently; hence, Stage 3. He was able to identify and describe the problem. He also understood what to do when facing the problem and solved it using his own ideas.

Anecdotal Notes 2:
Ethical Leadership—Sound Decision Making
Name: Chase

Grade: 4–5
Date: October 14, 2023
Context: Social studies project: Mission launching
Topic: Rights, Obligations, and Responsibilities. Students work collaboratively to decide on a narrower focus of the topic and make it their mission.

Explanation: As a leader, Chase suggested narrowing down the topic of "rights, obligations, and responsibilities" into a problem students face in their daily lives.

Chase started the discussion by sharing how his mom had to scold him to wake him up and then asked his teammates to take turns sharing other examples. As the discussion moved along, Chase gathered more information from other classmates. He compared data from four of his friends and found that three of them faced the same problem—time management. Based on this majority, he decided that time management would be the problem the team focused on for the project. The group agreed and they continued to the next steps, finding more data about how to manage time effectively.

Conclusion: Chase decided on a solution based on the generalization of the problems his teammates face. He compared data from everyone in the team and made a decision based on the data. He also asked for his teammates' opinions when making the final decision. His independence when executing his task as a leader shows that he is at Stage 3.

Student Products

Student products, with their concrete demonstration of skill application, are an important source of assessment data. Consider the following examples.

Keisha, a Grade 2–3 student, created two products for her Making Good Choices project in science as part of a unit on simple machines. First, she made a toy car for her brother, using lids from cans as the wheels and chopsticks as the axles. She also designed what she called "Knives and Scissors Super" (a product we featured in Chapter 3 on Creativity and Innovation). After observing that cooks in her father's restaurant needed a long time to chop vegetables, she decided to design an improved version of the vegetable-cutting machine they were using, applying ideas common in simple machines: "knives as the wedge" and "scissors as the lever." She acknowledged that the original idea came from her dad, but that she had made it better—faster and safer—by adding scissors and an on/off button.

Keisha's two products—the toy car and the improved vegetable-cutting machine—serve as one of the multiple pieces of evidence that she has reached Stage 3 of the Beginning level for the element of *novelty* in the essential skill of Creativity and Innovation. She has also reached Stage 3 for the element of *risk taking* in her novel use of materials, and for *beneficial contribution* by considering a need she had noticed in her father's restaurant. Her products also showed Adaptability and Agility as she was able to apply her skills and knowledge from Science to build a toy car for her brother and a more efficient machine for her dad.

Another example of the value of student products in assessing skill development levels comes from Reuben, the Grade 8–9 student whose waste management project has been described in several other chapters. Reuben's goal was to understand the different features of automated trash bins and apply his understanding to address the problem of trash in the school cafeteria. He used Audience-Centered Communication, specifically the *strategic reading* element, to conduct the literature research on waste management that would inform his design solution. Here are the questions Reuben wrote to help himself organize what he was learning as he read:

- What important information do I need to better understand automated trash bins?
- How can I determine what information is most useful?
- What are the most important features of automated trash bins?
- How can I categorize the important features of trash bins?
- Which evidence supports the information?
- What are the similarities and differences in types of automated trash bins?

This evidence shows that Reuben is at Stage 3 for the element of *strategic reading* within Audience-Centered Communication—capable of applying critical reading strategies and drawing conclusions without the teacher's help.

Finally, let's consider how Reuben approached a reading comprehension task in social studies. From his teacher, Reuben received the article "The Essentials of Democracy" by Dana-Marie Seepersad. To help ensure his understanding, Reuben listed a series of questions in a graphic organizer (Figure 9.4) and created a mind map that included the key points from the article (Figure 9.5, p. 218).

In his summary, Reuben concluded that democracy is important because it makes the relationship between citizens and government better, and it helps ensure the rule of law and the rights of individuals. Based on this evidence, we can conclude that Reuben has achieved Stage 3 for the element of *strategic reading* in Audience-Centered Communication.

FIGURE 9.4
A Grade 8–9 Student's Completed Graphic Organizer for Reading Response

BEFORE Reading	DURING Reading	AFTER Reading
• What will this article explain? • What do we need to create a good democracy? • Why is democracy essential? • How important is democracy? • How will we use democracy?	• Does the information presented explain why democracy is beneficial and how it has been implemented? • How important is citizen participation in a democracy?	• How many principles of democracy are there, based on the text? • In what ways is democracy vital to maintaining the government?

Student Reflection Essays

As part of their portfolio, students prepare a reflection essay at the end of each term that describes their projects and their performance on each. Students reflect on the planning process, what they learned, the thinking skills they used, the mistakes they made, and how they would create a better plan in future projects. Figure 9.6 (see p. 219) is an example of a reflection essay from a Grade 4–5 student. In it, the student explains how her purposeful products (an "ecobrick" and a sugar substitute) will benefit both her and others. She describes how systems thinking helped her accomplish her project and how feedback from her friends and teacher improved her skills and allowed her to achieve her goal. The student also realized that she needed to improve her research skills. Based on this evidence, she has reached Stage 3 of all the Meta-Level Reflection elements and of the *systems thinking* element of Expert Thinking.

Figure 9.7 (see p. 220) is another example of a student's reflection essay, this time from a student in Grade 8–9. The student describes how she achieved the targeted behavior for Meta-Level Reflection. She explains how she demonstrated conscious planning by developing thoughtful and responsible plans to make a video campaign based on her passion: the ocean and its ecosystems. She outlines her use of analytical and critical thinking using the Meta-Level Reflection rubric, describes how she compared and contrasted the pros and cons of various aspects of her solution, and acknowledges that

FIGURE 9.5
A Grade 8–9 Student's Mind Map on the Essentials of Democracy

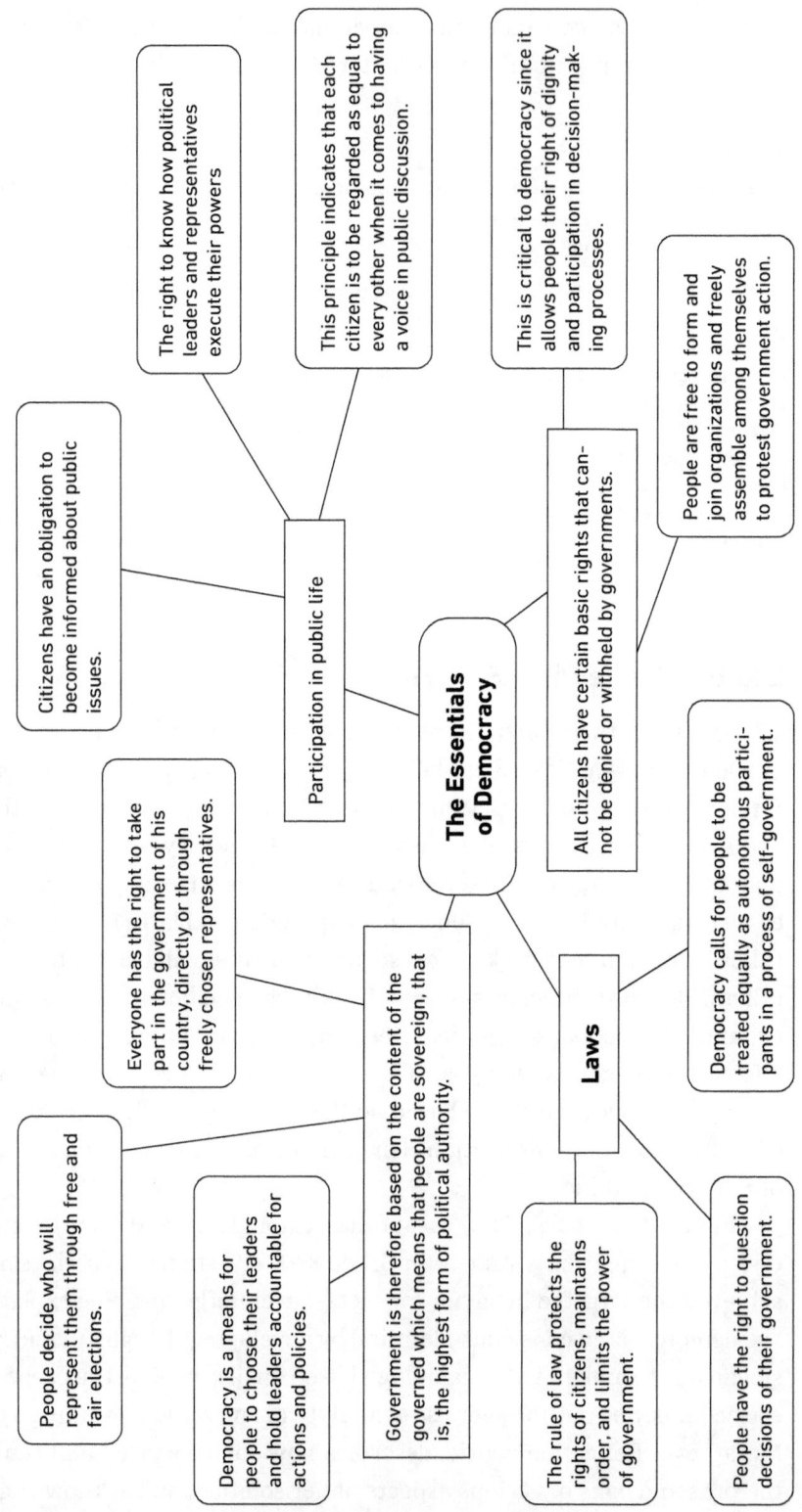

FIGURE 9.6
A Grade 4–5 Student's Reflection Essay

> My goal of this term is to make meaningful product and I was able to achieve it because I gather information from the people who will use my product before I design it. My purposeful interests of this term were science and experimenting. I really enjoyed exploring new things and testing ideas. The learner outcomes skills I want to learn in this term was Analytical thinking. When I look back on all of my projects (Science, Social Studies, Math, etc.) in this term, I think I have made a good choice because the product I created are beneficial for others, like my ecobric and my sugar replacement solution. I made those products based on a clear objective of recycling plastic bags at my house and creating a healthier version of sugar for my mom.
>
> The benefit of my goal for this term for myself was that I learned to use my time better and worked based on the timeline I have set in the beginning. The benefit of my goal for this term for others is that they can learn to recycle their plastics, and also to eat healthier by reducing sugar. The knowledge, values, and skills I used to achieve my goal were my knowledge from science and I also submit the projects on time that reflects my responsibility. Here are the procedures to achieve my goals: identifying the problem, think of the hypothesis, interview the people who will use my product, compare the information, and create the conclusion.
>
> When I was working on my project, the thinking skills I used to process the information were systems thinking. I identified the big picture of the digestive system, and then I study the elements that influence the digestive system. That's how I understood the impact of eating too much sugar or artificial sweeteners, and I search for healthier sugar replacement for my mom. When I was working on my project, I had to make some decisions such as deciding how to recycle plastic bags at my house. I found some options like bringing the plastics to recycling bank, reusing the plastic to create some arts and crafts, or create an ecobric. I decided to create an ecobrics based on my experience, knowledge, and skills. I know that I can't always bring the plastics to the recycling bank, and I also don't always have inspiration to create art and craft using recycled plastics. So I know that creating the ecobrics is my best choice because I can always do it at home and it's useful. I found some problems when I was making the ecobrics, I couldn't push the plastic bags hard enough inside the plastic bottle, so I solve the problem by asking for my dad's help. I also need more bottles for my ecobrics, as I ran out of bottles and I still had so many plastic bags. So my solution is to ask for used plastic bottles from my neighbors.
>
> I think that feedback from teachers, friends, and parents were important to improve my skills, knowledge and efficient to achieve my goals, because it helped me to make the best decision for my projects this term. My mom gave me the feedback that she like using honey for her pancakes, but she doesn't like it in her smoothies. So I found the other sugar replacement for her smoothies, and that is to use dates fruit to sweeten the smoothies. My teacher also gave me feedback to do more research to find other options for sugar replacements. The tools I used to help me carry out my thinking tasks were cause and effect and compare and contrast graphic organizer and steps to show the sequence. The celebration of my project management skills for this term are my time management and my useful solution. Next time I need to improve my research skills by consulting with my teachers.
>
> _____
>
> *Note:* This essay has not been edited for grammar, punctuation, or spelling.

FIGURE 9.7
A Grade 8–9 Student's Reflection Essay

My purposeful interests were making videos, and I'm also passionate in conserving the ocean/sea ecosystem. My chosen learning goals were improving my Creativity and Innovation. I proposed a creative solution to reduce overfishing for my MSC project. My plan to achieve my goal based on my interest and learner outcomes was understanding the expected outcomes, applying and improving my skills and knowledge in conducting research, assessing the benefit of my proposed solution for myself and the community, and also managing my time.

I supported the plans with arguments of making sure that I fulfill all the making good choices criteria in my projects, which are having clear objectives, having contribution for myself and or the community, and using my knowledge and skills.

The procedures I did to achieve my plans were understanding the subject and learner outcomes. Then, I found the problems to work with followed by researching possible solutions. I conducted research using various resources and proposed some ideas to develop a hypothesis to be tested. From the research and experiments, I can draw my conclusion.

I used my learned knowledge of ecosystem and my skills of observation, comparing and contrasting, conducting research using valid resources and proposing a hypothesis to ensure adaptive approaches to achieve goals. I also use the skills of reading, writing, speaking, and listening. My visual art skill supports me in designing the infographic as also my digital literacy skill in creating video. In the end, after testing my hypothesis, I came to a conclusion. I applies expert thinking, audience-centered communication, and creativity and innovation. I am also able to manage my time well.

When I look back on ALL of my projects this term, I think I have made a good choice because I can apply my knowledge and skills, I have a clear objective which is to solve problems in my community. I regulate myself by developing an agenda to manage my projects. When working on my projects this term, I made decisions on the best solution from several alternatives based on my literature research, survey, and interview.

When working on my projects this term, I made decisions on the best solution from several alternatives by considering the pros and cons of each solution. The thinking skills and process I engaged in this process is comparing and contrasting the solution from different aspect such as time and beneficial contribution.

The feedback I gained during working was having revision on the timeline and the scientific method of measurement for post-test. I used the feedback to ensure the attainment of an effective and efficient process toward the goals by changing the method. I have utilized steps to show sequence as well as the graphic organizer as the appropriate tools and strategies to carry out a thinking task based on the goals.

The celebration of my project management skills for this term is that I could accomplish the goal in this term as what I have planned in the timeline. I improve my creativity and innovation by thinking in a novel way and creating a project that is beneficial to my community. I am also improving my impactful writing skills in the part of writing based on the purpose. My plans to improve for the next project are to research more to gain more information and to make the product better. I also plan to improve my creativity and innovation in the part of risk-taking, by learning new skills to enrich the ideas on how I can propose a solution.

Note: This essay has not been edited for grammar, punctuation, or spelling.

she needs to improve her risk-taking skills to enrich her ideas for a solution. Her essay shows that she has achieved the targeted behaviors in Stage 3 for Meta-Level Reflection at the Developing level, as well as some of the indicators for Expert Thinking.

A third example of a student's reflection comes from Melissa, a Grade 12 student who reflected on the process she used to draft her senior thesis on the topic "Instagram's Negative Impact on Mental Health and Teenagers." Before capturing her reflection on video, Melissa handed in her script (see Figure 9.8, p. 222), which shows that she is at Stage 3 for the element of reflecting for future improvement in Meta-Level Reflection. She carefully and thoughtfully planned her thesis to ensure that it would be meaningful to the intended readers. In her writing, she presented reasoned arguments, citing the resources she had used and elaborating points, as necessary. She also acknowledged the identified areas for improvement and created an action plan for improvement.

Responses to Academic Prompts

Another source of evidence for assessment is the academic prompt. We design academic prompts that integrate natural and social phenomena as a context to assess students' achievement on essential life skills and related concepts, both subject-specific and more general. Students answer the academic prompt using an essay format. Figure 9.9 (see p. 223) is an example of an academic prompt for Grade 6–7 students, with related concepts and essential life skills.

Here is one student's response to the prompt:

As we are approaching the summer holiday, we could use this momentum to rebuild the tourism industry in Bali. A number of marketing strategies have been floating around the market for some time now. To make the strategies more fitting to my business, I would expand certain business strategies by:

1. Expanding the flexibility of Book Now Stay Later promo to the year 2023. Based on my research, some of the hospitality industries in Southeast Asia applied "Book Now Stay Later Promo" where foreign travelers can pay and book their stay now and choose their staying dates later on up to six months ("20 Promo, 'Book Now, Stay Later'"). However, having the flexible promo within six months won't be enough to cover the loss of income for Bali's local community. As we can see from Chart 1, in December 2020, the visitors of Bali decreased

FIGURE 9.8
Reflection Video Script from a Grade 12 Student

> Today I will reflect on how my process in creating my senior thesis project. My chosen topic for my senior thesis is "The Negative Impacts of Instagram on Mental Health and Teenagers."
>
> Before I finalize my decision on the topic, I had to consult with Mr. Rob and what he thought about my topic. I provided three topics that caught my interest which speaks about mental health in general. Throughout the discussion process, I was advised to make my topic to be more specific and narrow down the criteria on what to research on. For example, one of my options for topics before was how applying makeup could produce hormones that make it addicting and promote confidence. Mr. Rob advised me not to take that topic, as it has already been proven. The topic I chose I can back it up with proof and evidence, yet it isn't necessarily "proven," and it isn't necessarily accepted as a fact yet.
>
> So after choosing a topic and finalizing my topic decision I move on to the next step which is planning. This is the most crucial and important step because this is what really organized my thoughts to set a thoughtful plan with clear measurement criteria so that this thesis will be useful for the targeted readers, and also to raise awareness on the impact of social media for our mental health. I think this topic will be very beneficial especially for teenage readers around my age.
>
> When I chose this topic, I thought that I already had all of my arguments in mind, up until I had to work on the proposal. When I created my thesis statement to explain how important it is to address this topic in the significance part, I would like to include five argument points which involve beauty standards, anxiety and other mental health issues related.
>
> I used expert thinking when I summarized my argumentative points and the refutations on how I would refute my counterarguments. I also provided three refutations and the bibliography to cite all of the resources I used. This is also very important for me because one of the main points that I would not want to include in my thesis paper is plagiarism. Citing it ensures I will avoid plagiarism.
>
> The next stage is the writing process itself. This stage is when I need to elaborate all of my primary research results which for me includes the survey and the expert interview. This is why the planning proposal part is very important because once I get to the writing stage, I need to have all the information I need and organize my thoughts in a structured way.
>
> However, when I evaluate my writings, I still need to improve on my writing skills and how I elaborate the resources I have to explain the main points that I wish to answer, background refutations and my argumentative points as well as resources. So repeatedly evaluating my planning is important because it prepares me for the writing stage of the thesis itself. With everything that I have on the thesis, I will need some additional research because along the way as I write, I might notice that I need some data or statistics that I would like to include in the presentation, but other than that all of the information has already been researched and included in the thesis. Therefore my action plan is to add analytic data from reliable resources to support my arguments on how Instagram affects Mental Health and Teenagers. In addition to it, I also have to improve my writing skills on how to elaborate main points. The whole process of reflection certainly helps me to achieve my learning goals as I am consciously aware of my learning goals and how to achieve and improve them.
>
> _____
>
> *Note:* This essay has not been edited for grammar, punctuation, or spelling.

FIGURE 9.9

Example of a Grade 6–7 Academic Prompt, with Related Concepts and Essential Life Skills

Academic Prompt	Related Concepts and Essential Life Skills
Bali, whose economy depends largely on the tourism sector, was hit the hardest by the economic impact of the pandemic, which left hotel occupancy down to nearly zero and many people unemployed. Even though Bali recovered swiftly from past crises, both natural and man-made, including the Bali Bombing (2002), there are concerns that this COVID-19 crisis could be different. 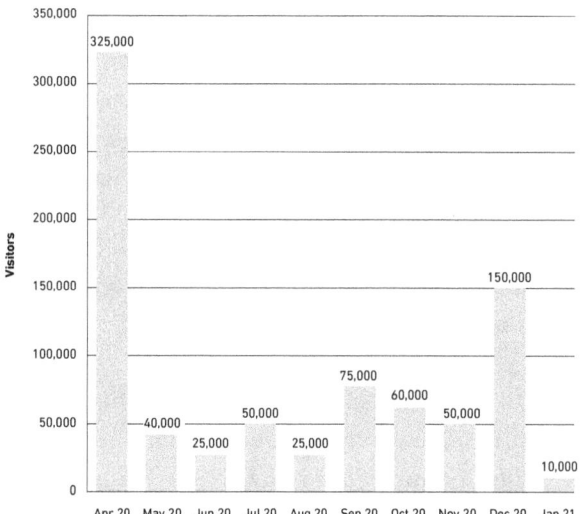 Number of Foreign Visitors to Bali During COVID-19 Pandemic Adapted from: Badan Pusat Statistik in Lidwina, 2021. A different approach may now be needed to save the tourism industry. If you were a Bali domestic small business owner, how would you create a new business approach (ideas) based on existing ideas as an opportunity to make your small business survive in this pandemic? Based on your understanding of the concept of cause and effect, explain how your approach (ideas) affects other perspectives (e.g., perspectives for communities, economies, environments, or health protocols). Select information from multiple and varied resources about how different countries managed tourism during the COVID-19 pandemic. Use your findings to support your reasoning and evidence.	**Concepts:** Cause-effect A relationship between events or things, in which one is the result of the other or others. This is a combination of action and reaction. When one decision has been made, it creates something else that follows. **Essential Life Skills:** Expert Thinking—*Critical Thinking*: • Compares, questions, and selects information from a range of (primary and secondary) sources of information and explains the reasons for choosing. • Identifies errors in information, procedures, and systems. Creativity and Innovation—*Novelty*: • Creates an innovation based on a combination of original ideas (content and/or form) and investigation of the surroundings. Creativity and Innovation—*Beneficial Contribution*: • Creates products that attempt to efficiently solve problems related to sustainability that are accepted by the surroundings, using relevant technology and materials.

more than half of the amount of the minimum foreign visitors before the pandemic hit. In this case, we need to gain as much as possible in order to help Bali's local community to survive. By expanding the promo to 2023, it will cater to the uncertainty for international travelers, while the income for Bali's local community will still be fulfilled up to 2023.
2. Creating promo for domestic tourism and working with the Bali government to make sure that most people in Bali have been vaccinated and make Bali a green zone area to visit. It is still risky to travel during this uncertain time; as responsible business owners, we need to build trust in the community by fulfilling requirements to standardized hygiene protocols ("Rebuilding Tourism for the Future"). We don't know how long this pandemic crisis will take before things truly come back, but what we can do is to stay optimistic and adapt towards the current situation.

Sources:
OECD. (2020, December 14). Rebuilding tourism for the future: COVID-19 policy responses and recovery. https://www.oecd.org/coronavirus/policy-responses/rebuilding-tourism-for-the-future-covid-19-policy-responses-and-recovery-bced9859/.
Rahadiansyah, C., & Amira, A. (2020, December 29). 20 promo "book now, stay later" di Bali. *DestinAsian Indonesia*. https://destinasian.co.id/13-promo-book-now-stay-later-di-bali/.

This student's response to the academic prompt shows he selected information from multiple sources. However, he didn't explain his reasons for selecting those resources, nor did he identify any errors. He created an innovative business strategy to help Bali tourism survive the pandemic crisis by combining multiple ideas. His business strategies expanded the "book now stay later" promo and created advertising based on the safety of traveling to Bali during the pandemic. His strategies also used relevant technology and materials. This student's response can be one source of evidence for the Expert Thinking element *critical thinking*, and for the Creativity and Innovation elements *novelty* and *beneficial contribution*.

Cross-Referenced Evidence

Evidence from one context can be used for more than one essential life skill by cross-referencing. Cross-referencing may require rephrasing to highlight the evidence from different angles, depending on what is expected or described in the rubric description for the various skills. It is also possible that even when using the same evidence, a student can be rated as being at different stages, depending on the expectation in the description. In the case description that follows, evidence from Reuben is used across elements of different life skills—namely, the *decision making* element of Ethical Leadership and the *individual accountability* element of Synergistic Collaboration.

Example 1: Ethical Leadership—Sound Decision Making

The rubric for Ethical Leadership describes how students at the Developing level can decide on the best solution from several alternatives by considering team members' perspectives and surrounding factors. Here is the sample of evidence for Reuben:

Name: Reuben
Grade: 8–9
Context: Science project
Topic: Waste Management. As part of a collaborative project, Reuben and his team tried to solve the problem of solid waste management in the school cafeteria from the perspective of tools. Their goal was to create an automated tool that could raise awareness of the need to keep the cafeteria clean. Each member had to research characteristics that represent the best features for waste management tools. A teacher monitored the students' progress.
Explanation: Reuben read several articles and came up with a generalization related to the best automated trash bins, based on data he gathered from the resources and focused specifically on the perspectives of design, materials, and features. He concluded that all automated trash bins have features such as sensors, an automatic lid, and voice activation. They are also made of stainless steel, which is durable and easy to clean. However, he did not consider the ideas of his team members, who came up with different kinds of materials and features.

Teacher: How did you include your team members' ideas in your decision?
Reuben: Actually, I had difficulty putting our ideas together. When we distributed our roles, each of us was responsible for researching different aspects to find the best features for tools to help with waste management. I did research on automated trash bins. Bella did research on tools to segregate different types of waste, and Carlos did research on tools to manage organic waste. Acting on our combined ideas would mean making lots of modifications to our existing manual trash bins. Our main goal

was to utilize the waste management tool for social campaigns, which is only possible with automation. That's why automation needs to be the main feature.
Teacher: How complex would the modification be?
Reuben: Well, if we only take my idea to automate trash bins, it would be as easy as adding a sensor tool and recorded voice to notify "Thank you's." But to add segregation would require adding different containers for different types of waste. I think we can do something about that. Adding a composting system is even more complex. Proper composting requires a good balance between "green" and "brown" elements. I'm not sure we can create such advanced coding or even a robot to take care of it.
Teacher: Well, Reuben—first, not all ideas have to be accepted. With more discussions and analysis, you can decide which one is feasible and which one is not. Second, remember that you're a team, so decide this as a team.
Reuben: I get what you mean. OK, I'll discuss my considerations with Bella and Carlos, and I'll listen to their opinions, too.

Reuben got back to his teammates and considered different possibilities and the pros and cons of each idea. Together, they came up with the analysis shown in Figure 9.10.

As the sample of evidence shows, after guidance from his teacher, Reuben decided to have more discussion with his teammates so they could agree on a solution together. He considered different alternatives to decide which one could help the team reach their goal—namely, to use the waste management tool for a social campaign to address the problem of trash in the school cafeteria. Because he needed a bit of support from the teacher to include his team members' perspectives, Reuben is at Stage 2 of the *sound decision making element* of Ethical Leadership.

Example 2: Synergistic Collaboration— Individual Accountability

The evidence just described can be cross-referenced for the *individual accountability* element of Synergistic Collaboration. As a student at the Developing level on the rubric for Synergistic Collaboration, Reuben is expected to understand his own role and to have a full sense of responsibility in completing the task to ensure effective and efficient approaches toward the group goal. Reuben's statements show that he understood that he needed to consider his team members' ideas to draw a conclusion, but he had difficulty doing that. When the teacher guided him with prompting questions,

Reuben was able to fulfill his task as a leader. This shows that, as was the case for *sound decision making* in Ethical leadership, Reuben is at Stage 2 for the element of *individual accountability* for Synergistic Collaboration.

FIGURE 9.10
Example of a Student Analysis

Goal	Utilize the waste management tool for social campaigns		
Options	Automated trash bin	Waste segregation	Composting System
Pros	Sensor and coding (with recorded voice) enables social campaign: • Opening trash bin is not disgusting anymore because its sensor detects our hand and opens the lid automatically. • The recorded voice says thank you or other acknowledgment to remind students to put the trash where it belongs.	• Students get to separate waste in different bins. • The classification helps the waste collection officers collect the trash more easily.	Organic waste will be better organized.
Cons	Without trash segregator, will not solve waste problem.	Needs to add different types of containers and "glue" them together.	Needs a very complex coding system for automation. Not feasible.
Ideas to minimize cons	Place existing trash bins next to each other and put stickers of different colors to inform which bin is for which type of trash.	Place existing trash bins next to each other and put stickers of different colors to inform which bin is for which type of trash.	
Conclusion	• Automated trash bins with coding can be added with a waste segregation feature as a simple solution. • Composting system is not feasible and might be more suitable as a separate project.		

Reporting

Our school mission is "to help students develop totally—academically, interpersonally, interpersonally, and physically—and to be competitive internationally." More specifically, we want our students to become self-regulated, forward-thinking leaders who possess and demonstrate all the essential life skills.

To provide an accurate picture of students' acquisition of these skills, we created a reporting system to record their personal development and academic growth. We use this "Summary of the Learning Journey" to provide information for monitoring students' progress and achievement, to celebrate their successes, and to guide continuous development.

We use a bar graph to report students' progress on the essential life skills through the five continuum levels: Early, Beginning, Transition, Developing, and Expert (see Figure 9.11). It communicates a student's current position and the progress made since the previous year in a visual, reader-friendly way. Provided to both students and parents, the bar graph presents an overall picture of where the students are on their learning journey.

To determine the level of progress shown on a student's bar graph, teachers follow the procedures outlined in Figure 9.3 (see p. 211). Three teachers rate the same essential life skills, based on the continuum level and stages. Each teacher also provides at least one piece of evidence to support the rating given. Here, for example, is the evidence cited by one of Reuben's teachers:

> Reuben compared and contrasted types of trash bins into two superordinate categories: "manual" and "automated." He added subordinate categories under them: "existing trash bins with a lid," "automated trash bins with a sensor," and "advanced trash bins with a sensor and coding." He identified the pattern and interconnectedness with a bit of guidance from the teacher before finally coming up with the final solution. He also addressed the possibility of a counterargument that people might find the idea too pricey or too cheesy. He voiced his opinion on it. Based on this evidence, Reuben is at Stage 2; he needed a bit of guidance to identify the pattern and interconnectedness in his analysis. Other than that, he fulfilled the description in the rubric independently.

During the parent conference, teachers describe what students can do in each essential life skill, again citing evidence to support their description.

Process, Progress, and Product

Tom has described three categories of learning criteria for grading and reporting (Guskey & Bailey, 2001):

1. *Product criteria* explain what students know and can do at a particular point of time.

2. *Process criteria* describe behaviors that enable or facilitate learning.
3. *Progress criteria* explain what students have gained or how much improvement they have made.

To ensure accurate representation of essential life skills development, our reporting system includes these three types of criteria. If you look at the bar graph in Figure 9.11, you'll note that student progress toward the development of each of the eight life skills is charted over time: the lighter shade shows previous achievement, and the darker shade shows the year's progress toward the current achievement level.

FIGURE 9.11
Essential Life Skills Report

Student	Reuben	Year	2020–2021
Grade	8–9 C	Term	Term 4/8
Subject	English 8–9		

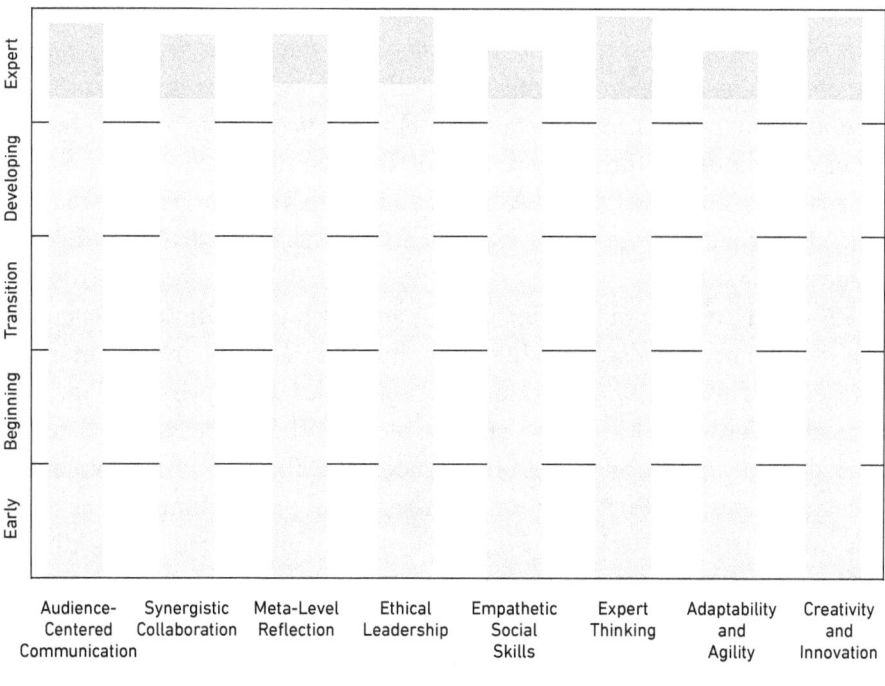

Integrating Essential Life Skills in Learning Content and Process

Our grading and reporting system for the essential life skills reflects the journey of our student's learning experience. In developing the essential life skills, we integrate learning *content* and *process*, based on the ideas set forth by Benjamin Bloom and colleagues (1956), who stressed that content and process *cannot be separated* in establishing learning goals. That is, for every element of content, educators must decide what students are to do with it (i.e., process or skill). Similarly, process *must* be related to some content. For example, to use thinking skills, you need something to think about, as Howard Gardner (2015) stressed when he noted, "You can't think outside of the box unless you have a box! And that box contains the disciplined knowledge that you have acquired, often over a significant period of time" (para. 12). This is why we use academic content as the context for life skills development.

With intention, a Grade 8–9 science teacher, for example, can ensure that a group project requiring students to compare and contrast the human body systems with animal and plant body systems helps them not only master the subject outcome (*be able to generalize how living organisms maintain homeostasis by explaining patterns, trends, relationships, and interconnectedness*) but also develop the *analytical thinking* element of Expert Thinking (*be able to explain the patterns, trends, relationships, and interconnectedness found in the analysis and develop arguments/hypotheses/conclusions/generalizations/solutions with reasons and evidence and addresses the counterclaims*). The collaborative nature of the group project further requires students to practice Synergistic Collaboration and Ethical Leadership. In other words, students can master subject outcomes via learning experiences that *also* develop essential life skills.

As you have seen in this chapter, our approach to grading and reporting the development of essential life skills involves using analytic, criterion-referenced rubrics that reflect authentic abilities and specific behavioral indicators for each skill. These rubrics, along with the bar graph displays, provide a meaningful description of students' abilities and promote a fair assessment system. Furthermore, our assessment process emphasizes regular, descriptive feedback, allowing students to demonstrate their skills in various forms and reflect on their progress. By adopting this comprehensive, multidimensional model, we empower students to focus on their growth, foster a genuine love of learning, and promote the development of self-regulated learners and future-ready leaders.

Conclusion

Educators throughout the world recognize the need to help students develop essential life skills. All acknowledge that students' success in school and in their lives beyond school depends on important qualities and skills that are seldom reflected in the typical school curriculum. What educators have lacked is a clear understanding of what life skills are most important; how to integrate the development of those skills into current school curricula; and how to assess, evaluate, and report students' progress in developing those skills.

Our purpose in developing this book was to describe the work we have done to address this crucial need in education even as we acknowledge that our program to help students develop essential life skills is still a work in progress. Although every year we see improvements in the performance of our students and experience new levels of success, every year we also find things we need to change and make better. We don't claim that our program is an exemplary model that other schools should emulate directly. Rather, we present the program here as the work of a group of dedicated educators committed to providing our students with the best possible educational experiences.

We hope that our description has helped you feel encouraged and confident that you and your teaching colleagues can help your students develop similar essential life skills within your existing curriculum, classroom structure, and assessment routines. Ours is but one approach that we hope provides a useful framework. Yours can and should be different, adapted to your curriculum, community, circumstances, and context.

Some of what we advocate may seem to require a lot of extra time and work for teachers, especially to those who find developing students' life skills a new and unfamiliar idea. But we suspect that many of you are already engaged in work similar to what we have described. Recognizing the importance of these and other essential life skills, you have begun practices similar to those we recommend and are observing how students respond. Although the work adds somewhat to teachers' already lengthy list of responsibilities, you have likely begun to see the benefits. You also recognize that for many students, these essential life skills do not develop by chance, but need to be specifically, intentionally, and effectively taught. And because little in most teachers' backgrounds or experience has prepared them to teach these skills, they need detailed and practical guidance on how to make the adjustments in their instructional routines necessary to address the essential life skills you identify. Still, we feel confident that you and your colleagues will quickly find that the extra time and effort you devote are truly worthwhile.

We also believe you will quickly discover how teaching essential life skills has enduring effects and helps students prepare for, face, and successfully manage future challenges. A surprisingly large number of our alumni have told us that working on essential life skills not only helped them succeed in their college and university studies but also in the workplace. They report how important they have found the ability to communicate based on the audience, to make sound decisions, to think critically, and to solve interpersonal issues.

One of our students graduated and went on to university, attained her medical degree, and today is a respected physician. Recently she wrote to us, sharing this message:

> I learned a great deal in HighScope, particularly life skills. Communication skills, public speaking, and logical and critical thinking served me well in college, while pursuing my master's degree, and in my current position as a physician in the emergency room. We were given opportunities to conduct group discussions and assume leadership roles in high school, so we are confident in making sound decisions in real life.

Another of our graduates described the benefits he gained from developing "learn-to-learn" skills as part of Meta-Level Reflection:

> The most useful skill I learned in high school was project management. At HighScope, I learned how to manage a project and how to think critically through doing the Plan-Do-Review system. It taught me how to actively think about all the relevant situations during the planning stages of a project.

These and similar notes that we have received from our alumni confirm our belief that learning and applying essential life skills by design helps students enter an uncertain and unpredictable future better prepared to succeed. When essential life skills become an integral part of the curriculum and learning process, students gain an intellectual, social, and emotional foundation they can rely upon for the rest of their lives. Helping students develop that foundation will be a long and sometimes difficult journey. But it will definitely be worth your time and effort because you will see your students become future-ready citizens, prepared to face whatever challenges they may encounter in their lives.

Acknowledgments

We would like to express our sincere gratitude and appreciation for the amazing individuals who made this book possible. At the top of our list are The Think Tank team, for enduring endless discussions of this work and helping us face challenges together, and the many busy teachers who provided us with glimpses of their classroom implementation.

We would like to thank the following people in particular:

- The Training, Research, and Development team at HighScope Indonesia Institute, composed of Titiasari Indayani, Citra Cininta, Diana Kartika, Triwidiastuti, Yuannita Rahmani, Aisyah Daulay, and Astri Juliasari. Thank you for your insights, valuable contributions, continuous support, hours of discussions, brainstorms, and writing sessions.
- Harry Susianto, PhD, of the University of Indonesia. Thank you for your constant guidance and insights from the earliest days of the Essential Life Skills development.
- The committed teachers of Sekolah HighScope Indonesia: Adisty Damaranti, Akhmad Sekhuri, Bayu Marsetyawan, Eka Dewi Maya, Irene Deborah, Lies Utami, Martina Ramirez, Pujiastuti, Rahmawati, Rifát Syauqi, Rizky Achyar, Stephanus Setia, Taqwa Gunawan, Tya Moulita Irwan, Wardhina, Yiska Tesalonika, and others who have supported us in this journey. Thank you for taking the time to provide us with crucial evidence of your successful classroom implementation.
- S. M. Naimah, for the fruitful brainstorming sessions in various phases of the Essential Life Skills rubric development, assessment system, and instructional strategies; Patrick W. Houterman, for assisting us with the proofreading process since the beginning of the rubric development; Jossy Soenarjo, from the Quality Monitoring team, who makes sure the teachers in our school apply the instructional strategies and assessments with quality; and Wahyuni Ratna Lingga, for her unwavering support throughout this entire journey.

- The principal team of Sekolah HighScope Indonesia TB Simatupang: Eva Tantri Mahastri, Hani Amalia, Iko Septo Nughroho, Indriani Rusydi, and Nur Wahida Zuchrifah. In developing the book, we relied on your excellent support and the invaluable data you contributed.
- Alejandra Barraza, PhD, the president of HighScope Educational Research Foundation, for supporting our work.
- The ASCD editorial team, for their patient and unfailing support in helping us turn our manuscript into an enjoyable and helpful read for all educators.

References

Adams, W., Wieman, C., & Schwartz, D. (2008, July 30). *Teaching expert thinking*. Carl Wieman Science Education Initiative, University of British Columbia.

Berk, L. E. (2017). *Development through the lifespan* (7th ed). Pearson.

Bierman, K. L., Greenberg, M. T., Coie, J. D., Dodge, K. A., Lochman, J. E., & McMahon, R. J. (2017). *Social and emotional skills training for children*. Guilford.

Bloom, B. S., Engelhart, M. D., Furst, E. J., Hill, W. H., & Krathwohl, D. R. (1956). *Taxonomy of educational objectives. Handbook I: Cognitive domain*. McKay.

Blumenfeld, P. C., Marx, R. W., Soloway, E., & Krajcik, J. (1996). Learning with peers: From small group cooperation to collaborative communities. *Educational Researcher, 25*(8), 37–40.

Bouchard, M. (2005). *Comprehension strategies for English language learners: 30 research-based reading strategies that help students read, understand, and really learn content (teaching strategies)*. Scholastic.

Bradberry, T., & Greaves, J. (2012). *Leadership 2.0*. TalentSmart.

Buehl, D. (2014). *Classroom strategies for interactive learning* (4th ed.). International Reading Association.

Caine, R., N., Caine, G., McClintic, C., & Klimek, K. J. (2009). *12 brain/mind learning principles in action: Developing executive functions of the human brain*. SAGE Publications.

Cambridge Dictionary. (n.d.). Synergistic. https://dictionary.cambridge.org/dictionary/english/synergistic

Cash, R. (2016). *Self-regulation in the classroom: Helping students learn how to learn*. Free Spirit.

Center on the Developing Child at Harvard University. (2019, February 22). *A guide to executive function*. https://developdevhcdc.wpengine.com/a-guide-to-executive-function/

Daniels, H., & Zemelman, S. (2014). *Subjects matter: Exceeding standards through powerful content-area reading* (2nd ed.). Heinemann.

Dweck, C. S. (2006). *Mindset: The new psychology of success*. Random House.

D'Zurilla, T. J., & Goldfried, M. R. (1971). Problem solving and behavior modification. *Journal of Abnormal Psychology, 78*, 107–126. http://dx.doi.org/10.1037/h0031360

D'Zurilla, T. J., Nezu, A. M., & Maydeu-Olivares, A. (2004). Social problem solving: Theory and assessment. In E. C. Chang, T. J. D'Zurilla, & L. J. Sanna (Eds.), *Social problem solving: Theory, research, and training* (pp. 11–27). American Psychological Association. https://doi.org/10.1037/10805-001

Emmerling, R. J., & Goleman, D. (2003, October). Emotional intelligence: Issues and common misunderstandings. *Issues and Recent Developments in Emotional Intelligence, 1* (1).

Fountas, I. C., & Pinnell, G. S. (2011). *The continuum of literacy: Grades preK–2*. Heinemann.

Fountas, I., & Pinnell, G. S. (2017). *Guided reading: Responsive teaching across the grades*. Heinemann.

Frayer, D. A., Frederick, W. C., & Klausmeier, H. G. (1969). A schema for testing the level of concept mastery (Technical Report No. 16). University of Wisconsin.

Gallo, A. (2018, January 3). Why we should be disagreeing more at work. *Harvard Business Review*. https://hbr.org/2018/01/why-we-should-be-disagreeing-more-at-work

Gardner, H. (2006). *Five minds for the future*. Harvard Business School Press.

Gardner, H. (2015, November 5). *Howard Gardner interviewed by Korean newspaper "Joongang Daily."* https://www.multipleintelligencesoasis.org/blog/tag/korea

Goldberg, E., & Podell, K. (1999). Adaptive versus vertical decision making and the frontal lobes. *Consciousness and Cognition, 8*(3), 364–377.

Grotzer, T., Forshaw, T., & Gonzalez, E. (2021, July). *Developing adaptive expertise for navigating new terrain: An essential element of success in learning and the workplace*. Project Zero, Harvard Graduate School of Education. http://www.pz.harvard.edu/resources/developing-adaptive-expertise-for-navigating-new-terrain-an-essential-element-of-success

Guskey, T. R. (2015, June). Why glorify failure to enhance success? *Educational Leadership, 57*(6). https://www.ascd.org/el/articles/why-glorify-failure-to-enhance-success

Guskey, T. R., & Bailey, J. M. (2001). *Developing grading and reporting systems for student learning*. Corwin.

Guskey, T. R., & Brookhart, S. M. (Ed.). (2019). *What we know about grading: What works, what doesn't, and what's next*. ASCD.

Hargie, O. (2006). *The handbook of communication skills*. Routledge.

Hasso Plattner Institute of Design at Stanford University. (n.d.). *Get started with design thinking*. Author. https://dschool.stanford.edu/resources/getting-started-with-design-thinking

Hill, B. C. (2001). *Developmental continuums: A framework for literacy instruction and assessment K–8*. Christopher-Gordon.

Hohmann, M., Weikart, D. P., & Epstein, A. S. (2008). *Educating young children*. HighScope.

Jensen, E. (1994). *The learning brain*. Turning Point.

Jordan, J. (2020, April 6). Lessons in agility from a dancer turned professor. *Harvard Business Review*. https://hbr.org/2020/04/lessons-in-agility-from-a-dancer-turned-professor

Kallick, B., & Zmuda, A. (2017). *Students at the center: Personalized learning with habits of mind*. ASCD.

Levy, F., & Murnane, R. J. (2004). *The new division of labor: How computers are creating the next job market*. Princeton University Press.

McCloskey, G., Perkins, L. A., & Van Divner, B. (2009). *Assessment and intervention for executive function difficulties*. Routledge.

Meltzer, L. (Ed.). (2018). *Executive function in education: From theory to practice* (2nd ed.). Guilford.

Meyer, J. (1994, November 22). *Teaching through teams in communication courses: Letting structuration happen.* Paper presented at the 80th annual meeting of the Speech Communication Association, New Orleans, Louisiana.

Olweus, D. (1994). Bullying at school: Long-term outcomes for the victims and an effective school-based intervention program. In L. R. Huesmann (Ed.), *Aggressive behavior: Current perspectives* (pp. 97–130). Plenum. https://doi.org/10.1007/978-1-4757-9116-7_5

Palmer, E. (2014). *Teaching the core skills of listening and speaking.* ASCD.

Partnership for 21st Century Learning. (2019). *Framework for 21st century learning definitions.* https://static.battelleforkids.org/documents/p21/p21_framework_definitionsbfk.pdf

Sawyer, R. K., John-Steiner, V., Moran, S., Sternberg, R. J., Feldman, D. H., Nakamura, J., & Csikszentmihalyi, M. (2003). *Creativity and development.* Oxford University Press.

Schweinhart, L. J., Barnett, W. S., & Belfield, C. R. (2005). *Lifetime effects: The High/Scope Perry Preschool study through age 40.* HighScope.

Scipioni, J. (2019, October 23). *10 principles for great leadership, according to Disney's Bob Iger.* CNBC. https://www.cnbc.com/2019/10/23/disney-ceo-bob-igers-principles-for-great-leadership.html

Springer, L., Stanne, M. E., & Donovan, S. S. (1999). Effects of small-group learning on undergraduates in science, mathematics, engineering, and technology: A meta-analysis. *Review of Educational Research, 69*(1), 21–51. https://doi.org/10.3102/00346543069001021

Sternberg, R. J., & Grigorenko, E. L. (2003). Teaching for successful intelligence: principles, procedures, and practices. *Journal for the Education of the Gifted, 27*(2/3), 216. https://files.eric.ed.gov/fulltext/EJ787926.pdf.

Swartz, R., & Parks, S. (1994). *Infusing the teaching of critical and creative thinking into content instruction: A lesson design handbook for the elementary grades.* Critical Thinking Press and Software.

Timperley, H. (2010). Using evidence in the classroom for professional learning. *ResearchGate.* https://www.researchgate.net/publication/242475272_Using_Evidence_in_the_Classroom_for_Professional_Learning

Zenger, J. (2015, July 16). Taking responsibility is the highest mark of great leaders. *Forbes.* https://www.forbes.com/sites/jackzenger/2015/07/16/taking-responsibility-is-the-highest-mark-of-great-leaders/?sh=6918b8ab48f2

Index

The letter *f* following a page locator denotes a figure.

accountability
   individual, 125–131, 125*f*, 140, 141*f*
   nurturing, 190–191
Adaptability and Agility
   assessing and measuring, 83, 84*f*, 85–89
   defined, 2, 73
   importance of, 73–75
   integrating into curriculum and classroom practice, 89–90
Adaptability and Agility, key elements
   agile mindset, 76–78
   defined, 75*f*
   versatility, 80–82
Adaptability and Agility rubric, 84*f*
adaptive and agile individuals, 74–78, 75*f*, 80–82
agile mindset, 75*f*, 76–78
agile mindset rubric, 84*f*
agility. *See* Adaptability and Agility
analytical thinking, 32*f*, 35–42
analytical thinking rubric, 46–47*f*
annotation, text, 100
assessment
   Adaptability and Agility, 83, 84*f*, 85–89
   Audience-Centered Communication, 107, 108–110*f*, 111
   Creativity and Innovation, 66, 67–68*f*, 69–72
   Empathetic Social Skills, 170, 171–173*f*, 174–178
   essential life skills, 210–212, 211*f*, 230
   Ethical Leadership, 194, 195–196*f*, 197–201

assessment—(*continued*)
   Expert Thinking, 45, 46–47*f*
   habit in self-learning, 9, 11
   Meta-Level Reflection (MLR), 21, 22–23*f*, 24
   Synergistic Collaboration, 139–140, 141–142*f*, 143–147
atmosphere allowing creativity and innovation, 53, 55
Audience-Centered Communication
   assessing and measuring, 107, 108–110*f*, 111
   defined, 2, 91
   in group settings, 122
   importance of, 91–92
   integrating into curriculum and classroom practice, 119, 121
   nurturing the skill of, 134
   producing effective, clear, and persuasive communication, 93
   understanding the audience in, 92–93
Audience-Centered Communication, key elements
   defined, 94*f*
   listening, active, 95–97
   reading, strategic, 97–100
   speaking, effective, 100–102, 103*f*
   writing, impactful, 104–105, 105*f*, 106*f*, 107
Audience-Centered Communication rubric, 108–110*f*

beginning level (grades K–3) rubrics
   active listening, 48*f*

beginning level (grades K–3) rubrics—(*continued*)
    adaptability and agility, 48*f*
    adaptive social problem solving, 172–173*f*, 175
    agile mindset, 48*f*
    analytical thinking, 46–47*f*
    audience-centered communication, 48–50*f*
    beneficial contribution, 48*f*
    conscious planning, 22*f*
    creativity and innovation, 47–48*f*
    critical opinion, 142*f*
    critical thinking, 47*f*
    developing healthy relationships, 172*f*
    effective speaking, 49*f*
    empathetic social skills, 171–173*f*
    ethical leadership, 195–196*f*
    expert thinking, 46*f*, 48–49
    group cohesiveness, 141*f*
    growth mindset development, 196*f*
    impactful writing, 49–50*f*
    individual accountability, 141*f*
    novelty, 47*f*, 67*f*
    personal integrity, 195*f*
    reflection for future improvement, 23*f*
    risk taking, 47*f*
    sound decision making, 195*f*, 197–198
    strategic reading, 48*f*, 108*f*, 111–114, 112*f*, 113*f*
    synergistic collaboration, 141–142*f*
    systems thinking, 46*f*
    taking charge of personal safety, 171–173*f*
    thoughtful learning, 22*f*, 25–26
    versatility, 84*f*, 85
    virtual collaboration, 142*f*, 143
big picture thinking
    nurturing, 33–34
    in systems thinking, 32
brain, the human, 181
bullying, 158

caring, nurturing the concept of, 132–134
cause and effect
    identifying, 34
    in systems thinking, 32

challenges, viewing as natural part of life, 76–78, 77*f*
changes, viewing as natural part of life, 76–78, 77*f*
character, cultivating good, 181–182
choices, making good, 12–13, 13*f*, 14*f*
classification, 35–37, 39–40, 39*f*
classrooms
    atmosphere allowing creativity and innovation, 53, 55
    clean-up time, 132–133
    democratic, 55
    shared control, 55
clean-up time, 132–133
cohesiveness, group, 125*f*, 131–134, 133*f*, 140, 141*f*
collaboration, synergistic. *See* Synergistic Collaboration
collaboration, virtual, 125*f*, 136–139, 140, 142*f*
communication. *See also* Empathetic Social Skills
    critical opinion in, 134–136
    giving suggestions with sound arguments, 136
    problem solving and, 152
    speaking up, having the courage for, 135–136
    virtual, 136–139, 138*f*, 140, 142*f*
communication, audience-centered. *See* Audience-Centered Communication
compare and contrast
    in analytical thinking, 35–37
    graphic organizer, 26*f*, 37*f*, 49*f*
conclusions, drawing in analytical thinking, 38–42
conflict resolution, 80, 152–153, 162–163, 167–168. *See also* problem solving
connections and patterns in information, 30
Constructive Friends Protocol, 96
content, crafting for effective speaking, 100–101, 101*f*
contribution, beneficial
    in creativity and innovation, 56*f*, 63–66
    poster reminder for, 60*f*
    rubric, 68*f*
conversation, 100–101
courage to speak up, 135–136

Creativity and Innovation
    assessing and measuring, 66, 67–68*f*, 69–72
    atmosphere allowing, 53, 55
    defined, 2, 53
    in effective, clear, and persuasive communication, 93
    importance of, 53
    integrating into curriculum and classroom practice, 72
    intrinsic motivation in, 53–54
Creativity and Innovation individuals, 53, 61
Creativity and Innovation key elements
    beneficial contribution, 63–66
    defined, 56*f*
    novelty, 55–60
    risk taking, 61–62
Creativity and Innovation rubric, 67–68*f*
critical thinking, 32*f*, 42–45
critical thinking rubric, 47*f*

decision making
    adaptive, self-thought and, 180–181
    with Expert Thinking, 31
    sound, 183–188, 184*f*, 195*f*
delivery of content, effective, 102, 103*f*
developing level (grades 6–9) rubrics
    active listening, 48*f*
    adaptability and agility, 48*f*
    adaptive social problem solving, 172–173*f*, 176–178*f*
    agile mindset, 48*f*
    analytical thinking, 46–47*f*
    audience-centered communication, 48–50*f*
    beneficial contribution, 48*f*
    conscious planning, 22*f*
    creativity and innovation, 47–48*f*
    critical opinion, 142*f*
    critical thinking, 47*f*
    developing healthy relationships, 172*f*
    effective speaking, 49*f*
    empathetic social skills, 171–173*f*
    ethical leadership, 195–196*f*
    expert thinking, 46*f*, 50
    group cohesiveness, 141*f*
    growth mindset development, 196*f*

developing level (grades 6–9) rubrics—(*continued*)
    impactful writing, 49–50*f*
    individual accountability, 141*f*
    novelty, 47*f*, 67*f*, 70–71
    personal integrity, 195*f*
    reflection for future improvement, 23*f*
    risk taking, 47*f*
    sound decision making, 195*f*, 199–200
    strategic reading, 48*f*, 108*f*, 116–118, 117*f*
    synergistic collaboration, 141–142*f*
    systems thinking, 46*f*
    taking charge of personal safety, 171–173*f*
    thoughtful learning, 22*f*, 27
    versatility, 84*f*, 86–87
    virtual collaboration, 142*f*, 145–147
differences, nurturing respect for, 124, 158–159
discipline, 54

early level (preschool–K) rubrics
    active listening, 48*f*
    adaptability and agility, 48*f*
    adaptive social problem solving, 170, 172–173*f*, 172*f*, 174–175
    agile mindset, 48*f*
    analytical thinking, 46–47*f*
    audience-centered communication, 48–50*f*
    beneficial contribution, 48*f*
    conscious planning, 22*f*
    creativity and innovation, 47–48*f*
    critical opinion, 142*f*
    critical thinking, 47*f*
    developing healthy relationships, 172*f*
    effective speaking, 49*f*
    empathetic social skills, 171–173*f*
    ethical leadership, 195–196*f*
    expert thinking, 46*f*, 48
    group cohesiveness, 141*f*
    growth mindset development, 196*f*
    impactful writing, 49–50*f*
    individual accountability, 141*f*
    novelty, 47*f*, 67*f*, 69–70
    personal integrity, 195*f*

early level (preschool–K) rubrics—
(*continued*)
    reflection for future improvement,
        23*f*
    risk taking, 47*f*
    sound decision making, 195*f*, 197
    strategic reading, 48*f*, 108*f*, 111
    synergistic collaboration, 141–142*f*
    systems thinking, 46*f*
    taking charge of personal safety,
        171–173*f*
    thoughtful learning, 22*f*, 25
    versatility assessment, 83, 84*f*
    virtual collaboration, 142*f*, 143
eggmotions, 153
elements in systems thinking, 32
emotions
    evaluating, 17, 17*f*
    managing, 152–153
    monitoring, 14–16, 16*f*
Empathetic Social Skills
    assessing and measuring, 170,
        171–173*f*, 174–178
    conflict, growing from, 152–153
    defined, 2
    emotions, managing, 152–153
    importance of, 149–153
    integrating into curriculum and
        classroom practice, 179
    key behaviors in, 150
    poster reminder for, 167*f*
Empathetic Social Skills, key elements
    adaptive social problem solving,
        164–165, 166*f*, 167–168, 169*f*, 170
    defined, 154*f*
    healthy relationships, 151, 157–163
    personal safety, 153–157, 154*f*, 155*f*
Empathetic Social Skills rubric,
    171–173*f*
empathy
    nurturing, 133
    in problem solving, 12
    producing effective, clear, and per-
        suasive communication, 93
    in risk taking, 61–62, 62*f*, 63*f*
environmental sustainability, 182–183
errors, ability to evaluate, 43–46
Ethical Leadership
    assessing and measuring, 194,
        195–196*f*, 197–201

Ethical Leadership—(*continued*)
    character, cultivating good, 181–182
    defined, 2, 180
    environmental sustainability,
        182–183
    expert thinking, nurturing, 184–186
    importance of, 180–183
    integrating into curriculum and
        classroom practice, 202
    respect and responsibility toward
        others, 182–183
    self-thought and adaptive decisions
        in, 180–181
Ethical Leadership, key elements in
    defined, 184*f*
    growth mindset in developing one-
        self and others, 191–194
    personal integrity, 188–191
    sound decision making, 183–188
Ethical Leadership rubric, 195–196*f*
excellence, nurturing, 192–194
executive function, developing, 181
Exhibition of Learning, 102
expertise, adaptive, 81–82
expert level (grades 9–12) rubrics
    active listening, 48*f*
    adaptability and agility, 48*f*
    adaptive social problem solving,
        172–173*f*, 176–178
    agile mindset, 48*f*
    analytical thinking, 46–47*f*
    audience-centered communication,
        48–50*f*
    beneficial contribution, 48*f*
    conscious planning, 22*f*
    creativity and innovation, 47–48*f*
    critical opinion, 142*f*
    critical thinking, 47*f*
    developing healthy relationships,
        172*f*
    effective speaking, 49*f*
    empathetic social skills, 171–173*f*
    ethical leadership, 195–196*f*
    expert thinking, 41–42, 46*f*, 50–51
    group cohesiveness, 141*f*
    growth mindset development, 196*f*
    impactful writing, 49–50*f*
    individual accountability, 141*f*
    novelty, 47*f*, 67*f*, 71–72
    personal integrity, 195*f*

expert level (grades 9–12) rubrics—
  (*continued*)
    reflection for future improvement,
      23*f*
    risk taking, 47*f*
    sound decision making, 195*f*,
      200–201
    strategic reading, 48*f*, 108*f*, 118–119,
      120*f*
    synergistic collaboration, 141–142*f*
    systems thinking, 46*f*
    taking charge of personal safety,
      171–173*f*
    thoughtful learning, 22*f*
    thoughtful learning assessment,
      22*f*, 27–28
    versatility, 84*f*, 87, 87*f*, 88, 88*f*, 89
    virtual collaboration, 142*f*, 147
Expert Thinking
  assessing and measuring, 45, 46–47*f*
  better decision making with, 31
  defined, 2, 29
  filtering information in, 30–31
  importance of, 30–31
  integrating into curriculum and
    classroom practice, 51–52
  patterns and connections in, 30
  poster reminder for, 40*f*
  producing effective, clear, and per-
    suasive communication, 93
Expert Thinking, key elements
  analytical thinking, 32*f*, 35–42
  critical thinking, 42–45
  defined, 32*f*
  systems thinking, 31–34
Expert Thinking rubric, 46–47*f*

feedback, 193
feelings and processes
  evaluating, 17, 17*f*
  monitoring, 14–16, 16*f*
FEOF technique, 60
friendship, healthy, 157–158
function, understanding, 63–64, 64*f*

generalizations in analytical thinking,
  38–42
goals, shared, 123–124, 126–128, 131
grades
  authenticity in, 203

grades—(*continued*)
  reliability in, 203, 207
  reporting systems, 227
  subjectivity in, 203
  as temporary, 203–204
  validity in, 207
grading
  for an agile mindset, 74
  fair and meaningful, 210
  of process, 229
  of product, 215–217, 217*f*, 218–220*f*,
    228
  of progress, 229, 229*f*
grading and reporting, 203–212,
  228–229
grading and reporting rubric, 206*f*
grading evidence, gathering
  academic prompt responses, 221,
    223*f*, 224
  cross-referenced, 224–227
  observations, 213–215
  product, 215–217, 217*f*, 218*f*
  reflection essays, 217, 219–220*f*, 221,
    222*f*
  sources for, 212
  student portfolios, 213
graphic organizers
  based on text structure, 115*f*
  changes and challenges, brainstorm-
    ing responses to, 77*f*
  compare and contrast, 26*f*, 37*f*,
    49*f*
  Frayer model for integrity, 190*f*
  interviewing potential users of inno-
    vations, 62*f*
  PREP, 101*f*
  preschool safety activity, 156*f*
  project focus question, brainstorm-
    ing, 64*f*
  project planning, 82*f*
  reflection for future improvement,
    19*f*
  reliability and reasonableness of
    information, evaluating, 44*f*
  reviewing a plan and considering its
    effectiveness, 15*f*
  rights and responsibilities, 163*f*
  strategic reading assessment, 112*f*,
    113*f*, 115*f*
  systems thinking, 33*f*

graphic organizers—(*continued*)
    thinking process awareness, developing, 8, 9*f*
    vocabulary detective, 41*f*, 59*f*
    writing stages, 104–105, 105*f*, 106*f*
grit, adaptive and agile individuals, 74–75
group work. *See* Synergistic Collaboration
growth mindset, developing oneself and others with a, 184*f*, 191–194, 196*f*

ideas
    determining reasonableness of, 42–45
    original, nurturing, 55–60
    synthesis of baseline, 57–60
imagination, 58
information
    clarifying, 35
    connections and patterns, 30
    filtering, 30–31
innovation. *See* Creativity and Innovation
integrity
    Frayer model graphic organizer, 190*f*
    personal, 184*f*, 188–191, 195*f*
interconnectedness in systems thinking, 32
internet, interacting safely online, 150–151, 156

kindness, 150, 161–163, 161*f*
knowledge transfer, 78, 79*f*

leaders, self-regulated, 29. *See also* Ethical Leadership
learning, thoughtful, 14–17, 22*f*, 24–28
life skills, essential. *See also specific skills*
    assessing and measuring, 210–212, 211*f*, 229*f*, 230
    developing, importance of, 231
    integrating in learning content and process, 230
    integrating into curriculum and classroom practice, 231–232
listening
    active, 94*f*, 95–97, 108*f*
    attentive, 95–96

listening—(*continued*)
    Constructive Friends Protocol, 96
    to verbal and nonverbal cues, 95–97

Making Good Choices log, 13*f*, 14*f*
Making Good Choices project, 12–13, 75
mediation, peer, 162–163, 169*f*
Meta-Level Reflection (MLR)
    assessing and measuring, 21, 22–23*f*, 24–28
    benefits of learning, 232–233
    defined, 2, 7
    importance of, 7
    integrating into curriculum and classroom practice, 28
    producing effective, clear, and persuasive communication, 93
    self-learning habits, 9
    thinking process awareness, 8, 9*f*
    working agreement reminder, 10*f*
Meta-Level Reflection (MLR) journals, 81–82, 82*f*
Meta-Level Reflection (MLR), key elements
    conscious planning, 10–11
    defined, 11*f*
    graphic organizer, 12*f*
    reflection for future improvement, 18–21, 19*f*, 20*f*, 21*f*, 23*f*
    thoughtful learning, 14–17
Meta-Level Reflection (MLR) rubric, 22–23*f*, 24–28
monitoring habit in self-learning, 9, 11
Monitoring My Own Thinking Parking Lot poster, 17*f*
motivation, intrinsic and extrinsic, 54

netiquette, 137–139, 138*f*
nonverbal cues, responding to, 95–97
novelty, 55–60, 56*f*, 60*f*
novelty rubric, 67*f*

objectives, achieving, 8, 9*f*
observations, in grading, 213–215
opinion, critical, 125*f*, 134–136, 140, 142*f*
optimism, adaptive and agile individuals, 74–75

patterns and connections in information, 30

patterns of behavior
    identifying, 34
    in systems thinking, 32
persistence in risk taking, 62
personalization of knowledge, 40
perspectives, multiple or interdisciplinary, considering
    adaptive and agile individuals, 74
    in conscious planning, 10, 12–14, 13f
    nurturing the ability for, 186–188
    versatility and, 80–81
Plan-Do-Review (PDR), 11, 18, 75
planning
    conscious, 10–13, 11f, 13f, 14f, 22f
    habit in self-learning, 9, 11
plans, detailed with good choices, creating, 10, 12–14
portfolios, grading with, 213
praise, 192
presentations
    crafting, 101f
    delivery of content, effective, 102, 103f
problem solving. *See also* conflict resolution
    adaptive, 152
    adaptive expertise in, 81
    adaptive social, 164–165, 167–168, 169f, 170, 172–178
    communication and, 152
    considering multiple or interdisciplinary in, 80
    thinking process awareness, developing, 8, 9f
product, grading, 215–217, 217f, 218–220f
productive skills in language strategies, 101f
progress, grading, 229, 229f
prompt responses, academic, 221, 223f, 224
public speaking, 102, 103f
punishment and rewards, 192

Random Acts of Kindness Cards, 161–163, 161f
reading
    shared, 95–96
    strategic, 94f, 97–100, 108f

reading comprehension strategies, 99–100, 99f
reading goals, 97–99
Recall Time, 20
reflection. *See also* Meta-Level Reflection (MLR)
    for future improvement, 18–21, 19f, 20f, 21f, 23f
    nurturing the ability for, 18–19
reflection essays, grading with, 217, 219–220f, 221, 222f
reflection journals, 81–82, 82f
relationships
    establishing and maintaining, 151
    healthy, developing, 157–163, 172f
    rights and responsibilities in, 162–163, 163f
resources, determining reliability of, 42–45
respect
    for different perspectives, 186–188
    nurturing, 151, 158–159
    teaching, 182–183
responsibility
    nurturing, 190–191, 192–194
    toward others, teaching, 182–183
rewards and punishment, 192
risk taking
    in creativity and innovation, 56f, 61–62, 62f
    poster reminder for, 60f
risk taking rubric, 67f

safety, learning to take charge of one's own, 150, 153–157, 154f, 155f, 171f
same and different, 36
SCAMPER technique, 60
school, historically, 1
self-learning, 9, 11
Self-Reflection Card for Group Cohesiveness, 133f
self-respect, 183
skills transfer, 78, 79f
SOAPS analysis, 119, 120f
social problems, defined, 164
social problem solving, adaptive, 164–165, 166f, 167–168, 169f, 170
social skills, empathetic. *See* Empathetic Social Skills

sort and classify in analytical thinking, 35–37, 39, 39*f*
speaking, effective, 94*f*, 100–102, 103*f*, 109*f*. *See also* communication
speaking up, having the courage for, 135–136
structure in systems thinking, 32
success, requirements for, 231
suggestions, giving with sound arguments, 136
Synergistic Collaboration
    assessing and measuring, 139–140, 141–142*f*, 143–147
    Audience-Centered Communication, nurturing, 134
    concept of caring, 132–134
    defined, 2, 122
    flexible grouping, 124
    giving suggestions with sound arguments, 136
    importance of, 122–124
    integrating into curriculum and classroom practice, 147–148
    multiage settings, 124
    positive, strategies to maintain, 123–124
    project mission, 126, 127*f*
    roles and task descriptions in, 128–131, 129*f*, 130*f*
    shared goal and responsibility in, 123, 126–128, 131
    speaking up, having the courage for, 135–136
Synergistic Collaboration, key elements
    critical opinion, 134–136, 140, 142*f*
    defined, 125*f*
    group cohesiveness, 131–134, 133*f*, 140, 141*f*
    individual accountability, 125–131, 140, 141*f*
    virtual collaboration, 136–139, 138*f*, 140, 142*f*
Synergistic Collaboration rubric, 141–142*f*
systems thinking, 31–34, 32*f*, 33*f*
systems thinking rubric, 46*f*

technology, interacting safely online, 150–151, 156
technology application, nurturing, 139–140
text annotation, 100
thinkers, novice, 29
thinking, expert. *See* Expert Thinking
thinking process awareness, developing, 8, 9*f*
thinking processes and feelings
    evaluating, 17, 17*f*
    grading, 229
    monitoring, 14–16, 16*f*
transition level (grades 3–6) rubrics
    active listening rubric, 48*f*
    adaptability and agility, 48*f*
    adaptive social problem solving, 172–173*f*, 175–176
    agile mindset, 48*f*
    analytical thinking, 46–47*f*
    audience-centered communication, 48–50*f*
    beneficial contribution, 48*f*
    conscious planning, 22*f*
    creativity and innovation, 47–48*f*
    critical opinion, 142*f*
    critical thinking, 47*f*
    developing healthy relationships, 172*f*
    effective speaking, 49*f*
    empathetic social skills, 171–173*f*
    ethical leadership, 195–196*f*
    expert thinking, 46*f*, 50
    group cohesiveness, 141*f*
    growth mindset development, 196*f*
    impactful writing, 49–50*f*
    individual accountability, 141*f*
    novelty, 47*f*, 67*f*, 70
    personal integrity, 195*f*
    reflection for future improvement, 23*f*
    risk taking, 47*f*
    sound decision making, 195*f*, 198–199
    strategic reading, 48*f*, 108*f*, 114, 115*f*, 116
    synergistic collaboration, 141–142*f*
    systems thinking, 46*f*
    taking charge of personal safety, 171–173*f*
    thoughtful learning, 22*f*, 26–27
    versatility, 84*f*, 85–86
    virtual collaboration, 142*f*, 143–145

21st century skills
    defined, 1–2
    designing for, 3–6
    the essential, 2–3

value added concept, 63–66
values transfer, 78, 79*f*
verbal cues, responding to, 95–97

versatility, 75*f*, 80–89
versatility rubric, 84*f*
Vocabulary Bingo, 187, 187*f*

workforce preparedness, 1–3
writing, impactful, 94*f*, 104–105, 105*f*, 106*f*, 107, 109–110*f*

About the Authors

Antarina S. F. Amir, SE, MSc, MBA, is founder and president of HighScope Indonesia Institute. A graduate of the University of Pittsburgh and an instructor at the University of Indonesia, she is passionate about improving education in Indonesia. Believing that education should focus on what is truly best for children, Amir established the HighScope Early Childhood Education Program in Jakarta in 1996. After extensive study, consultation with education experts, and numerous visits to schools in the United States and other countries, she expanded the program to be a comprehensive K–12 education institute. The aim of the program is to provide integrated and inclusive learning experiences that help students become self-regulated leaders, equipped with the skills needed to be successful and thrive in their lives. Contact her by email at antarina@sch.highscope.or.id.

Thomas R. Guskey, PhD, is professor emeritus in the College of Education, University of Kentucky. A graduate of the University of Chicago, he began his career in education as a middle school teacher and later served as an administrator in Chicago Public Schools. He is a fellow in the American Educational Research Association and was awarded the Association's prestigious *Relating Research to Practice Award*. Guskey's most recent books include *Implementing Mastery Learning*; *Get Set, Go! Creating Successful Grading and Reporting Systems*; and *What We Know About Grading: What Works, What Doesn't, and What's Next*. Contact him by email at guskey@uky.edu, on Twitter/X at @tguskey, or at www.tguskey.com.

Contributing Authors

Henny Astuti, ST, began her journey in education as an elementary teacher, delivering mathematics lessons, before becoming vice principal at Sekolah HighScope Indonesia. Four years later, as a member of the Training, Research, and Development Department at HighScope Indonesia Institute, she became a teacher trainer, responsible for developing the school's music and mathematics curriculum. She currently serves as coordinator of training and research development, responsible for overseeing all academic research and development activities for the innovative education approach of HighScope Indonesia Institute. Contact her by email at heni.astuti@sch.highscope.or.id.

Ilsa Nurina, BC, is chief human capital and academic development officer at HighScope Indonesia Institute. A graduate of Edith Cowan University in Australia, she began her career as a middle school teacher, and later became a trainer and quality monitoring specialist. Nurina continued her career as a research and development coordinator, where she learned from many education experts and best practice schools in Indonesia, the United States, and Australia. Her genuine passion for human development continues to grow and keeps her excited about the potential of education and the power of educators. Contact her by email at ilsa.n@sch.highscope.or.id.

Piesesha Hartiyana, SPd, MM, is a language arts and visual arts specialist at the HighScope Indonesia Institute. Her journey in education began as a kindergarten and preschool teacher, followed by assuming the role of a mentor teacher. Presently, she serves as a specialist in the Training, Research, and Development department. When she first joined the department, Hartiyana was a part of the development team for the Essential Life Skills Assessment System. This book is particularly special as it serves as a medium for her to channel her fervor for knowledge sharing and nurturing personal growth in others. Contact her by email at piesesha.h@sch.highscope.or.id.

 **Ratih Larasati, MPsi,** is a clinical child and adolescent psychologist practicing in Jakarta, Indonesia. After graduating from the University of Indonesia and the University of Queensland in Australia, she began her career in education as a special education teacher at Sekolah HighScope Indonesia. Larasati firmly believes that our future depends on our children and that an education system that equips them with essential skills is key. Motivated by her desire to make a lasting impact, she subsequently became a training, research, and development specialist at the HighScope Indonesia Institute, where she co-develops the Essential Life Skills Assessment System and helps to empower children with the skills they need to navigate the challenges of the future. Contact her by email at ratih.l@sch.highscope.or.id.

Related ASCD Resources: Social-Emotional Learning and Life Skills

At the time of publication, the following resources were available (ASCD stock numbers in parentheses).

All Learning Is Social and Emotional: Helping Students Develop Essential Skills for the Classroom and Beyond by Nancy Frey, Douglas Fisher, and Dominique Smith (#119003)

Curriculum 21: Essential Education for a Changing World edited by Heidi Hayes Jacobs (#109008)

The Formative Five: Fostering Grit, Empathy, and Other Success Skills Every Student Needs by Thomas R. Hoerr (#116043)

Social Emotional Learning and the Briain: Strategies to Help Your Students Thrive by Marilee Sprenger (#121010)

Students at the Center: Personalized Learning with Habits of Mind by Bena Kallick and Allison Zmuda (#117015)

Students Taking Action Together: 5 Teaching Techniques to Cultivate SEL, Civic Engagement, and a Healthy Democracy by Lauren M. Fullmer, Laura F. Bond, Crystal N. Molyneaux, Samuel J. Nayman, and Maurice J. Elias (#122029)

Taking Social Emotional Learning Schoolwide: The Formative Five Success Skills for Students and Staff by Thomas R. Hoerr (#112014)

Teaching for Deeper Learning: Tools to Engage Students in Meaning Making by Jay McTighe and Harvey F. Silver (#120022)

Teaching Students to Decode the World: Media Literacy and Critical Thinking Across the Curriculum by Chris Sperry and Cyndy Scheibe (#122006)

For up-to-date information about ASCD resources, go to **www.ascd.org.** You can search the complete archives of *Educational Leadership* at **www.ascd.org/el.** To contact us, send an email to member@ascd.org or call 1-800-933-2723 or 703-578-9600.

WHOLE CHILD
TENETS

HEALTHY
Each student enters school healthy and learns about and practices a healthy lifestyle.

SAFE
Each student learns in an environment that is physically and emotionally safe for students and adults.

ENGAGED
Each student is actively engaged in learning and is connected to the school and broader community.

SUPPORTED
Each student has access to personalized learning and is supported by qualified, caring adults.

CHALLENGED
Each student is challenged academically and prepared for success in college or further study and for employment and participation in a global environment.

ascd whole child

The ASCD Whole Child approach is an effort to transition from a focus on narrowly defined academic achievement to one that promotes the long-term development and success of all children. Through this approach, ASCD supports educators, families, community members, and policymakers as they move from a vision about educating the whole child to sustainable, collaborative actions.

Life Skills for All Learners relates to all five tenets. For more about the ASCD Whole Child approach, visit **www.ascd.org/wholechild**.

Become an ASCD member today!
Go to www.ascd.org/joinascd
or call toll-free: 800-933-ASCD (2723)

DON'T MISS A SINGLE ISSUE OF ASCD'S AWARD-WINNING MAGAZINE.

If you belong to a Professional Learning Community, you may be looking for a way to get your fellow educators' minds around a complex topic. Why not delve into a relevant theme issue of *Educational Leadership*, the journal written by educators for educators?

Subscribe now, or purchase back issues of ASCD's flagship publication at **www.ascd.org/el**. Discounts on bulk purchases are available.

To see more details about these and other popular issues of *Educational Leadership*, visit **www.ascd.org/el/all**.

2800 Shirlington Road
Suite 1001
Arlington, VA 22206 USA

www.ascd.org/learnmore

www.ingramcontent.com/pod-product-compliance
Lightning Source LLC
Chambersburg PA
CBHW060418010526
44118CB00017B/2273